Eliane Saadé

The Concept of Justice and Equality

Practical Philosophy

Edited by
Herlinde Pauer-Studer, Neil Roughley,
Peter Schaber, and Ralf Stoecker

Volume 20

Eliane Saadé

The Concept of Justice and Equality

On the Dispute between John Rawls and Gerald Cohen

DE GRUYTER

D82 (Diss. RWTH Aachen University, 2013)

ISBN 978-3-11-044719-4
e-ISBN (PDF) 978-3-11-044890-0
e-ISBN (EPUB) 978-3-11-044740-8
ISSN 2197-9243

Library of Congress Cataloging-in-Publication Data
A CIP catalog record for this book has been applied for at the Library of Congress.

Bibliografische Information der Deutschen Nationalbibliothek
Die Deutsche Nationalbibliothek verzeichnet diese Publikation in der Deutschen Nationalbibliografie; detaillierte bibliografische Daten sind im Internet über http://dnb.dnb.de abrufbar.

Druck und Bindung: CPI books GmbH, Leck
♾ Gedruckt auf säurefreiem Papier
Printed in Germany

www.degruyter.com

To my husband Elie and my children Adriana and Andreas
To all persons with Apert syndrome

Foreword

This book is based on the doctoral dissertation that I wrote at the RWTH Aachen University. It would not have been possible to write this doctoral thesis without the help and support of the kind people around me.

First and foremost, I would like to thank my supervisor Prof. Dr. phil. Markus Stepanians for his time, advice, and patience. I appreciate all his contributions to make my Ph.D. experience so motivating. He has taught me the importance of a clear and coherent thinking in order to provide intelligible ideas. It has been a pleasure to work under his supervision.

I am also very grateful to my second supervisor, Prof. Dr. phil. Wulf Kellerwessel. I appreciate his support during the period of my work.

I am thankful to my friends in Aachen, who became a part of my life, for time spent with them, and to my friends in Lebanon and elsewhere who always provided me with their encouragements and never failed to support me in all my pursuits.

Lastly, I would like to thank my dearest family, who live in Lebanon, for all their love, encouragement, and for their financial support in the first years of my studies. For my parents who always believed in my capabilities. For my mother, brother and sister who visited me in Aachen. And most of all, for my loving, encouraging husband, Elie Al Nahri, whose faithful support and great patience during my Ph.D. experience is so appreciated. Thank you.

Contents

Introduction

The Role of Political Philosophy

Political philosophy[1] is one of the branches of philosophy that began in antiquity with the pre Socratic philosophers. The fundamental concepts and questions at the root of all subsequent concepts and philosophical theories, were determined by ancient philosophers. They questioned the universe hence highlighting fundamental philosophical problems that became subjects of different philosophical fields, such as political philosophy, moral philosophy or ontology. The basic questions of political philosophy concern, for example, the virtue of justice or the set of rights and liberties. However, the development of political philosophy is kept alive in intense discussions about essential questions in political matters.

Because of these debates, a prominent role is given to contemporary scholars and thinkers, who contemplate the main questions of political philosophy. Contemporary philosophers, who still ask similar philosophical questions as their ancient forbears, have the duty to determine, according to their own reasoning, what is right and what is wrong in all these disputes. This responsibility is in some way imposed on them by the current problems that the world of today is faced with. Although ancient philosophers, for example, never explored the phenomenon of terrorism, they nonetheless enabled contemporary thinkers, by using the concepts defined within the sphere of political philosophy, to deal with contemporary problems.

The Question of Justice

However, within political philosophy, the central question focuses on the merits of justice, as all other political topics, such as what is the best political system, where are the limits of political obedience, what is the best educational system and the correct set of rights and liberties, depend on just this question. Moreover, the question of justice seems to enjoy a certain primacy over other questions within political philosophy, because the selection of the best political system or the correct set of rights and liberties, or the best educational system

1 This work examines the role of western political philosophy, as influenced by ancient philosophy.

presupposes a profound understanding of the concept and the meaning of justice, against which these political questions should be explored.

Yet, the philosophical question that examines the idea of justice – "What is justice?" – asked by ancient and modern political philosophers has different and sometimes opposing answers, which has been subject to many philosophical disputes. Most theories stipulate that an equal distribution of rights and liberties to all members of society is a judicial requirement, whereas the equal distribution of resources does not find the same understanding. Recently a particularly instructive philosophical disagreement on justice between John Rawls's definition of justice and its principles and Gerald Cohen's treatment of the same concept came to light. Rawls and Cohen agree that an equal distribution of rights and liberties is just, but they disagree on the distribution of income and wealth. The discrepancy in their ideas can be traced back to their intellectual upbringing; the different schools they come from. Rawls belongs to the liberal school of thought focusing on the importance of liberty and equal rights. He compiled a contractarian theory of justice whose principles must be accepted by all members of society in order to be applied. As to Cohen, he argues in favour of socialism and criticizes Rawls's conception of justice. But if justice involves a conviction about distributive justice, what is the reasoning about justice that underlies this conviction? What is justice? Is it a principle, a norm, or an ideal? Is it a harmony, a divine command, or a human creation? Is it a natural law or a mutual agreement? Which theory reveals what justice really is?

On the one hand, the Rawlsian theory of justice is a theory of a social contract agreed upon by members of a society, who agree on the most suitable principles for their social collaboration. Following Rawls, those principles which promote equal rights and liberties, equality of opportunity and fair distribution of social and economic benefits express the idea of justice because they are chosen under fair conditions. He believes that an unequal distribution of social and economic advantages is unjust, unless it improves the socioeconomic situation of the most deprived members of society. Rawls justifies the principles of justice within the original position device. His method consists of assembling representative members, who are to select what they think are the best principles of justice under certain conditions of knowledge and ignorance. In the process these persons should deliberate and choose the principles of justice according to their understanding of the idea of justice based on factual information about human nature and the human condition. They opt for just institutions, which should distribute rights, liberties and social and economic advantages according to the principles of justice.

On the other hand, Cohen examines our understanding of justice in our system of beliefs when he asks: What is justice? In order to answer this question, he suggests that we make use of the conceptual analysis method, which is a way to inspect all concepts in the structure of our beliefs and our principles. Everyone is invited to apply the Cohenian method of conceptual analysis if the person knows the principles, objects of belief, and the grounds for holding them. Cohen concludes that fundamental normative principles are principles that do not reflect facts and are therefore the foundation of all other normative principles, which do reflect facts. So, fundamental principles of justice do not reflect facts about human nature or the human condition, but rather the virtue of justice, which is independent of those facts. However, since Cohen's ideas on justice imply that rights and liberties should be distributed equally, he views an unequal distribution of social and economic advantages not affected by a person's choice or responsibility unfair and thereby unjust. Nothing can justify or remove this injustice.

The Approaches to Justice

In the second part of his book *Rescuing Justice and Equality* (RJE), Cohen investigates the fundamental concept of justice by asking what justice is. His examination of the concept of justice is meta-ethical in the sense that it does not concern substantial issues about distributive justice[2], but rather our thinking about justice and other virtues, our understanding of justice, our idea of justice, or as he puts it: our concept of justice.

In order to explore the idea of justice, Cohen analyzes the concepts and the principles of moral and political philosophy, which presupposes on the reader's part an "understanding of the sort of principle that a principle of justice is" (RJE: 7). The reader should intuitively[3] recognize normative principles of justice,

---

2 Distributive justice is an understanding of the concept of justice, which applies to society's institutions by allocating rights, liberties and goods that result from social cooperation to members of society.

3 The understanding of the principles of justice is intuitive in the sense that it lacks a specific method to determine these principles. They are recognized by intuition to express the virtue of justice.

such as the principle formulated by Polemarchus in Plato's *Republic*, which says that justice is "to give each his due" (Republic, VI-VII: 331-e).[4]

Cohen's conceptual analysis is a method of practicing philosophy, which he says is preferred by many "Oxford types"[5] (RJE: 4) of philosophers like himself. He uses this method not only as a general approach to philosophy, but in particular in his examination of the form and substance of justice. According to this conception, normative principles are determined after individual normative judgements regarding particular cases have been investigated, based on the knowledge that general principles supported by individual judgements maintain priority, although they might contradict principles held by other judgements. "In my philosophically conservative view, that is the only way to go" (ibid.). Cohen affirms that through this method, we will reach and uncover "our deepest normative convictions" (ibid.), which are presented in a competitive display. However, Cohen concedes that it may not be humanly possible to reach a completely satisfactory theory:

> Discursively indefensible trade-offs are our fate. I do not say that such an intellectual predicament is satisfactory. But I do say that it is the predicament that we are in (ibid.).

The method of conceptual analysis in philosophy is criticized by John Rawls, in *A Theory of Justice* (TJ) as being unsatisfactory and lacking an explicit method, which determines the priority rules for the selection of principles. The conceptual approach to philosophy adapted by Cohen is said to be "radical pluralist"[6] because of the plurality of conflicting normative principles thus making the conflict between them even more fundamental and the selection of the normative principles more intuitive. On a practical level, Cohen's intuitive procedure

---

4 There are different conceptions of this principle of justice that reveal different ways to determine what is due to people. However, those views, which are irrelevant for the argumentation at hand, are not discussed here.

5 In the introduction of RJE, Cohen stresses a list of disagreements between himself and the Rawlsians. One of those disagreements is the fact that Cohen studied at the University of Oxford and Rawls taught at Harvard University. Both philosophical traditions have, according to Cohen, different viewpoints about the status of philosophy and its relation to practice. "Oxford people of my vintage do not think that philosophy can move as far away as Harvard people think it can from pertinent pre-philosophical judgement" (RJE: 3).

6 It is very interesting to note that this expression of "radical pluralism" is used by both philosophers, but in different ways. Whereas Rawls attributes it to society, which is marked by the fact of "reasonable pluralism", where every member is free to have their own beliefs, Cohen refers to the plurality of conflicting normative principles present in everyone's mind, and which makes the conflict between these principles radical or fundamental.

consists of intuitively negotiating, weighing and balancing a plurality of (opposing) normative convictions, until the best intuitive trade-off or the foremost principle is reached. Yet, to what normative principle would the Cohenian philosophical method lead, if it were applied to justice?

After investigating the shape and the logical implications of his deepest convictions about justice, Cohen affirms that his firm conviction in political philosophy with respect to justice is that of a distributive justice. This conviction implies

> that an unequal distribution, whose inequality cannot be vindicated by some choice or fault or desert on the part of (some of) the relevant affected agents, is unfair, and, therefore, pro tanto, unjust, and nothing can remove that particular injustice (RJE: 7).

So, Cohen questions the "justice" of unjustified inequalities that result from unequal distributions. He concludes that unjustified inequalities are *pro tanto* unfair and thereby unjust, which describes his view of the relationship[7] between equality, fairness and justice. However, although they are unjust, unjustified inequalities could be part of a distributive policy that is "more just than any other" (ibid.). Yet, the fact that a policy is more just than another policy of distribution still does not make it just: "But it does follow that any package that contains that kind of unfairness cannot be through-and-through just" (ibid.).

According to Cohen, any theory which aims at realizing a virtue in society should not rely on contingent facts, but rather on purely normative principles, and ultimate normative principles are fact-insensitive. Normative principles can take facts into account if and only if doing so is justified by more ultimate principles, which do not depend on contingent facts. So, any normative principle which responds to facts should also respond to a superior normative principle which is fact-insensitive. The relationship between the normative principle responding to the fact and the fact itself is grounded in another normative principle which is a fact-insensitive principle. For example, principles for human beings should not be based on facts about human life. They should be built upon ultimate principles irrespective of life's realities.

The way Cohen approaches political philosophy and the nature of justice in particular leads him to a certain view about distributive justice. This conviction about distributive justice, which implies the distribution of rights, liberties, income and wealth among members of society, is also shared and formulated by Rawls in his theory of justice in the form of the two principles of justice. Both

---

7 This relationship in particular is discussed later on in this chapter.

philosophers proceed with different methods to examine the nature of justice. Nonetheless it seems that they agree, in principle, on the normative principle of distributive justice. This agreement between the two thinkers raises the question whether the Cohenian idea of distributive justice is really opposed to the Rawlsian idea.

In TJ Rawls questions the meaning and the role of justice in liberal societies. In *Justice as Fairness: a Restatement* (JF), Rawls summarizes, reformulates and rectifies some elements of the theory he developed in his first book, TJ. He makes use of the idea of a social contract based on a set of principles that should realize justice. Such a contract is a consensus between citizens of the same society on the assignment of rights and liberties, on the treatment of social and economic inequalities as well as on the distribution of income and wealth. This consensus is to be put into practice in a liberal democratic society according to the set of principles of justice proposed by Rawls. The idea of a social contract expresses Rawls's view that citizens of liberal democratic societies should share a common understanding of the conception of justice that rules their society, and a common commitment to those principles.

A liberal democratic society in the Rawlsian understanding is obtained when a group of free and equal citizens live together in "a fair system of cooperation" ordered by principles of justice. These persons, who live together in the same society, are called "citizens" because they are engaged in social cooperation and committed to the same laws and social institutions under the same political conception of justice that orders their social system. In a liberal democratic society, basic rights and liberties should be equally secured for all members. Being free and equal persons, they should agree on a political conception of justice that regulates their system of cooperation.

According to Rawls, free and equal citizens have two moral powers: a sense of justice and an understanding of what is good. Free and equal citizens should understand and apply the conception of justice that rules their society and pursue a conception of the good they believe in. The conception of justice should be commonly accepted and pursued by all, regardless of how each citizen understands the idea of good, which might differ from their beliefs and convictions. Yet, they are called equal persons because they know that each person possesses and uses the moral powers that enable them to participate in the cooperation. The conception of the good each of them pursues does not affect their social identity as citizens engaged in social cooperation, even if their beliefs related to this good change. In a liberal democratic society, people are free to choose any conception of what they believe is good. However, no matter to what religion they belong or what doctrine they support, members of a liberal democratic society should agree on *one* conception of justice that rules their cooperation.

Although citizens live under the same political conception of justice, they normally differ in many other respects. They are differently gifted by nature and belong to different social classes. They may belong to a well-off social class by birth, or they may have natural talents, such as intelligence, beauty, physical force or capacities such as good will and good health. Besides, members of a society often receive different educations, so that their skills develop differently. As a result, they have different expectations and future plans for life and different opportunities to realize them. Thus, the different determination of expectations often depends on differences or inequalities of income, wealth as well as natural and social abilities. Expectations on life are determined according to the capacities to achieve them. For example if Paul lives in a liberal society and wants to be a doctor, he should like people; he should have good learning abilities and he should be able to afford a university education. If he lacks one or more of these elements, he will not be able to achieve his studies and he will not envisage such a life plan. Hence, the feasibility of any future prospect depends to a large degree on a person's natural, social and economic abilities.

Yet, in a liberal society, there are always differences, sometimes even gross differences in people's prospects, which are limited by natural, social and economic inequalities. Some citizens are able to fulfill their expectations while others are not. However, in "a fair system of social cooperation", ruled by a reasonable conception of justice, everyone should have an equal chance to maximize their expectations of an accomplished life. Everyone should be able to pursue their aims.

It is important to mention that, according to Rawls, even in rich societies where all citizens could be able to achieve their prospects, the profit and advantage that results from social and economic inequalities should be ruled by a conception of justice. The application of justice depends on the nature of justice – "the first virtue of social institutions" – and not on the economic status of the citizens in a society. Even if social and economic differences between citizens of the same society determine their social and economic situation or social class, these differences do not have any influence on the nature, role and application of justice.

People's social and economic situations can be classified as more or less advantaged. The least advantaged members of society are "those belonging to the income class with the lowest expectations" (JF: 59). Respectively, the most advantaged would be those who belong to the income class with the highest expectations. According to Rawls, the use of social and economic inequalities should be regulated by the conception of justice, so that the expectations of the least advantaged citizens are maximized.

> [V]iewing society as a fair system of cooperation between citizens regarded as free and equal, what principles of justice are most appropriate to specify basic rights and liberties, and to regulate social and economic inequalities in citizens' prospects over a complete life? These inequalities are our primary concern (TJ: 41).

Unlike Cohen, who questions the nature of justice with his method of conceptual analysis, Rawls is content to describe the role of justice in a social cooperation and thereby the character of social institutions: "Justice is the first virtue of social institutions, as truth is of systems of thought" (TJ: 3). According to him, many things, such as laws, institutions, personal decisions and judgements are commonly said to be just or unjust. But Rawls's interests are narrower: On the one hand, the Rawlsian topic concerns only social justice, or precisely the way in which society's main institutions distribute rights, duties and social and economic benefits. On the other hand, his theory is a theory of a social contract, whose principles are subject to an original agreement made between free and rational persons wanting to promote their own interests. Members of a society agree that they need a set of principles for distributive justice. Moreover, they "agree that institutions are just when no arbitrary distinctions are made between persons in the assigning of basic rights and duties and when the rules determine a proper balance between competing claims to the advantages of social life" (TJ: 5).

Like Cohen, Rawls admits that these normative ideas express his conviction of the primacy of justice. But he finds Cohen's intuitive approach unsatisfactory, insofar as it does not present any method that justifies the selection of normative principles. Thus, "in any event I wish to inquire whether these contentions or others similar to them are sound, and if so how they can be accounted for. To this end it is necessary to work out a theory of justice in the light of which these assertions can be interpreted and assessed" (TJ: 4).

> Conceptions of justice are to be ranked by their acceptability to persons so circumstanced. Understood in this way the question of justification is settled by working out a problem of deliberation: we have to ascertain which principles it would be rational to adopt given the contractual situation. This connects the theory of justice with the theory of rational choice (TJ: 17).

So, Rawls does not only describe the role of justice and the character of social institutions, he also attributes a fundamental responsibility to members of society in determining the just and unjust distribution of liberties and benefits. For the task he imagines the "original position"[8], which is a procedure for generating principles. It is a hypothetical situation of equality, where free and equal representative members of society stand behind a "veil of ignorance". From this position of superficial knowledge and ignorance of specific conditions, everyone can choose just rules and principles for their social cooperation. Representatives know the general character of human nature and the laws of sociology and economics, but are ignorant about particulars, such as the social class they represent and to which social class they belong once the veil of ignorance is removed. Rawls argues that no one should be advantaged or disadvantaged by social circumstances in the choice of principles. "For example, if a man knew that he was wealthy, he might find it rational to advance the principle that various taxes for welfare measures be counted unjust; if he knew that he was poor, he would most likely propose the contrary principle" (TJ: 19). So, the principles selected in the hypothetical situation of equality are just because they are chosen under fair conditions. Rawls, who calls his conception of justice "justice as fairness", sketches, in his turn, a relationship between justice, fairness and equality.

The method that Rawls proposes for choosing the principles of justice consists of searching in the original position for reasonable requirements of justice. These requirements are shared by representative members of society, until the appropriate distributive principles for the basic structure[9] of society are identified and which should match the personal convictions about justice. "Our convictions about principles are much less firm and assured; so we look to our firmest convictions for guidance where assurance is lacking and guidance is needed" (JF: 42). However, the Rawlsian approach to justice is constructivist, which means that normative principles of justice are "constructed" or created in the original position, since the persons who select the principles should themselves choose what is just and unjust for their social cooperation. The term "constructivist" entered the recent philosophical debate with Rawls. In his article "Kantian Constructivism in Moral Theory" (1980) he examines the Kantian variant of constructivist moral conceptions, which is justice as fairness. This conception of justice, adopted by Rawls in TJ, finds its roots in Kantian constructivism.

---

8 For a further discussion of the original position device see chapter 1.

9 The basic structure of society represents all main institutions, which are in charge of assigning rights, liberties and social and economic advantages that result form social cooperation. For a further presentation of the basic structure, see chapter 1.

> [I]t specifies a particular conception of the person as an element in a reasonable procedure of construction, the outcome of which determines the content of the first principles of justice. [...] [T]his kind of view sets up a certain procedure of construction which answers to certain reasonable requirements, and within this procedure persons characterized as rational agents of construction specify, through their agreements, the first principles of justice (Collected Papers: 304).

Thus, Rawls calls his conception of justice "justice as fairness". He postulates that the representatives in the original position decide that basic rights and liberties are equally assigned. Inequalities in income and wealth should be tolerated and permitted, but only if they benefit the least advantaged citizens. The result of this social consensus is Rawls's two principles of justice.

> [1.] Each person has the indefeasible claim to a fully adequate scheme of equal basic liberties, which scheme is compatible with the same scheme of liberties for all; and
> [2a.] Social and economic inequalities are to satisfy two conditions: first, they are to be attached to offices and positions open to all under conditions of fair equality of opportunity; and second, [2b.] they are to be to the greatest benefit of the least-advantaged members of society (the difference principle) (JF: 42-43).

The first principle of justice prohibits inequalities in the assignment of basic liberties. Every member of society holds the same right to basic liberties. The second principle of justice deals with social and economic inequalities, which Rawls does not aim at removing. Inequalities are allowed within a liberal democratic society if certain conditions are met. For Rawls, their existence is not considered unfair or unjust, if they are regulated by the following principles:

2a. Offices and positions should be accessible to all citizens no matter what their social class is. "Accessible to all" means that everyone – no matter to what social class they belong – should have the same chance to attain them. If Paul is sufficiently intelligent and motivated to learn but out of money, he should get help to be able to pay for his university education. The social class to which Paul belongs must not affect Paul's opportunity to climb the social ladder. If the situation is different and Paul is a well-off citizen, he should not have a better chance than others – who are less advantaged than himself – to attain a specific position.

2b. The second part of the second principle of justice is named by Rawls "the difference principle as a principle of a distributive justice" (JF: 61). Rawls assumes that social cooperation is always productive so that there is always something to be distributed. The difference principle allows social and economic inequalities among citizens. However, if the social product increases the prospects of the most advantaged, the resulting inequalities should also increase the expectations of the least advantaged members. Everyone is allowed to produce more in order to earn greater returns, if the most disadvantaged benefit from this increase as well. However, since the economic situations of all social classes are tightly connected the expectations of all would decrease if the expectations of the most advantaged declined. The "incentives argument" – implicit in the difference principle – states that the most advantaged persons, would be unwilling to produce more unless they received more returns. The increase of income would serve as an incentive to motivate the privileged to increase their production. An economic improvement can be accepted and permitted, but only if it also improves the situation of the least advantaged members of society. In this case, Rawls considers inequalities that result from greater returns to some citizens as just because everyone, especially the least advantaged benefit from them.

So, Rawls decides that social and economic inequalities are unjust, unless they benefit the most disadvantaged individuals in society.[10] Socioeconomic inequalities, caused by morally arbitrary circumstances, are, however, tolerable and therefore just, if and only if they promote to the maximum possibility[11] the advantage of the least advantaged social classes. These vested inequalities would function as necessary incentives to motivate privileged people to increase their productivity, and thereby benefit underprivileged persons.

> [T]he difference principle requires that however great the inequalities in wealth and income may be, and however willing people are to work to earn their greater shares of output, existing inequalities must contribute effectively to the benefit of the least advantaged. Otherwise the inequalities are not permissible (JF: 64).

Cohen criticizes the constructivist approach[12] to social justice insofar as it identifies the content of justice with the best rules that regulate social living. Justice

---

10 For a further presentation of the principles of justice, see chapters 1 (first principle) and 4 (second principle).

11 Rawls indicates that the advantages of the least advantaged persons should be maximized, without giving precise explanations of that maximization. However, he means that the situation of the least favoured members is better under a distribution with socioeconomic inequalities, than under an equal distribution of benefits, because these inequalities would motivate the well-off persons to increase their production. As a matter of fact, more income and opportunities will be distributed than under an equal distribution of goods. Therefore, inequalities of unequal distributions are justified.

12 Cohen rejects the constructivist approach to social justice in general. His critique also "applies to Scanlonian constructivism, to Gauthier's contractarianism, and to Ideal Observer theory, where each is recommended as a procedure for identifying what justice, in particular, is" (RJE: 275).

is, in this manner, identified as the output of a “privileged choosing situation” (RJE: 3), which is the original position device; and the selected normative principles would not only reflect the pure virtue of justice, but rather facts about human nature and conditions of life, which assure the feasibility of the principles. “That being so, justice, itself, could not be what is specified by such rules” (ibid.). However, Rawls’s principles of justice, which are chosen in the original position (the hypothetical device for the selection of the principles of justice), are supported by facts about the human condition. According to Cohen, the principles thus do not refer to fact-insensitive rules, but rather to facts. Representative persons equally positioned in the original position choose the principles of justice for their society, provided with the general facts about the human liberal condition. According to Rawls’s conception, the choice of the principles of justice would be a direct response to the question: What would be the best principles of justice that suit our human condition? Yet, this question is strikingly different from the central question asked by Cohen: What is justice and what are its fundamental principles isolated from the human condition?

Cohen’s thesis is that fundamental principles of justice should not respond to the finite human factual situation. The fundamental principles of justice must be defined according to what justice is and not according to what individuals create if they want to act in a just way. The principles of justice selected by Rawls are fact-sensitive principles, which according to Cohen must be justified by fundamental principles of justice, but not be confused with them. Fact-sensitive principles reflect fundamental principles but remain separate from them. Even though the selected principles of justice are the best feasible principles, they are not to be mistaken for fundamental principles of justice.

According to Cohen, in Rawls’s theory of justice, the question as to which principles we should adopt given our human condition is more important than the question about the nature of justice. Rawls tries to find principles that humans are able to apply in concrete circumstances. His initial starting point is not justice but the human condition and capacity to apply justice. As Cohen says, Rawls’s principles of justice have been mistaken for fundamental principles of justice. The principles accepted in the original position are fact-sensitive, and as such are not fundamental principles of justice.

Cohen concludes that the Rawlsian approach to the substance of social justice is mistaken. On the one hand, it is incorrect, in order to guarantee their feasibility, to make normative principles of justice preconditioned by facts about human nature and condition; fundamental normative principles are not sensitive to facts and therefore they cannot be determined by facts. On the other hand, it is a central error in constructivism to pervert the nature of justice by failing to distinguish it from other virtues; optimal principles which regulate the basic structure of society are shaped by values that do not only reflect the point of view of justice.

> A failure to make this distinction with clarity and force, in the right place, is central to the error in constructivism that I claim to discern, the error which means that the very concept of justice must be rescued from constructivism, whatever the content of justice may turn out to be (RJE: 21).

In his approach, Cohen conceives that Rawls does not answer the essential philosophical question: 1) What is justice? And he charges Rawls with confusing it with the question: 2) What are the right principles for the regulation of social life? Yet, following Cohen, the first question concerns the nature of justice and the answer to the second, if taken to be an answer to the first question, mistakes what justice is. In general, his criticism of constructivism is that the answer to the second question could not answer *his* question, which is the right question about the concept of justice: What is justice?

Hence, Cohen believes that Rawls's philosophy changes the meaning of justice and therefore justice should be "rescued" from the Rawlsian treatment. Furthermore, the meta-ethical rescue of the concept of justice supports, according to Cohen, the rescue of the egalitarian thesis, which he attempts in the first part of RJE. Why does the rescue of justice support the rescue of equality? What is the relationship between justice and equality so that a critique of the Rawlsian approach to social justice constitutes by the same fact a critique of Rawls's egalitarianism, and a rescue of distributive justice? If the rescue of justice is a rescue of the concept, would the rescue of equality be a rescue of the content of that concept?

The Relationship between Justice and Equality

According to Cohen, in a society in which distributive justice is applied, people's material chances should be equal; "distributive justice does not tolerate the deep inequality, driven by the provision of economic incentives to well-placed people" (RJE: 2), which Rawls's difference principle, however, condones. Furthermore, Cohen thinks that justice *requires* equality; equality is then an important component of the content of justice. Without equality, justice can neither be defined, nor achieved.

> To the extent that justice is distinguished from other values, the case for the thesis that justice requires equality is strengthened, because other values than justice tend against

> equality. […] Accordingly, the rescue of justice that distinguishes it both from other values and from implementable rules of regulation supports (≠ establishes) the claim that justice requires equality (RJE: 3).

If justice requires equality, then an unequal distribution of benefits is in that way *pro tanto* unjust. This is the idea behind the Cohenian conviction about distributive justice indicated earlier. Unequal distributions, whose inequality is not justified by any choice or fault or merit, are unfair and thereby unjust, and nothing can remove this injustice or unfairness. Vice versa, a fair distribution of benefits is an equal distribution and accordingly just; justice is fairness, and fairness requires equality. Fairness is either realized by a justification of inequality (by some choice or fault or merit) or by an equal distribution.

For these reasons Cohen criticizes the Rawlsian difference principle, which endorses the justice of unjustified inequality that results from unequal distributions. "More generally, the Rawlsian approach denatures justice since it cannot recognize that if something is unfair, then it's to that extent unjust: the identification of the best-all-things-considered rules of regulation with the principles of justice excludes that recognition" (RJE: 8). Whereas Cohen considers an unfair distribution unjust to that extent, Rawls justifies this unfairness (inequality) as just, if it improves the situation of the least advantaged members of society.

So, justice, fairness and equality are strongly related, if not causally related with one another. Hence, a critique of Rawls's treatment of the concept of justice supports or even implies a critique of his treatment of the egalitarian thesis. What are the elements of Cohen's critique of Rawls's egalitarianism? Where are the common points and divergences of both "egalitarian" theories?

The Principles of Distributive Justice

Before focusing on the common points and disagreements of both theories, it is important to acknowledge the ideological disagreement generated by the different philosophical backgrounds of the two philosophers. On the one hand, Cohen shares Karl Marx's non-liberal socialist conviction that the achievement of "human emancipation"[13] implies that freedom and equality are expressed in

---

13 "Human emancipation will only be complete when the real individual man has absorbed into himself the abstract citizen; when as an individual man, in his everyday life, in his work, and in his relationships, he has become a *species-being*; and when he has recognized and organized his own powers (*forces propres*) as social powers so that he no longer separated his social power from himself as *political* power" ("On the Jewish Question" 1978: 46).

people's daily life in the form of an egalitarian ethos[14], so that individual economic choices and decisions reflect the egalitarian principle of distributive justice. Moreover, there is a difference between the ideal liberal society and the ideal socialist one. Whereas in the Rawlsian conception society's main institutions are supposed to realize a certain form of justice according to a certain economic scheme, there is, in the ideal socialist society, an egalitarian ethos that informs people's daily life and economic choices, so that the duality between the justice of social institutions and the justice of personal economic decisions would wither away.

> The Marx-inspired question is whether a society without an ethos in daily life that is informed by a broadly egalitarian principle for that reason fails to provide distributive justice. To that question, Rawls, being a liberal, says 'No': here is the deep dividing line between us (RJE: 2).

Beyond the philosophical disagreement due to different philosophical traditions and backgrounds, and the methodological disagreement that manifests itself in different approaches to philosophy and particularly to justice, the Cohenian and the Rawlsian results share fundamental viewpoints. Is it possible that both theories do not contradict each other but that they in fact complement each other?[15] Is Cohen simply a bit more egalitarian than Rawls?

> Some people think that I exaggerate the difference between what Rawls offers and what I counter-offer. If they were disposed, as a result, to call me a left-Rawlsian, I would neither disavow nor dislike the description. There is a strong egalitarian element in Rawlsianism that I try to train against its inegalitarian conclusions (RJE: 12).

In fact, both theories are theories of distributive justice. Rawls as well as Cohen are both driven by the same conviction with respect to justice, which is a conviction about distributive justice. Rights, duties, liberties, and social and economic benefits that result from social collaboration should be distributed according to the principles of distributive justice that each theory, explicitly or not, aims to provide.

Besides, even if Cohen does not accept the Rawlsian justification of the choice of the principles of justice in the original position procedure, he seems to agree with the content of the first selected principle. This distributive principle reflects the belief of an equal distribution of rights and liberties among all

---

14 The idea of the egalitarian ethos is explained later on in this chapter.

15 One of the aims of the next chapters of this work is to give an answer to this question.

members of society. "Each person has the same indefeasible claim to a fully adequate scheme of equal basic liberties[16], which scheme is compatible with the same scheme of liberties for all" (JF: 42). Cohen spares the substance of the Rawlsian first principle of justice from his critique. So, while there is a conceptual and methodological disagreement between both theories about justice and the way principles of justice are arrived at, there is apparently a fundamental conformity about the egalitarian distribution of rights and liberties.

The Cohenian Critique of the Difference Principle

Rawls's endorsement of inequalities as manifested in his principle of distributive justice is exactly what Cohen rejects in RJE. Cohen questions the Rawlsian concepts of justice and equality and endeavors, in both parts of the book, to rescue them from Rawls's liberal thought. How can inequalities be just if their causes are unjust? Causes of inequalities are unjust because no one earns their natural endowments and starting place in society. Cohen criticizes what he thinks is Rawls's use of unjust inequalities which effect only greater inequalities. Even those inequalities considered just in Rawls's view because the least advantaged benefit from them, appear unjust to Cohen. He thinks that the difference principle could be – in the best reading of it – a good policy to regulate already existing inequalities, but he rejects it as being one of the principles of justice. Cohen questions its nature, its meaning, and Rawls's choice to count it among the principles of justice. He concludes that it can neither be a principle of justice nor a defensible normative principle at all as it justifies the use of social and economic inequalities to achieve greater benefits.

It is assumed by Rawls that the increase of production *can* benefit all members of society including the least advantaged because there would be more income and wealth to be distributed, and it is just, when it does. This idea is expressed in the difference principle, which is a principle of distributive justice. The difference principle endorses unequal distributions in the name of justice, if these distributions meet certain conditions. According to Cohen, the difference principle expresses the will of the most privileged persons. He rejects the incentives argument. Although on the one hand, inequalities resulting from the increase of production and income are considered necessary for the most advantaged citizens to produce more, they should not be accepted by the least advantaged; on the other hand, inequalities are permitted and endorsed as just

16 The set of equal basic liberties is presented in chapter 1.

in virtue of the Rawlsian difference principle, because they benefit the least advantaged members of society. Following Cohen, affluent persons are able to produce more – even if they are not motivated by more returns – but they do not *want* to produce more. In an example, Cohen compares the arguments formulated by the most advantaged persons with the arguments raised by a kidnapper, who does not want to release the kidnapped person unless he is paid. "The incentives argument has something in common with the kidnapper argument, although there are major differences between withholding a hostage and withholding labor until one gets the money one desires" (RJE: 41). Like Rawls, Cohen thinks that every political principle should be accepted by all members of a community.[17] Yet, according to Cohen, if the privileged members of a community were questioned by the least advantaged citizens, they would find it difficult to justify their behaviour. Cohen concludes that if citizens were educated differently, they would choose an equal distribution. "[T]he proportioning of remuneration [...] is highly expedient; and until education shall have been entirely regenerated, is far more likely to prove immediately successful, than an attempt at a higher ideal" (RJE: 85). Why should citizens choose the difference principle in the original position, which favours unequal distribution – which is unjust, based on injustice – at the expense of an equal distribution which would be just? Why would a principle of distribution of resources that favours the economic interests of the most advantaged members of society, be fair towards all its members?

Cohen questions the choice of the difference principle and tries to show that Rawls sacrifices equality by choosing the difference principle. "Rawls establishes equality as the only prima facie just basis of distribution" (RJE: 87). But then, Rawls moves from an equal distribution to an unequal distribution according to the difference principle. The distribution achieved by following the difference principle allows inequalities that benefit people at the bottom or the least advantaged citizens. Yet, Cohen criticizes two points in that move. Rawls replaces an equal with an unequal distribution although he apparently acknowledges that equality is the only "prima facie" just basis of distribution. But, Rawls argues that as long as unequal distributions benefit all citizens including those at the bottom, they are just. "My object is to show that the two-stage argument [moving from equality to inequality and endorsing its justice] does not establish the justice of the inequalities that Rawls thinks are just" (RJE: 88). Why does Rawls move from an equal to an unequal distribution? With regard to the nature

17 A community is a group of people that accept to live under certain norms.

of inequalities that the difference principle allows, Cohen believes they are unjust because they are based on "morally arbitrary contingencies". In fact, talented individuals or the upper-classes have better expectations in life because they are naturally and socially better endowed. The fact that the endowment differs from one person to another is morally arbitrary insofar as there is no relevant normative reason why this person is thus endowed. After all, they have not done anything to merit or deserve it. Yet, the difference principle allows the use of morally arbitrary contingencies in order to create more inequalities that are according to Cohen also morally arbitrary. How could the application of a principle of justice be based on an unequal distribution of goods that promotes the justice of morally arbitrary inequalities?

However, Rawls's second principle of justice, with its second part that concerns the difference principle is the subject of the great dispute between Rawls and Cohen, and lays open their ideological and methodological disagreements. Before discussing the elements of the Cohenian critique, it is necessary to explain why the difference principle cannot be a common fundamental principle in both theories. Why is Cohen bothered by the idea of the difference principle?

The difference principle allows an unequal distribution of social and economic benefits, whose inequality is caused by morally arbitrary contingencies. It appears to violate the principle of equality and is to that extent unjust. To justify this *pro tanto* unequal (unjust) distribution, Rawls makes it part of a social package that assures an efficient productivity, from which almost all citizens benefit. After justifying the difference principle in the light of an overall efficient social scheme, Rawls argues that it is, despite the resultant inequality, whose cause is still morally arbitrary, not unjust when all things are considered. On the contrary, he concludes that this principle thereby becomes just. If the Rawlsian efficient social distribution seems acceptable to Cohen for economic considerations, he definitely refuses to justify these inequalities as just. "Thus, to take a central example, the difference principle, which in the Rawlsian conception, endorses the distributions that satisfy it as just plain just, in fact, [...] tolerates a certain form of injustice" (RJE: 7). Besides, Cohen argues that Rawls's justification of unequal incomes, only endorses the motivation of the most advantaged persons, who, although they are in the position to produce social goods, require extra financial incentives to do so. But then, instead of an unequal distribution of socioeconomic advantages, Cohen thinks that an equal distribution[18] would be feasible, if the affluent classes *wanted* to act in an egali-

18 This corresponds to the distribution D3 that Cohen proposes and discusses its feasibility. For a further discussion see chapter 7.

tarian way. So, Cohen, who proposes an egalitarian distribution of the benefits resulting from social cooperation, seems to be more egalitarian than Rawls. But how does Cohen prove the feasibility of an equal distribution of economic benefits according to the difference principle, which he criticizes? What is missing in the Rawlsian version of the difference principle?

As indicated earlier, the difference principle is the second part of the second principle of justice, chosen in the original position. The Rawlsian second principle of justice focuses on the treatment of social and economic inequalities. On the one hand, it promotes the principle of a fair equality of opportunity, which states that social offices and positions should be accessible to all members of society. On the other hand, it advances the difference principle, which states that inequalities, which are to the benefit of the least advantaged citizens, are to that extent justified and thereby just. But, on what grounds should the representative members in the original position choose the difference principle?

According to Rawls, representative members who are behind the veil of ignorance and do not know which social class they represent in real life, would try to minimize their own risk as much as possible: What if they belonged to the least advantaged social class? Their decisions should strive for the maximum welfare of the least favoured persons, by maximizing their share.[19] In this way, Rawls does not only justify undeserved inequality, but also its use as an improvement of the socioeconomic situation of the most disadvantaged people and renders it, to that extent, just. Here is the core of the dispute with Cohen. "I claim that that pattern of justification is far more problematic than is generally supposed" (RJE: 15).

In fact, the Cohenian critique of the difference principle has two aspects. It questions, on the one hand, the restricted application of the Rawlsian difference principle and, on the other hand challenges the principle itself. It is through the first critique, that Cohen attempts to save the difference principle by correcting the requirements of its application. He, in a further move, endeavours to prove the incoherence of the argument that underlies the difference principle:

> 1. Inequalities are unjust unless they are necessary to make the worst off people better off, in which case they are just. 2. Unequalizing incentive payments to productive people are necessary to make the worst off people better off. 3. Therefore, unequalizing incentive payments are just (RJE: 19).

19 See Markus Stepanians's (2009) „Gerechtigkeit als Fairness" p. 18.

The Cohenian critique of the "restricted" application of the difference principle, challenges the premises 2 and 3 in the aforementioned reformulation of the Rawlsian argument for the different principle.

Indeed, the application is restricted in the sense that the difference principle, properly understood, should not only apply to society's basic structure, but also to the choices of individuals in their daily lives. Personal economic decisions should therefore be formed on the basis of an egalitarian ethos of justice. "Now, many Rawlsians resist that extension of the difference principle into the personal domain" (RJE: 8). But, this is not Rawls's point of view, who assigns to individuals a set of "natural duties", the application of which depends on individuals rather than on the state; "and that include the duty to respect others, to uphold and foster just institutions, to do a great good when the cost of doing so is not excessive" (RJE: 9).[20] But, following Cohen, Rawls distinguishes the task of the state, which is to apply the principles of justice, from the "non-task of the individual, which is to do as she pleases within that framework" (ibid.). Whereas Rawls restricts the demands of distributive justice to the impersonal standpoint (state), Cohen believes that these demands should inform personal decisions as well.

> But the individual who affirms the difference principle must have some regard to it in his economic choices, whatever regard, that is, which starts where her personal prerogative stops. Yet the state, too, must have regard, in its legislation, to the personal prerogative of the individual (RJE: 10).[21]

So, individuals, acting according to the difference principle in their daily lives, should find a balance between the requirements of that principle and their own legitimate prerogatives.

Besides the fact that it is restricted in Cohen's view, he criticizes the application of the difference principle, which gives support to unequalizing incentive payments said to be crucial for the increase of productivity. Cohen argues that in the light of Rawls's own understanding of a just society, in which citizens live in "full compliance" with the principles of justice, "the difference principle does not justify incentive-based inequality *as a feature of a just society*" (RJE: 15). Yet, Rawls assumes that every member in society has a sense of justice, which enables them to observe the principles of justice in a well-ordered society, in which

---

20 See TJ §19.

21 Following Cohen, the personal prerogative provides each person "the right to be something other than an engine for the welfare of other people: we are not nothing but slaves to social justice" (RJE: 10).

the values of mutual respect, reciprocity and fraternity prevail. Accordingly, if incentive seekers chose to act in their daily lives in conformity with the Rawlsian conception of justice, they would not ask for unequal payments in order to induce production. Hence, unequalizing incentives are not *strictly* necessary and the Rawlsian endorsement of incentives' inequality represents the abandonment of the difference principle properly understood.

Furthermore, Cohen seeks to refute another Rawlsian argument for inequality, justified by the difference principle. Rawls starts by assuming that, in a just and well-ordered society[22], an appropriate understanding of the ideal of equality of opportunity requires equality.

Whether fault or choice or merit of their own, no person deserves, by no fault, choice or merit to have more resources than another person. However, Rawls imagines a social scheme of unequal incomes, under which everyone, including the worst-off people, would be better-off.[23] Therefore, he abandons the starting point of equality by justifying an inequality that makes everyone better-off. Cohen, however, wants to show that "if the case for an initial equality is sound, then it undermines the case for replacing that equality by an inequality" (RJE: 16). He, therefore, proposes a more egalitarian social scheme, according to which incomes are equally distributed. His idea of an egalitarian system is only feasible if, and only if, the individual choices are informed by an ethos of justice. He argues that a just society must be cultured by an egalitarian economic ethos, which affects the behaviour of the members of society in a way that they become more egalitarian. So, following his chain of arguments, the demands of distributive justice cannot be achieved solely by the basic structure of society or by citizens' compliance with the laws of the state.

> A society that it is just within the terms of the difference principle, so I conclude, requires not only just coercive rules, but also an ethos of justice that informs individual choices. Citizens do not qualify as fully committed to the difference principle unless that principle influences not only their voting behaviour but also some of their behaviour within the structure that their vote creates (ibid.).

Yet, Cohen challenges not only its application, but the difference principle itself, by trying to prove the incoherence behind the first premise in the above indicated syllogism. This premise states that unequalizing money incentives are unjust, unless they improve the social and economic situation of the lower classes.

---

22 For a further explanation of the Rawlsian understanding of this idea, see chapter 1.

23 This is the Pareto move, which is discussed in chapter 4.

As indicated earlier, Cohen accuses Rawls of inconsistency by 1) taking equality as a starting point for justice, based on the argument that nobody deserves more than anybody else, and then 2) abandoning equality on the grounds that under an unequal social scheme everyone would be better-off, and 3) declaring that the final inequality is just. Moreover, Cohen considers the inequalities that the difference principle endorses unjust, because they are caused by morally arbitrary circumstances. If no one deserves to be better endowed or more privileged than anyone else, unequal distributions might be efficient but cannot be considered just. Therefore, the difference principle cannot endorse the arbitrariness of a naturally and socially unequal distribution. It cannot justify these unjustified differences as just, on the grounds that they benefit the worst-off people.

The Thesis

So, both philosophers present two different approaches to social justice. Their approaches cannot be complementary, unless considered on a practical level, where a precise distribution of social and economic benefits is chosen. Both philosophers might agree on a reasonable distribution, even if they would justify their choice with different reasons.[24] However, from a philosophical viewpoint, it is difficult to perceive both theories as complementary, as they are not. The present disagreement about justice and its principles calls for a choice, for a precise viewpoint, which opts either for the Rawlsian theory or for the Cohenian one. What is the more plausible approach to social justice?

This work aims to defend Cohen's position in the light of two considerations. On the one hand, it answers the philosophical question about the analysis of the idea of justice, which puts the virtue of justice in its philosophical context. On the other hand, it presents a method everyone can apply in order to arrive at the fundamental principles of justice by employing the power of reason. Moreover, on a practical level, this theory does not only imply just institutions but also just persons, who take just decisions in their daily lives. A just society is therefore a society where just persons and just institutions exhibit the virtue of justice.

Beyond Rawls's and Cohen's disagreement about the idea of justice, a plausible approach to justice must distinguish between a theoretical and a practical

24 See RJE p. 319.

level. On the theoretical level, justice as a philosophical concept should be explored and the fundamental principles of justice defined accordingly. Yet, the practical level, which concerns human conduct in society, should be informed by the understanding of justice arrived at on the theoretical level. If the concept of justice is analyzed by philosophers, the understanding of justice thus reached should inform everyone's actions and decisions within society. Now, the philosophical question that explores the idea and the concept of justice is: What is justice? Beyond the disagreement about the answers to this question, the fundamental philosophical question about justice remains. Thus, a plausible approach to justice should start by asking this essential question rather than the pragmatic question of the best principles to live by. Furthermore, an analysis of the concept of justice based on the power of reason should seek to uncover the ultimate nature of justice, which is independent of facts and of other virtues. Once exposed, the understanding of justice arrived at should inform social institutions and determine people's daily decisions. The Cohenian approach might be more interesting insofar as it provides a philosophical method to define the concept of justice by analyzing the role of this concept in the structure of our beliefs and principles. This concept exists independently of facts about the agent analyzing this concept. The philosophical examination of this concept does not imply any conviction about it, such as the Cohenian conviction that involves the ideas of equality and distributive justice. So, the difference between the concept of justice and the content of it explored in RJE reveals the philosophical character of Cohen's thesis, and it is defended in this work. But, to what extent is the Cohenian critique of the Rawlsian theory justified?

Is the Cohenian Critique Justified?

Cohen criticizes the Rawlsian difference principle, which (from his point of view) justifies unjust inequalities as just, and the constructivist approach to social justice, which does not lead to the pure concept of justice. Both critiques are related in the sense that the rescue of the concept of justice from the Rawlsian treatment supports the rescue of the idea of equality. But, it is the thesis about the relationship between facts and fundamental principles in general, applied to the extent of the virtue of justice in particular that shows Cohen's philosophical originality and makes his thesis attractive. The critique of the constructivist approach, which is not exclusively directed against Rawls's constructivism, is justified because it aims to isolate the concept of justice from the facts of the world and from other considerations such as the feasibility of the principles of justice. A philosophical approach to justice should not worry about the feasibility of the principles of justice more than about the idea of justice itself, unless the task is to select the best feasible principles that should regulate social life. However, in that case the selected principles are not the fundamental principles of justice.

Concerning the critique of the Rawlsian principles of justice, Cohen challenges the incentives argument and the Pareto argument, with which the difference principle is justified. The difference principle rejects social and economic inequalities, unless they benefit the least advantaged members of society. Now, the incentives argument supposes that, if affluent people were entitled to the difference principle, they would not need special monetary rewards in order to increase their productivity. Hence, the refusal of the upper-classes to increase their productivity, – whose benefits would be distributed among members of society – means that they are committed neither to the difference principle nor to the values of fraternity and reciprocity. In order to consolidate his point, Cohen uses (what he calls) “the interpersonal test”, which is meant to illustrate the incentives argument with a conversation between a rich and a poor man. The well-off person is shown to be unable to justify the special money incentives required in order to maintain or to increase productivity. Now, without defending Rawls's position about the incentives argument, and even if the need for money incentives required by the well-off should prove that they are more committed to advancing their interests rather than to acting upon the principles of justice, it could still be the case that the use of the interpersonal test to reject the incentives argument is exaggerated, if not inappropriate. The test only confronts two particular citizens and judges the justice of the incentives argument from their viewpoints and according to the way it affects their socioeconomic situation. Whereas Cohen personalizes the Rawlsian theory, Rawls warns of such interpersonal comparisons and designs his theory for institutions, not persons. Let us remember that, according to Rawls, the justice of a social scheme is realized when social institutions function according to the principles of justice, without the need to compare people's economic situations.

As to the Pareto argument, Cohen criticizes what he considers to be the Rawlsian move from justice as equality to justice as inequality, in the case that this inequality improves the situation of the underprivileged. The Cohenian viewpoint is justified, in the sense that, even on a practical level, where an unequal distribution based on socially arbitrary contingencies could be considered more reasonable or more efficient, it remains unjust and nothing can remove or change this injustice into justice. As indicated earlier, even if both philosophers do not agree, in theory, to the treatment of the idea of justice, they might agree (albeit for different reasons) to the same distribution of the goods. Their views could therefore be considered, by accident, complementary on a practical level.

In sum, this work defends the Cohenian method of conceptual analysis in order to reach the fundamental principles of justice as well as his thesis about the relationship between facts and fundamental principles. The philosophical question behind the Cohenian thesis addresses the idea and the concept of justice, which rescues it from the facts considered in the Rawlsian pragmatic approach to social justice. Even if both philosophers seem to largely agree on a practical level on the distribution of goods, the respective theories seem to have very little in common. The Rawlsian approach, which believes common sense is a valid instrument for the definition of justice, does not query the fundamental concepts. The Rawlsian definition of justice depends upon facts about the human condition and considerations about the feasibility of a "just" social scheme. Is the Rawlsian theory of justice, which is widely read and examined, simply overestimated?

> I agree with the Socrato-Platonic view that led Socrates to reject illustrations of, for example, just behaviour as providing a proper answer to the question 'What is justice?' [...] Until we unearth the fact-free principle that governs our fact-loaded particular judgments about justice, we don't know why we think what we think just is just. And we have to retreat to (what we consider to be) justice in its purity to figure out how to institute as much justice as possible inside the cave (RJE: 291).

This work is divided into three parts. The first part focuses on the virtue of justice, as examined by Rawls and Cohen, the different methodologies and approaches both philosophers employ in order to explain the idea of justice, and their different conceptions of justice. Chapter 1 presents the Rawlsian conception of justice "justice as fairness", and the Rawlsian system built on related ideas. A just society is conceived as a fair system of social cooperation between free and equal citizens, who live according to the principles of justice. Social institutions are also ordered by these principles, so that rights, liberties and social goods are distributed fairly among members of society. Chapter 2 introduces the Cohenian meta-ethical theory, which examines the structure of beliefs and principles, and the way they are organized in people's minds. Cohen's thesis about the relationship between facts and principles, his argument and defense of the thesis, are explained. Chapter 3 shows how Cohen's meta-ethical theory is applied to the concept of justice, which pushes Cohen to rescue justice from the Rawlsian treatment that he takes to alter its nature. The rescue of justice from constructivism is the subject of the third chapter.

The second part of this work considers the idea of equality and its ties to the idea of justice. Although equality is a very important component in achieving social justice, it is defined and understood in a different way in both theories. If equality is a criterion for selecting the principles of justice in the Rawlsian conception of justice, it is much more than this in the Cohenian egalitarian idea about justice. Even if both philosophers share the same practical convictions about the factual outcome of distributive justice, the difference principle advanced by Rawls is subject to the Cohenian critique and rescue. Chapter 4 highlights the difference principle as different from the Pareto principle, the Rawlsian interpretation of it and Rawls's argument for it. Chapter 5 describes the Cohenian rescue of the idea of equality from the Rawlsian theory, from the incentives argument used by the privileged in the interpersonal test in order to achieve greater benefits. Cohen's rescue proposes two readings of the difference principle, which show the underlying contradiction between the values of fraternity and reciprocity promoted by this principle and the incentives argument that advances the benefit of people already more advantaged than others due to morally arbitrary circumstances. The rescue is completed by a critique of the Pareto principle. Chapter 6 scrutinizes the Cohenian argument and explores some challenges, distinguishing three levels of any conception of justice. It confirms the rejection of the difference principle as a principle of justice, but not as a reasonably efficient policy of distribution. The Cohenian alternative to the difference principle, which proposes an egalitarian distribution of social goods, is presented in chapter 7. Yet, the feasibility of this distribution called D3 depends on the will of the citizens, whose daily interactions should be informed by an ethos of justice. A just society is obtained when just people, who make just social and economic decisions, live according to just principles, which also inform society's main institutions. The Cohenian model proposes that just people *and* just institutions achieve social justice and is thus to be favoured over the Rawlsian pattern of a just society based on basic institutions functioning justly.

The third part of the work discusses the results obtained in the first two parts. Besides the disagreement on the approach to justice, Rawls and Cohen also disagree on the definition and role of fundamental principles. This is the subject of chapter 8 as well as a discussion of the role of facts, explored at the end of the chapter. The disagreement on the status of facts is discussed in chapter 9. Whereas Rawls searches for a just social system, Cohen questions the concept of justice and the structure of principles and beliefs. The chapter compares the two philosophers' approaches, terminologies and even questions, and shows that the Rawlsian question is a factual question that needs a factual and pragmatic answer. Therefore, facts about the world and human nature should be available to the selectors of the most suitable principles of justice. But Cohen's question is a conceptual one rooted in the philosophical Socrato-Platonic tradition that searches for an answer to the question, "what is justice?". The selected principles should not be "suitable" to persons, but should represent the virtue of justice. Chapter 10 concludes that both philosophers have different understandings of justice, which implies different treatments of it. They also have different conceptions of society and attribute different roles to moral feelings and education. The constructivist Rawlsian approach and Cohenian conceptual analysis method are opposite approaches which arrive at different types (fact-dependent in the Rawlsian case and fact-free in the Cohenian case) of fundamental principles. These profound disagreements lead to a discord on the principles of distributive justice. Against the difference principle, Cohen presents an egalitarian distribution, whose feasibility will also be discussed.

1 The Rawlsian Theory of Justice

One of the aims of Rawls's TJ is to provide an alternative to utilitarian theories[1] of justice which in anglophile philosophy predominated in the 19th and 20th centuries, and whose influence has been profound within political philosophy. Utilitarianism is a theory in normative ethics, which judges the moral value of an action by the "utility" of its consequences. Bentham's classical version of this theory defines the utility of an action by the "greatest happiness of the greatest number" of sentient beings resulting from it, which is evaluated by the sum of pleasures and pains, satisfactions or dissatisfactions.

> Nature has placed mankind under the governance of two sovereign masters, pain and pleasure. It is for them alone to point out what we ought to do. [...] By the principle of utility is meant that principle which approves or disapproves of every action whatsoever according to the tendency it appears to have to augment or diminish the happiness of the party whose interest is in question: or, what is the same thing in other words to promote or to oppose that happiness. (An Introduction to the Principles of Morals and Legislation: 1)

Like individuals, who balance their gains and losses in order to pursue and to fulfill their desires, society balances the satisfaction and dissatisfaction of its members in order to realize their welfare. In keeping with utilitarian theories, the social institutions of a just society should be ordered in such a way that they satisfy "the principle of utility" known as "the greatest happiness principle". This principle states that society should realize the greatest happiness – the predominance, on overall balance, of pleasure or satisfaction over pain or dissatisfaction – of the biggest number of its members. However,

> for it is by the conception of the impartial spectator and the use of sympathetic identification in guiding our imagination that the principle for one man is applied to society. It is this spectator who is conceived as carrying out the required organization of the desires of all persons into one coherent system of desire; it is by this construction that many persons are fused into one (TJ: 27).

So, if one of the goals of traditional utilitarianism is that the greatest possible number of individuals in society maximize the fulfillment of their desires, the

1 There are many forms of utilitarianism, which are not all presented here. Rawls represents his theory of justice as an alternative to utilitarian thought in general. Besides, "the contrast between the contract view and utilitarianism remains essentially the same" (TJ: 22) in all its versions. Therefore, only the classical utilitarianism, as considered by Rawls is presented in the following.

utilitarian theory of justice would allow then the interests of some members in society to remain "fused into one", unspecified and thereby unrealized. Would it be fair to surrender the desires of some individuals for the welfare of the larger part of society? Why should such a theory of justice be accepted and put into practice by everyone in society if it treats the interests of some citizens unfairly? From the perspective of justice, it seems that not only the sum of satisfaction of the rational desires of the individuals matters, but also the distribution of this satisfaction between all individuals. In his search for an alternative to utilitarian theories of justice, Rawls focuses on the importance of the interests of each member of a society. Whereas "utilitarianism does not take seriously the distinction between persons" (TJ: 27) but emphasizes instead the importance of the welfare of the whole society, Rawls thinks it important to stress that "[e]ach person possesses an inviolability founded on justice that even the welfare of society as a whole cannot override" (TJ: 3). Each person has the equal right to achieve their desires. Therefore a society should be organized in a way that all its members can, in principle, realize their aims. A just society is not achieved when the greatest number of individuals satisfy their desires, but rather when each person in society has the same chance to realize what they strive for. "[Justice] does not allow that the sacrifices imposed on a few are outweighed by the larger sum of advantages enjoyed by many" (TJ: 4). Therefore, Rawls formulates in TJ and JF, a conception of justice that could be reasonably accepted by all members of a "liberal democratic society". His theory, terminology, and methodology are presented in the following by answering two main questions: 1. What are the necessary conditions for a theory of justice that does not sacrifice an individual's interests to the greater benefit of all? 2. Why do the Rawlsian principles of justice prove the most appropriate to regulate society's main institutions, which are in charge of the distributions of rights, duties, and benefits among members of society?

By calling the society "democratic" and "liberal", Rawls identifies the type of society that best suits his theory. Institutions of a liberal democratic society or "a reasonably just constitutional democratic society" (*The Law of Peoples*: 12) function under both ideals of liberty and equality while prioritizing liberty in the assignment of rights and liberties. In a liberal democracy, institutions are informed by the principle of equal liberty, so that citizens may live within social and economic inequalities, as long as they have equal basic rights and liberties, secured by the constitutional democratic regime.

> The only reason for circumscribing the rights defining liberty and making men's freedom less extensive than it might otherwise be is that these equal rights as institutionally defined would interfere with one another (TJ: 64).

Basic rights and liberties, which citizens of a just liberal democratic society equally have, include:

> political liberty (the right to vote and to be eligible for public office) together with freedom of speech and assembly; liberty of conscience and freedom of thought; freedom of the person along with the right to hold (personal) property; and freedom from arbitrary arrest and seizure as defined by the concept of the rule of law (TJ: 61).

This list presents two kinds of liberties: a positive liberty, which is the freedom to do something, and a negative liberty, which is the freedom from certain constraints imposed by others. Rawls explains the concept of liberty by a reference to three items: the agents, who are free to do something, the limitations to their freedom, and its object. "The general description of liberty, then, has the following form: this or that person (persons) is free (or not free) from this or that constraint (or set of constraints) to do (or not to do) so and so" (TJ: 202). The constraints are defined by law, so that liberty in the Rawlsian understanding is none other than a structure of institutions and public rules defining rights and duties. "The best arrangement of the several liberties depends upon the totality of limitations to which they are subject, upon how they hang together in the whole scheme by which they are defined" (TJ: 203). Thus the precedence of liberty corresponds to the priority of the system of equal basic liberties defined according to the principle of liberty that characterizes a liberal democratic society. Whereas exchanges between basic liberties and economic and social advantages are denounced, exchanges between basic liberties are permitted, only if a different basic liberty is protected and the system of liberties as a whole is thereby improved. However, Rawls distinguishes between liberty as a system of institutions, by which basic liberties are defined, and the worth of liberty. While liberty refers to the system of equal basic liberties, the worth of liberty "to persons or groups is proportional to their capacity to advance their ends within the framework the system defines" (TJ: 204). Although equal liberties are the same for all citizens, the value of liberty is not the same for all, insofar as some citizens due to natural and social differences have greater means and wealth to realize their ideas. But, if the worth of liberty is not the same for all members of society, this means that those individuals, who have finer abilities, are socially and by nature more advantaged than those individuals, with fewer abilities. The more advantaged citizens would reach their aims faster and easier. So, the basic difference regarding the worth of liberty is the cause of other social and economic differences. Thus, the Rawlsian inquiry is: How to realize a just society, even if the worth of liberty and its use differs from one person to another, where everyone would have, in principle, the chance to realize themselves?

Society is formed by a group of persons, who live together in social cooperation according to certain rules, in order to secure their welfare. Their decision to live and cooperate together is rational; through their collaboration, they achieve more benefits than each of them would achieve if they had to live on their own. Given that citizens aim at maximizing their benefits in a world in which resources are scarce, society is marked by a conflict of interests. This conflict occurs each time two or more competing citizens aim at securing the same positions or goods, or when the benefits of social cooperation are distributed. Rationally members of society always prefer a larger to a lesser share. Hence, Rawls endeavors to establish principles of justice that could over time regulate liberal democratic societies which are marked by conflicts of interests. His aim is to look for a conception of justice that regulates society and guarantees its relative stability and social justice over generations.

Rawls suggests that reasonable citizens of a liberal democracy would agree, regardless of their own interests and aims, to a just social contract that defines the terms of social cooperation. This social contract would ensure the good of all for a number of generations. He states that the social contract should determine the just assignment of rights and duties, as well as the fair distribution of income and wealth resulting from social collaboration. Both distributions, which are explored later in this chapter, reflect both ideals of liberty and equality and constitute the Rawlsian principles of justice. Rawls reverts the traditional conception of the social contract, as found in Locke, Rousseau, and Kant and aims at generalizing it at "a higher level of abstraction" (TJ: 3). The common idea of the social contract presupposes that people live in a state of nature, which is a hypothetical situation and precedes a state of society that is characterized by the creation of a government. In the state of nature, individuals would choose to agree with one another on a social contract in order to secure their primary natural rights[2] by delegating some of their natural rights and freedoms to the government and thereby entering the state of society. Locke formulates his theory of the social contract in the *Second Treatise of Government*, and argues that the government should preserve man's natural rights, liberties, and properties.

---

2 Note that some versions of the social contract consider that the state of nature is only marked by natural freedoms and not by natural rights. Besides, the definition of natural rights and freedoms differ from one version to another. However, if Thomas Hobbes suggests giving up the absolute liberties and consequently "the right to every thing" (*Leviathan*: 1, XIV) in the move towards a peaceful secure state of society, John Locke stresses the importance of preserving the primary rights, such as the right to life, liberty and property.

> Men being, as has been said, by nature all free, equal, and independent, no one can be put out of this estate and subjected to the political power of another without his own consent, which is done by agreeing with other men, to join and unite into a community for their comfortable, safe and peaceable living, one amongst another, in a secure enjoyment of their properties, and a greater security against any that are not of it (*Second Treatise of Government*: VIII, 95).

Jean-Jacques Rousseau also focuses on the importance of liberties in his conception of the social contract. But, he distinguishes between the natural liberties determined by the natural rights in a state of nature and the civil liberties identified by the social contract. The move into the state of society requires the loss of natural liberty and the gain of civil liberty. Furthermore he highlights a moral liberty greater than natural and civil liberties, and which is the obedience to law, acquired in the state of society.

> We might, over and above all this, add, to what man acquires in the civil state, moral liberty, which alone makes him truly master of himself; for the mere impulse of appetite is slavery, while obedience to a law which we prescribe to ourselves is liberty (*Social Contract & Discourses*: Book 1, Chap. VIII).

As to the property rights, unlike Locke, who thinks that the social contract should preserve property acquired in the state of nature, Rousseau explains that individuals have the right to property only through the social contract which establishes that right. The right of the first occupier is established only if necessary conditions are met: The land should not be inhabited, the occupier may only take what is necessary for his subsistence, and the occupier must take possession only by his labour and cultivation. Consequently, property is not a natural right, but rather a social benefit legitimized by the social consensus.

> In granting the right of first occupancy to necessity and labour, are we not really stretching it as far as it can go? [...] How can a man or a people seize an immense territory and keep it from the rest of the world except by a punishable usurpation, since all others are being robbed, by such an act, of the place of habitation and the means of subsistence which nature gave them in common? (Ibid., Chap. IX).

By institutionalizing private property, natural inequality among individuals in the state of nature would be strengthened by another material inequality in the state of society. Therefore, Rousseau describes the best system of legislation as a combination of both principles of civil liberty and equality according to what Rousseau calls the "general will". This is the sum of all individual wills, but which is different from these wills because "the general will" surpasses them in wisdom and always aims at the good and the just. On the one hand, Rousseau assumes that instead of eliminating natural inequality, the social contract would secure a moral equality for all members of society, so that they are all equal "by convention and legal right" (ibid.). On the other hand, he explains that equality does not refer to absolutely equal powers and riches;

> but that power shall never be great enough for violence, and shall always be exercised by virtue of rank and law; and that, in respect of riches, no citizen shall ever be wealthy enough to buy another, and none poor enough to be forced to sell himself which implies, on the part of the great, moderation in goods and position, and, on the side of the common sort, moderation in avarice and covetousness (Ibid., Book 2, Chap. XI).

Rawls approves Locke's general viewpoint about the importance of an agreement between all members of society, which would preserve their basic liberties, but he disagrees with him on the question of property rights. Regarding this point, he adopts Rousseau's philosophical position. Whereas, according to Locke, the government should safeguard property, a just society should, according to Rousseau, consider the material wealth of all its members, which should match the general will. Like Rousseau, Rawls agrees that property, among other things, is arbitrary, insofar as it depends on certain natural and social circumstances, which could advantage or disadvantage individual life opportunities. He also endorses Rousseau's point of view on natural inequality, which he does not want to see eliminated but substituted, by establishing moral equality as one of the principles of a civil society.

Even though the main ideas of the social contract found in Locke and Rousseau are adopted by Rawls, his version of the social contract is rooted in the Kantian political philosophy. Regarding the principle of equal liberty and the priority of equal basic liberties over other rights, Rawls on the one hand, assumes a "Kantian interpretation of the conception of justice from which this principle derives" (TJ: 251), based on Kant's concept of autonomy. An autonomous person acts upon principles "chosen by him as the most adequate possible expression of his nature as a free and equal rational being" (TJ: 252). So, free and equal persons should act autonomously and consent to moral principles selected on rational grounds, and applied to society's main institutions. These autonomous rational choices should not reflect people's economic and social circumstances, but rather a mutual recognition of their morally equal and equally free existence.

On the other hand, the Rawlsian principles of justice, selected to enhance the good of all members of society, "are also categorical imperatives in Kant's sense" (TJ: 253). Categorical imperatives in the Kantian understanding are principles of conduct that apply to rational free and equal persons unconditionally, without consideration of their aims or desires. Hence, Rawls's principles of justice are categorical imperatives insofar as they are universal, but they do not provide instructions for individual actions. They neither take into account the particular plans of life nor the particular circumstances to realize them, but rather the good of all free and equal citizens.

> To act from the principles of justice is to act from categorical imperatives in the sense that they apply to us whatever in particular our aims are. This simply reflects the fact that no such contingencies appear as premises in their derivation (ibid.).

In the Rawlsian theory of justice, the terms of social cooperation, settled within the social consensus, which have to be honored by almost[3] everyone within society, are fundamental in realizing justice in society. Rawls presents his social contract, as a "viable alternative" (TJ: 3) to all anterior ones.

> The main idea is that when a number of persons engage in a mutually advantageous cooperative venture according to rules, and thus restrict their liberty in ways necessary to yield advantages for all, those who have submitted to these restrictions have a right to a similar acquiescence on the part of those who have benefited from their submission (TJ: 112).

The conception of justice, which supports the Rawlsian social contract, is "justice as fairness". In the expression "justice as fairness", fairness qualifies justice as if Rawls affirms that the justice, he is looking for, is fairness. What is the just? Rawls would answer: The just is the fair. A just society, for example, where its members have the chance to realize their plans for life, is a fair society. But, before justifying the Rawlsian choice of justice as fairness, what does fairness imply?

> We are not to gain from the cooperative labors of others without doing our fair share. [...] [E]ach person receives a fair share when all (himself included) do their part (ibid.).

The Rawlsian understanding of fairness corresponds to the idea of "fairplay" in games or competitions.[4] The behaviour among the players or competitors is fair, not only when they follow the rules, but also when their dealings with one another are marked by mutual recognition and mutual respect. In a just society, citizens deal with one another in a fair way, which implies a mutual recognition

3 Persons that suffer from chronic illness may be excluded from social collaboration.

4 The Rawlsian concept of fairness is explained by Markus Stepanians (2009) in "Gerechtigkeit als Fairness, John Rawls' Theorie der Gerechtigkeit", p. 6-7.

and respect for the rights of others as free and equal persons with the same rights. Moreover, fairness implies an autonomous and fair choice of the principles which apply to the social system. It is an autonomous choice according to the Kantian interpretation of this notion, insofar as all representative members of society voluntarily consent to the most suitable principles, to which they would be committed. But,

> the essential point is that we need an argument showing which principles, if any, free and equal rational persons would choose and these principles must be applicable in practice (TJ: 255).

In order to justify the choice of the principles of justice, he imagines the original position, which corresponds to a hypothetical state of nature in other versions of the social contract. It is a reputed initial situation of equality, where representative members of society deal with one another in such a way that they attain the fairest principles of justice. The original position and the justification of their choice are explained further down.

Rawls argues that *any* social contract between members of society should be based on the idea of justice as fairness. He believes that by applying and adhering to the principles of the Rawlsian conception of justice, the mutual recognition of rights and the fair distribution of the benefits that result from social cooperation would be guaranteed. Once this has been established, citizens should be committed to the application of the principles of justice throughout their lives. What principles are most appropriate to rule the social system in a way that they realize social justice[5] and guarantee the rights of all?

> The problem of the choice of principles, however, is extremely difficult. I do not expect the answer I shall suggest to be convincing to everyone. It is, therefore, worth noting from the outset that justice as fairness, like other contract views, consists of two parts: (1) an interpretation of the initial situation and of the problem of choice posed there, and (2) a set of principles which, it is argued, would be agreed to (TJ: 15).

As already mentioned Rawls stresses the importance of a broad social consensus, which ensures that the interests of each member of society are taken into account, and which is accepted if it is fair. Individuals would not agree to an unfair theory that may, as it is the case in utilitarian theories, sacrifice their "happiness" on the altar of the greater good. Rawls builds his philosophical

5 According to Rawls, many things are said to be just, but his objective is about social justice. It is the way the main institutions of society distribute rights, duties and the division of income that result from social collaboration.

system for realizing social justice on the central idea of justice as fairness, but he relates it to six other fundamental ideas or requirements, so that the application of the first central idea – 1) justice as fairness – depends on the application of the other fundamental ideas. His political conception of justice is to be applied within 2) "society as a fair system of cooperation" by 3) "citizens as free and equal persons" on the 5) "basic structure" of 4) "a well-ordered society". As for the choice of the principles of justice that reflect the idea of justice as fairness, Rawls establishes what he regards as the most objective conditions for choosing them in a situation of hypothetical equality in the 6) original position. On a final level, he tests the acceptability and the stability of justice as fairness through the fundamental idea of 7) "public justification" and other ideas related to it, such as the "reflective equilibrium", the "overlapping consensus" as well as "public reason". These fundamental ideas in the Rawlsian theory are explored in the following.

1.1 Justice as Fairness

The first requirement of the conception of justice is that it is fair in order to be accepted and applied by all citizens of society. It is fair when it secures the rights and liberties of everyone as well as a fair distribution of a share of the benefits that result from social collaboration. The search for fairness is of primary importance because in a liberal democratic society, individuals may have to live with considerable, sometimes even gross, inequalities. For liberals, these inequalities are not morally bad in themselves as long as they were created justly. But they may have a deep influence on people's chances in life, their future plans and expectations. It is not morally bad in itself – how could it? – that some are more talented than others, but it is morally arbitrary. Social and economic inequalities result to a large degree from morally arbitrary circumstances. These circumstances are facts of two kinds. On the one hand the social contingencies, such as the social class into which citizens are born, and the natural contingencies, such as their innate talents and abilities, – such as, physical force, intellectual skills, good health, intelligence, beauty –, and on the other hand the good or bad luck they have in life. These endowments are morally arbitrary because there is no justification why some enjoy better endowments than others or why some are luckier than others. If natural and social advantages are not justified, it means they are undeserved. No one is entitled to being more endowed and no one deserves to be less endowed. Yet, individuals who are naturally and socially better endowed may use and improve their endowments to achieve greater benefits and to reach better positions than others.

Rawls aims at regulating and correcting, where necessary, in a fair way, inequalities based on morally arbitrary contingencies. Since the determination of the prospects in life depends to a large degree on social and natural endowments and the way they came about, there must be a conception of justice that mitigates the contingencies of natural endowment and social circumstance.

Moreover, according to Rawls, the expectations, for each individual, depend on a list of five different kinds of goods he takes to be "primary" and fundamental for a good life. Morally relevant inequalities among persons are differences in one or more of these primary goods. They could be called citizens' primary needs for complete engagement in society because they are what each person needs to be a fully cooperating member in society:

I. Basic rights and liberties.
II. Freedom of movement and thought, such as freedom from arbitrary arrest.
III. Powers of offices and positions of authority accessible to all, such as the right to be eligible for public office.
IV. Sufficient income and wealth distributed according to a fair policy.
V. The social bases of self-respect and self-confidence are the most important primary goods, because the agreement to a conception of justice for a liberal democratic society depends on each person's chances to satisfy their interests.

These are the primary goods that every citizen *needs* to be able to fully engage in social cooperation, where "need" suggests something necessary for a successful life in society. The principles of justice should regulate the assignment of primary goods in a way that secures equal basic rights and a fair distribution of income and wealth for all. The worth of liberty, – as defined in the beginning of this chapter – proportional to the capacities to achieve different aims and future plans, seems then to be proportional to the primary goods, which cover all these capacities. As a result, the least advantaged persons are those who have the lowest capacities and expectations in contrast to the most advantaged members, who have the highest capacities to realize their future plans.

Here another philosophical question arises regarding the treatment of inequalities resulting from morally arbitrary contingencies. As described before, for Rawls, natural and social endowments are arbitrary and undeserved, but what about the merits that result from improving and developing them? What would a fair treatment of morally arbitrary inequalities be, if no one merits the endowment they have or the position they reach through the improvement of these endowments? Although justice as fairness seeks to correct and nullify the effects of inequalities resulting from morally arbitrary contingencies, it does not aim at removing them. It hopes to realize justice within a "fair agreement on the basis of which those better endowed, or more fortunate in their social position, neither of which we can be said to deserve, could expect the willing cooperation of others when some workable scheme is a necessary condition of the welfare of all" (TF: 15). Rawls hopes that, through his conception of justice, the most and the least fortunate persons would be willing to collaborate upon fair terms of cooperation. The idea is that rational persons would agree to participate in social cooperation when it preserves their rights and liberties and their share of the distribution of income and wealth. Upon what terms does social cooperation ensure the rights and liberties as well as the parts of social and economic advantages for all?

1.2 A Fair System of Cooperation

Members of society should live – in the Rawlsian understanding of justice – within a fair system of cooperation. The idea of cooperation refers to the rational commitment of members of society to assist each other in order to create welfare for everyone. A scheme of collaboration is fair when citizens mutually recognize and respect the equality of rights possessed by all other participating citizens. They have to agree on rules and procedures fair to all. If social cooperation does not respect the rights of everyone, it is not fair and therefore neither accepted nor applied by everyone. Fair terms of cooperation should reflect the ideas of reciprocity and mutuality. Persons are situated as equals in relevant respects: Each participant knows that all participants, within their social cooperation, equally possess the same rights; each member has the right to pursue their own rational advantage. Thus, a democratic society is just when all members mutually collaborate upon fair terms of cooperation (mutuality), agreed to by all (reciprocity), in order to realize the interests of all. The Rawlsian conception of justice finds no application in non-democratic societies or in societies marked by unfair systems of cooperation. As an example of different cases of existing societies, which represent fair and unfair systems of social cooperation Germany, Turkey and Saudi Arabia will be compared in the following.

The Kingdom of Saudi Arabia, which is an absolute monarchy, with an Islamic government is characterized by discrimination against women. Saudi women do not have the same rights as men. They have fewer social and political rights. For example, in public every adult woman must be accompanied by a guardian, who is a close male relative (father, brother or husband). Although Turkey is a democratic constitutional republic, one of the reasons for withholding membership to the EU, is Turkey's poor human rights record; the Turkish government does not provide sufficient protection for religious minorities in the country. In both types of societies, Saudi Arabia and Turkey, human rights and liberties are not equally enforced for all members of society. Therefore, these societies cannot be regarded as fair systems of cooperation by all their citizens. A possible candidate, to which the Rawlsian theory of justice could be applied, is the German society. It is a society, where all citizens are free to pursue their rational advantage and claim the same human rights as all other citizens.

1.3 Free and Equal Citizens

In the Rawlsian conception of justice, citizens are conceived as free and equal persons. They are expected to be fully engaged in a fair system of social cooperation throughout their entire lives as detailed earlier in the example. To participate in social cooperation, citizens are required to apply their two moral powers. The first power affords a "sense of justice". It is the capacity to understand and to put into practice the principles of a conception of justice that specify the fair terms of social cooperation. The second power is the capacity to pursue an "understanding of the good". To cooperate fully in society, citizens need to exercise both moral powers. Members of a society are equal in so far as they possess, at least a minimum degree of the moral capacities that enable them to participate in social cooperation. While citizens are free to choose the conception of the good they want to pursue over their life, they have to agree on *one* conception of justice to put into practice, as a basis for mutual cooperation.

Although rational persons should consent to a political conception of justice in order to secure their benefits under fair terms of cooperation, Rawls conceives that they cannot be expected to agree on one mutual conception of the good to pursue in life. Indeed, a reasonable pluralism on the pursuit of the good is a defining feature of a democratic society. "This is the fact of profound and irreconcilable differences in citizens' reasonable comprehensive religious and philosophical conceptions of the world" (JF: 3). In American society, for example, Christians, Jews, Buddhists, Muslims, and Atheists live together in one system of cooperation, even though it is impossible for all groups to agree on one conception of the good as these different denominations all have different understandings of the good. They are, however, able to agree on a conception of justice for their society. So, in a reasonable pluralistic democratic society, citizens are *free* to choose their beliefs and convictions about what constitutes a good life although they are *equally* engaged in choosing and respecting the fair terms of social cooperation. Furthermore, Rawls distinguishes between reasonable and rational. Members of society are free and equal but also reasonable and rational. Reasonable persons are those who propose or accept and put into practice fair principles of social cooperation, agreed with others. They are ready to respect principles that are fair to all, even if doing so is sometimes detrimental to their own interests, whereas rational persons take advantage of their situation in society in order to realize only their own interests.

1.4 The Basic Structure of a Well-Ordered Society

A well-ordered society is a society ruled by a political conception of justice. Whereas the concept of a fair system of cooperation is about the collaboration between citizens upon a fair agreement, the concept of a well-ordered society refers to the social institutions that are organized by the political conception of justice. Society's main institutions should function according to the principles incorporated in the political conception of justice, i.e. justice as fairness in the Rawlsian case. Justice in the here relevant political sense does not apply to persons; it applies primarily to social institutions, which constitute the basic structure of a well-ordered society that Rawls defines as follows:

> For us the primary subject of justice is the basic structure of society, or more exactly, the way in which the major social institutions distribute fundamental rights and duties and determine the division of advantages of social cooperation. By major institutions I understand the political constitution and the principle economic and social arrangements (TJ: 7).

The choice of the principles of justice is made in the original position.

1.5 The Original Position

As indicated earlier, Rawls imagines a hypothetical situation where representatives of all social classes meet to negotiate and to choose the most reasonable principles of justice for their society. In this situation, they are equally positioned because they stand behind the "veil of ignorance". As already mentioned fairness implies the mutual recognition of the rights of other persons. But, fairness also corresponds to fair-play, which means the rejection[6] of every type of discrimination and egoism. Therefore, Rawls imagines the veil of ignorance

6 See Stepanians (2009), "Gerechtigkeit als Fairness", p. 10-11.

which would filter the information that leads to egoism and discrimination in the selection of the principles. Representatives, who stand behind the veil of ignorance, are uninformed of the social class they represent or whether they are advantaged or disadvantaged by social and natural contingencies.

> Although Rawls does not formulate it that way, we can imagine that the negotiators, when entering the original position, receive a serum injected, which causes, for the duration of the trial, a selective memory loss. After the application of the amnesia-serum, the parties have no longer certain information about themselves and the society in which they live. Among others, they have forgotten who they are, what sex they have, whether they are old or young, which religion and which ethnic group they belong to. Nor do they know whether they are rich or poor, what job they perform, and the economic and cultural state of their society. (Stepanians, Gerechtigkeit als Fairness: 11; my translation from the German).

They stand as free and equal persons who own the two moral powers and further powers and capacities that enable them to cooperate fully in society throughout their lives. As rational and reasonable persons, they have to decide about the principles that maximize their rights, liberties and the realization of their interests and ends, "ignoring any inclinations that might arise from envy" (JF: 88)[7]. The veil supposedly hides the information about particular interests, thus precluding any differences of interest among the members of society. Rawls divides the argument from the original position into two parts. Principles of justice are chosen in the first part. The representatives assume that the persons they represent "are not moved by the special psychologies (or attitudes)" (JF: 180), yet they have to select the most appropriate principles for society on the basis of human reason, shared by all citizens. Rawls argues that, because they do not know which social class they represent, they would decide to stay on the "safe side" by choosing the principles of justice that *secure* a maximum assignment of equal rights and liberties.

> It seems reasonable to suppose that the parties in the original position are equal. That is, all have the same rights in the procedure for choosing principles [...] the purpose of these conditions is to represent equality between human beings. [...] Together with the veil of ignorance, these conditions define the principles of justice as those which rational persons concerned to advance their interests would consent to as equals when none are known to be advantaged or disadvantaged by social and natural contingencies (TJ: 19).

---

7 Note that the Rawlsian conception of the representatives, who stand behind the veil of ignorance, "ignoring any inclinations that might arise from envy", has been extensively discussed and criticized by many philosophers. The emotion of "envy" is subject to many controversies, because of the complexity of its nature.

Representatives would also choose a principle for distributing the income and wealth that result from social cooperation. Moreover, according to Rawls, social and economic inequalities, which are morally arbitrary, would be regulated so that all members of society, from the most advantaged to the least advantaged, obtain a minimum (fair) share of income and wealth.

The second part of the argument from the original position concerns the question of the stability of the political conception of justice, justice as fairness. This question will be explored in the last part of this chapter.

The results of the social consensus reached in the original position are Rawls's two principles of justice.

1.6 The Principles of Justice

> [1.] Each person has the indefeasible claim to a fully adequate scheme of equal basic liberties, which scheme is compatible with the same scheme of liberties for all; and
> [2a.] Social and economic inequalities are to satisfy two conditions: first, they are to be attached to offices and positions open to all under conditions of fair equality of opportunity; and second, [2b.] they are to be to the greatest benefit of the least-advantaged members of society (the difference principle) (JF: 42-43).

It is important to mention the priority of the first principle over the second in the order of application, which reflects the priority of liberty over equality, discussed earlier in the chapter. The second principle, which is explored in the fourth chapter, should only be applied after the full application of the first. "The point is that if a political conception of justice covers the constitutional essentials[8], it is already of enormous importance even if it has little to say about many economic and social issues" (JF: 28). Moreover, this priority means that failures and omissions concerning equal liberty stated within the first principle cannot be compensated by social and economic advantages.

1.6.1 The First Principle of Justice

As to the first principle of justice, it states that all citizens have equal rights and liberties. This principle, which applies to the basic structure of society, requires institutions to accord basic rights and liberties equally to everyone. Citizens of a just society should hold the same set of basic rights and liberties. Their repre-

8 These are essential questions in political justice, such as the set of basic rights and liberties.

sentatives decide in the original position, once and for all, about the equality of the distribution of political liberty. Many of the primary goods to be secured by a just basic structure of society are taken into account by the first principle: the right to vote, together with the freedom of thought and movement, and protection from arbitrary arrest. As for the distribution of other primary goods, such as income and wealth, the equality of opportunity and the regulation of social and economic inequalities, they are included within the second principle of justice. The first principle is widely accepted even by the philosophical schools of thought that criticize the Rawlsian theory of justice, in contrast to the second principle of justice which has been the subject of fierce philosophical dispute.

1.6.2 Justifying the Principles of Justice

After choosing the principles of justice, Rawls justifies his choice through the fundamental idea of "public justification". It is a way of ensuring that the conception of justice adopted in the original position is also accepted, under the real-life conditions of a pluralistic democratic society, not limited by the veil of ignorance, by all citizens who follow different doctrines and have different convictions. Rawls wants to convince all "others" by "ways of reasoning" to accept his political conception of justice. "For justice as fairness to succeed, it must be acceptable, not only to our own considered convictions, but also of those of others" (JF: 27). By "others", Rawls refers to the citizens in society who do not have the same political points of view about questions such as the distribution of rights and liberties and the distribution of income and wealth. "If there is no conflict in judgment about questions of political justice [...] there is nothing to justify" (ibid.: 27). Rawls also refers on another level to the philosophical theories which disagree with him on the question of justice, such as the utilitarianism.

The public justification of the Rawlsian political conception of justice is successful when every member of a society, even if they hold different religious and philosophical views, agrees on the most essential questions: What fundamental principles should rule the basic structure of society? What are the equal basic rights and liberties of citizenship? The justification and acceptance of fundamental principles of justice, such as the set of basic rights and liberties that each citizen should have, constitute the essential elements of public justification. If these essentials are accepted by everyone, Rawls believes, their application will ensure the stability of a fair system of cooperation. He argues that each reasonable and rational member would accept the principles of justice as a safeguard for their basic rights and liberties:

> Clearly one leading aim of public justification is to preserve the conditions of effective and democratic social cooperation on a footing of mutual respect between citizens regarded as free and equal. Such justification depends on agreement in judgment at least on constitutional essentials (JF: 28).

Thus, the public justification seeks to justify the principles chosen for the social contract between members of society, who are expected from within their different conceptions of the good to agree on the conditions of fair social cooperation. If this aim is achieved, "we have an overlapping consensus of reasonable doctrines, and with it, the political conception affirmed in reflective equilibrium. It is this last condition of reasoned reflection that, among other things, distinguishes public justification from mere agreement" (JF: 29).

To explain the idea of "reflective equilibrium", Rawls starts from the idea of free and equal citizens, who are capable of exercising their two moral powers. If these powers are developed gradually over time, they can be exercised in many kinds of general judgements of justice concerning the basic structure of society as well as in everyday actions. The convictions of political justice – or what Rawls calls the considered judgements – are those developed when the two moral powers and the power of reason are exerted. However, judgements may differ from one person to another and may even be in opposition to other judgements that the same person has made on other occasions. "Many of our most serious conflicts are conflicts with ourselves" (JF: 30). But the aim is to achieve a reasonable agreement on questions of political justice. Each member of society should exercise his power of reason and moral powers to contemplate the questions of political justice. When achieving harmony between all their judgements and the political conception of justice of society, persons would be in a "narrow reflective equilibrium". This means that their own judgements are reflected in the political conception of justice. However, a person achieves the "wide reflective equilibrium" only after considering the arguments for many conceptions of justice. So, if citizens in society achieve the wide reflective equilibrium, they would, as Rawls argues, affirm justice as fairness[9] as the most appropriate political conception of justice for a liberal democratic society. Once they have mutually recognized that all citizens have achieved the wide reflec-

---

9 Citizens are ensured by justice as fairness to hold equal rights and liberties, guaranteed by the equal distribution of the same set of rights and liberties stated in the first principle of justice and a fair share of income and wealth, included within the second principle of justice.

tive equilibrium, they would reach the full reflective equilibrium. Whereas both the narrow and the wide reflective equilibrium should be reached by every citizen in society, the full reflective equilibrium is no other than the mutual recognition of all wide reflective equilibriums.

> The most reasonable political conception for us is the one that best fits all our considered convictions on reflection and organizes them into a coherent view. At any given time, we cannot do better than that. In justice as fairness, full reflective equilibrium is characterized by its practical aim [...]. In this way it meets the need for a basis of public justification on questions of political justice (JF: 32).

However, is it not utopian that all citizens – from within different and conflicting religious, philosophical and moral viewpoints – affirm the same political conception of justice?

It is obvious from the fact of reasonable pluralism that citizens affirm the same political conception of justice for many different reasons. "But this does not prevent the political conception from being a shared point of view from which they can resolve questions concerning the constitutional essentials" (JF: 32). The conception of justice does not contradict the different conceptions of the good that members of society pursue. It would therefore be supported by reasonable though conflicting views and affirmed in an overlapping consensus. Yet justice as fairness does gain the support of an overlapping consensus because "[i]ts requirements are limited to society's basic structure, its acceptance presupposes no particular comprehensive view, and its fundamental ideas are familiar and drawn from the public political culture" (JF: 33).

However, Rawls does not deny the possibility of a reasonable disagreement between members of society. He questions the sources of these disagreements and concludes that in such cases, many obstacles, – such as different epistemological positions, which make it sometimes hard to reason and evaluate – may hamper the correct use of the power of reason and the moral powers.

> [D]ifficulties are particularly acute in the case of political judgments in view of the great complexity of the questions raised, [...] and since we cannot eliminate these burdens, pluralism is a permanent feature of a free democratic culture. [...] Yet since we cannot as a democracy use state power, with its cruelties [...] to eradicate diversity, we look for a political conception of justice that can gain the support of a reasonable overlapping consensus to serve as a public basis of justification (JF: 36-37).

Thus, Rawls argues that, in a liberal democratic society characterised by a reasonable pluralism, citizens, who exercise their power of reason and moral powers from within their opposing religious, philosophical and moral convictions, would for many reasons affirm the same political conception of justice. This political conception of justice is not incompatible with their points of view. Rawls believes that justice as fairness can be supported and affirmed by all conceptions of the good in an overlapping consensus. In this reasonable agreement on the most appropriate way to rule society, different conflicting doctrines accept the Rawlsian conception of justice, which serves as a basis for public justification.

Moreover, equal citizens who exercise their power of reason and moral powers may impose rules on other citizens in order to convince them of the most appropriate political conception of justice. They should agree first on which criteria or public reason the principles of justice are selected. The primary agreement is mainly on the formal ways of reasoning (individual, associational, or political), the rules of evidence and the principles of inference as well as the relevant information and knowledge on questions of political justice. Every theory should be examined by public reason: "the knowledge and ways of reasoning, the plain truths now common and available to citizens generally" (JF: 89). The second agreement is on the principles of justice. If members of society consent to a fair political conception of justice, with the use of moral powers and power of reason according to public reason, they will apply the principles of justice. But what happens if disagreements arise?

Members of a democratic regime of free and equal citizens, enjoy a certain measure of power which is based on the power of the state. If disagreements arise on the essential societal principles of justice, citizens may use their coercive power in the light of public reason to force other members of society to accept the conception of justice: Citizens should learn and apply the concepts and principles of public reason which are part of common human reason.

> In sum, public reason is the form of reasoning appropriate to equal citizens who as corporate body impose rules on one another backed by sanctions of state power. As we have said, shared guidelines for inquiry and methods of reasoning make that reason public, while freedom of speech and thought in a constitutional regime make that reason free (JF: 92).

Likewise, the well-ordered society is to realize what Rawls calls the condition of full publicity as the political conception of justice has an educational function. The idea of full publicity refers to three mutual recognitions that citizens of a well-ordered society realize: The mutual recognition of the principles of justice and the belief that the main institutions of society apply these principles, as well as the mutual recognition of the general facts according to which they are selected; also the mutual recognition of the complete justification of justice as fairness through overlapping consensus. It would be possible to satisfy the condition of full publicity through the educational role of the political conception of justice. The Rawlsian hope is to achieve a society where the ideological consciousness, or the different illusions and delusions about the conceptions of person and society, is overcome.

> [T]hose who grow up in a well-ordered society will, in good part, form their conception of themselves as citizens from the public culture and from the conceptions of the person and society implicit in it. Since justice as fairness is worked up from fundamental intuitive ideas belonging to that culture, this role is central to it (JF: 122).

However, given that members of a society consent to the Rawlsian conception of justice, is justice as fairness able to "generate sufficient support for itself" (JF: 181)?

The question of the stability of justice as fairness depends on the one hand on whether different reasonable groups of society accept the conception of justice and on the other hand on its capacity to generate justice over time. The question of the acceptance of justice as fairness is examined within the overlapping consensus. The second question is whether citizens, who live and grow up under the principles of justice as fairness, would normally "comply with just arrangements and are not moved to act otherwise, say, by social envy and spite, or by a will to dominate or a tendency to submit" (JF: 181). The meaning of stability is that citizens act voluntarily in a way that secures justice over time. Is justice as fairness a stable political conception of justice?

Justice as fairness is a liberal conception to be applied in a democracy, characterized by reasonable pluralism, because it is endorsed as just with an overlapping consensus by conflicting religious, philosophical and moral doctrines. It is designed to gain the support of all conceptions of the good of society. Within its principles, it addresses each citizen's reason and satisfies their interests. Over time citizens will act according to the principles of justice, because the good they pursued after years of living under justice as fairness would be what justice requires.

> For in the well-ordered society of justice as fairness, the just and the good (as specified by that political conception) fit together in such a way that citizens who count as part of their good being reasonable and rational and being seen by others as such, are moved by reasons of their good to do what justice requires (JF: 202).

In sum, in his search for an alternative to utilitarian political theories of justice, Rawls suggests justice as fairness as the most appropriate political conception of justice for a liberal democratic society. This society is marked by reasonable pluralism, which is a characteristic of democratic societies. Rawls relates justice as fairness to other fundamental ideas in a fair system that distributes rights, liberties, and social and economic advantages. Justice as fairness should be applied to the basic structure of a well-ordered society according to the principles of justice. These principles are chosen in the original position. The aim is to agree, behind the veil of ignorance, on a maximum of rights and liberties, and a share of income and wealth. Representatives of all social classes would choose in the original position an equal distribution of rights and liberties and a fair distribution of income and wealth. Rawls argues that these principles are the most appropriate for governing a liberal democratic society. However, he justifies the choice of the principles through public justification. Each reasonable and rational citizen would accept justice as fairness, which secures everyone's rights and liberties. So, within an overlapping consensus, free and equal citizens, would affirm justice as fairness even if they hold opposing conceptions of the good, because after considering many conceptions of justice, justice as fairness secures every person's interests. Moreover, the stability of the Rawlsian theory depends on its acceptability, which depends on its fairness. Moreover, for justice as fairness to succeed, it should secure the preservation of justice over time from one generation to the next. Following Rawls, citizens, who grow up in a society ruled by the principles of justice, act from within justice. The good they pursued would be pursued under conditions of justice.

The first principle of justice is widely accepted because it guarantees the same set of basic rights and liberties for all. This seems plausible and has proven to be largely uncontroversial. However, the same cannot be said about Rawls's second principle of justice, which has been contested. Why has the second principle of justice, which includes fair equality of opportunity and regulation of social and economic advantages to the greatest benefit of the least advantaged members of society, been the subject of so much philosophical dispute?

2 A Meta-Ethical Theory: Cohen's Idea of Justice

Because of its enormous influence on political philosophy, Rawls's TJ has been widely scrutinized, defended and criticized. Cohen's monograph, RJE, may be considered the profoundest and most challenging critical work on Rawls's TJ. Cohen's book questions the justice of inequalities that result from unequalizing incentives. In fact, within the Rawlsian theory of justice, the most productive citizens are permitted to increase their productivity and are thus able to gain (greater) economic benefits. These benefits are intended as an incentive to encourage these more productive people to enhance their productivity from which the entire society would benefit. According to Rawls, the inequalities that result from the incentives are just, as long as the economic and social situation of the worst-off citizens is improved. Whereas Cohen recognizes the efficiency of such an unequal economic distribution, he does not think that the resulting inequalities are just. Therefore he does not accept that greater efficiency is compatible with justice: "[W]hile I could see that it might be sensible for all concerned to offer [those] unequalizing incentives [...] I could not see why that would make the resulting inequality just" (RJE: XV). Consequently, RJE aims at rescuing the concepts of justice and equality from the Rawlsian liberal argument that distorts their nature.

RJE is divided into two parts. In the first part, Cohen attempts to "rescue" the concept of equality from Rawls's treatment of it, by providing a sophisticated critique of the Rawlsian theory of justice, and focusing on the difference principle. According to Cohen, "in a society in which distributive justice prevails, people's material prospects are roughly equal: distributive justice does not tolerate the deep inequality, driven by the provision of economic incentives to well-placed people, that John Rawls and his followers think a just society displays" (RJE: 2).

The second part of the book endeavours to "rescue" the concept of justice from the Rawlsian liberal argument, which links it to the rules for social living, for which other values are relevant than justice. This is the constructivist treatment that Cohen conceives distorts the meaning of justice by unduly mixing its content with other values, such as feasibility and efficiency.

> On the constructivist view, the content of justice is identified by the rules for social living, the rules of regulation that would be chosen in a privileged choosing situation [...]. My rescue of justice denies the mooted identification on two grounds: if rules of social living are soundly based, they will reflect both values other than justice and practical constraints that restrict the extent to which justice can be applied. That being so, justice, itself, could not be what is specified by such rules (RJE: 3).

One must remember that the principles of justice within Rawls's theory are chosen in the original position. Representative members of all social classes within a society are behind a veil of ignorance, which masks all the truths about their economic and social situation as well as their psychological characteristics. The information they are provided with, and according to which they choose the most suitable principles of justice for their society, are facts about their human nature as well as general information about economics and human psychology. The results arrived at by the selected principles of justice thus reflect the reality of the human condition, as the most important information available to the representatives. The selected principles of justice are a direct and reasonable response to the general facts of life in such societies. Not only Rawls, but "most philosophers who provide an answer to the question whether principles are grounded in facts say that (sound) normative principles, as such (and, therefore, all of them), are (at least inter alia) grounded in the facts of human nature and of the human situation" (RJE: 229).

Apart from the rescue of the concept of justice from the Rawlsian treatment, Cohen presents in the second part of RJE his own understanding of justice and his own methodology to comprehend its principles. The rescue of justice from the Rawlsian theory directly follows from Cohen's idea and principles of justice. Thus, the part of RJE[1] that Cohen describes as "meta-ethical", concerns the meta-ethical thesis, which is about the relationship between facts and normative principles. The initial question asks what meta-ethical means?

In philosophy, meta-ethics is a self-reflective and theoretical branch of ethics, which seeks to understand the meaning and the nature of ethical evaluations and the foundation of moral judgements. Many meta-ethical theories and disputes deal with central questions in meta-ethics, such as, the origin and the nature of right and wrong, the objectivity or subjectivity of normative principles, and whether from an "ought" follows an "is".[2] However, Cohen's thesis is not meta-ethical in that sense; "although my thesis is undoubtedly meta-ethical, it is neutral with respect to what one may reasonably regard as the central question of meta-ethics" (RJE: 257). So even if it is not meta-ethical in the traditional fashion, since it is distinct from the questions that dominate the meta-ethical literature, the Cohenian thesis is meta-ethical in the sense that it

1 The meta-ethical part of RJE concerns chapters 6 and 7, where Cohen respectively presents his understanding of justice and the appropriate methodology to reach the fundamental principles of justice.

2 This main question in meta-ethics, whether from an "ought" follows an "is" is discussed later on in this chapter.

concerns the structure of a person's principle beliefs. His theory has a meta-ethical character, as it examines what is beyond and behind the sphere of ethics; it inspects and reflects upon the system of principles and the structure of people's beliefs. Moreover Cohen's inquiry is not about the substance of justice, but about the thinking and the very idea of justice in the structure of beliefs. Therefore, his rescue, in the second part of RJE, is not interested in the substance of justice, but rather the concept of justice and all other relevant concepts. What is the structure of principled beliefs? How are the principles connected with one another? Why does the Cohenian thesis that explores the relationship between facts and principles constitute a rescue of the concept of justice? These questions are answered in the following four sections by analyzing chapter 6 of RJE. The meta-ethical thesis is presented in the first section followed by an examination of the arguments which Cohen uses to defend the thesis in the second part. The last three parts investigate the thesis further and respond to possible critiques. Finally Cohenian conclusions on the concept of justice are presented as well as Thomas Pogge's critique of Cohen's meta-ethical thesis.

As indicated earlier, Cohen's thesis concerns the relationship between facts and normative principles. (It is worth noting that Cohen calls "normative principles" simply "principles", and that I will follow him in this practice). "A normative principle, here, is a general directive that tells agents what (they ought, or ought not) to do" (RJE: 229). For example, a normative principle of justice supposedly tells people what they should do and what they should not do in order to act in line with justice. However, "a fact is, or corresponds to, any truth, *other than (if any principles are truths) a principle*" (ibid.), such as the facts of human nature. Principles might be facts in the broader sense of "fact", where facts represent all truths including true principles.[3] But, in the narrower Cohenian understanding of facts and principles, normative principles are not facts; they are related to facts. Normative principles are general directives related to any truths one might suppose support these principles. According to Cohen, most philosophers believe that, in order to be justified, normative principles should be grounded in facts about human life. How does Cohen describe the relationship between facts and normative principles? Cohen argues that philosophers who believe that normative principles are grounded in the facts of

3 Cohen believes that his argument is "robust across permissible variations in the meaning of "fact", and it is also neutral across contrasting conceptions of the relationship of fact and value" (RJE: 230).

human nature and of the human situation are mistaken. The central aim of his thesis is to disprove this belief.

> The thesis to be defended here contradicts what many people [...] think, to wit, that our beliefs about matters of normative principle, including our beliefs about the deepest and most general matters of principle, should reflect, or respond to, truths about matters of fact: they should, that is, – *this is how I am using "reflect" and "respond to"* – include matters of fact among the grounds for affirming them (RJE: 231).

A normative principle is grounded in a fact, or responds to a fact, or is supported by a fact, or reflects a fact, or is justified by a fact, or is fact-sensitive, whenever the fact constitutes at least part of the grounds for affirming the principle. Therefore, facts constitute one of the reasons for affirming principles; it is because of definite facts, that certain normative principles are affirmed. That a principle is justified by a fact means that the fact corresponds to the "principle-grounding" of a principle and its "reason-providing power" (RJE: 234). Cohen accepts the grounding relationship between facts and normative principles, trying to find the reason (raison d'être) why a fact can in general ground a principle. But he disagrees with most philosophers who affirm that *all* sound normative principles should be grounded in facts. "I am happy for facts to be whatever my opponents in this debate, [...] (reasonably) understand them to be" (RJE: 231).

He illustrates his disagreement about the status of facts in grounding normative principles by referring to the constructivist approach to justice. According to Cohen, constructivists conceive that our beliefs about principles should reflect facts about human nature, for example,

> the fact that human beings are liable to pain, or the fact that they are capable of sympathy for each other, and also facts about human social organization, such as the tendency for people to encounter collective action problems, or for societies to be composed of individuals who have diverse interests and conflicting opinions (ibid.).

2.1 Cohen's Thesis

The Cohenian thesis includes two important affirmations that reveal his philosophical disagreement with most political philosophers, in particular with the constructivists. On the one hand, it cannot be true that all normative principles, which govern human life, are fact-sensitive. Some principles are fact-sensitive and others are fact-insensitive meaning that they do not respond to facts. On the other hand, Cohen states that a principle can respond to a fact, only because it is a response to a fact-insensitive principle. In other words, not all normative principles reflect facts; and principles reflecting certain facts should, in order to reflect these facts, reflect a principle, which does not reflect (those) facts. Cohen examines the principles grounded in facts and the facts that ground them. He does not aim to answer the question whether a principle can follow from a fact, but he explores the principles that are already grounded in facts. His questions are: What makes a principle a principle? What fact grounds a principle?

The Cohenian thesis should apply to every principle and to the structure of anyone's principles. Individuals should know what their principles are and the grounds for holding them. Cohen theorizes that on the basis of believing in F, which is a proposition that states a certain fact, a person affirms a principle P. If the constructivists think that fact F suffices for grounding and justifying the principle P, Cohen agrees that the fact supports the principle, but he wants to explain why; He upholds the thought's supportive, reason-providing power. According to him, a person affirms the normative principle P, which is, however, supported by the fact F, only because they affirm a more ultimate principle P1. This P1 is an ultimate principle in the sense that it "would survive the denial of *P* itself, a principle, moreover, which holds whether or not *F* is true, and which explains why *F* is a reason for affirming *P*: it is always a further principle that confers on a fact its principle-grounding and reason-providing power" (RJE: 234).

So, if a fact F grounds a principle P, this grounding relationship is possible only because another relationship between the principle P (sensitive to the fact F) and a principle P1 insensitive to F or any other facts. To illustrate the relationship between facts, fact-sensitive principles and fact-insensitive principles, one should look at the optical metaphors employed by Cohen and compare the principle P1 to a source of light. A principle P reflects a fact F, because of the light emitted by P1, which is the source of light. The light irradiates the relationship between P and F and facilitates the reflection between P and F by illuminating it and thus making it visible. The ultimate principle P1 is the light that makes the principle P reflect the fact F, and the light remains as it is, even if the principle P is denied and the fact F is not true. Cohen determines the way normative principles are connected with one another in the structure of principled beliefs: Some of them are sensitive, and some are insensitive to facts, but, it is always a fact-insensitive principle that confers on a fact its principle-grounding power. Cohen argues that "the original principle, *P*, presupposes a principle that is insensitive to *all* facts, a principle, that is, which is insensitive not only to *F*, but which is *altogether* fact-insensitive" (ibid.). In fact he believes there is a difference, between an original or a fundamental principle and a fact-insensitive principle. The fundamental principle is insensitive to all facts and cannot be derived from other principles. The fact-insensitive principle is insensitive to certain facts and sensitive to other facts, and can be derived from fundamental principles, which are not derived from other principles and which do not rest on factual grounds.

To see the difference between these two principles, an example employed by Cohen is presented and discussed in the following.[4] In his illustration, he imagines a person who affirms a principle P, on the basis of a fact F. This person "treats F as a reason of affirming P" (ibid.). Cohen holds the view that this is possible, only because the person affirms a more ultimate principle P1, "that holds whether or not F is true and that explains why F is a reason for affirming P" (ibid.). So, it is always an ultimate fact-insensitive principle P1, according to which a fact F can ground a principle P. The person affirms the principle P that we should keep our promises because of fact F, which states that only when promises are kept can projects be successfully pursued. The fact F is not the only ground for affirming the principle P, but it is a plausible one. According to Cohen, a person who believes that F supports P, "surely" believes also the principle P1, which says that we should help people pursue their projects. Cohen argues that

> it is *P1*, which makes *F* matter, which makes it support *P*, but the subject's affirmation of *P1*, as opposed to whether or not that affirmation induces her to affirm *P* itself, has nothing to do, essentially, with whether or not she believes that *F*. She would affirm *P1* even if she did not believe the factual statement *F*: *P1* is not, in her system belief, sensitive to whether or not *F* is true (ibid.).

So if a person finds fact F is false, they will modify their affirmation of the principle P, but not their affirmation of the principle P1, which remains unaltered. However, even if principle P1 is insensitive to fact F, it could still be sensitive to fact F1, which alleges that people can achieve happiness only if they are able to pursue their own projects. In this case, F1 supports P1, only in the light of a more ultimate principle P2, which says that "people's happiness should be promoted". But, "it is possible that there will be no [further] fact on which that principle, P2, is grounded" (RJE: 235). Yet F2 would support P2, only in the light of a more ultimate principle P3, which holds that we should express our respect for people. This principle P3 could be grounded in the fact F3, that "people possess what are thought to be respect-meriting characteristics" (ibid.). Cohen proceeds in analyzing the system of beliefs, until the relevant, basic, fundamental,

4 See the Cohenian illustrations, RJE p. 234-235.

fact-free principle is arrived at, called earlier the "original" principle. So, while a fact-free principle cannot reflect any facts at all, a fact-insensitive principle is relatively insensitive to certain facts but sensitive to other facts. An original principle or a fact-free principle is strictly insensitive to all facts.

> The relevant basic fact-free principle P4 may then be: one ought to respect beings, human or otherwise, who have the relevant characteristics. Note that P4 is immune to denials that human beings, or any beings, have the relevant characteristics. To be sure, P4 is inapplicable if no beings have such characteristics, but that certain beings do have such characteristics is nevertheless no ground for affirming P4 (ibid.).

So in order to examine the structure of a person's beliefs, principles, and the grounds for affirming them, we should proceed from fact-sensitive principles, which are supported by facts, to ultimate principles, which are either fact-insensitive, or fact-sensitive, until the original fact-free principle is arrived at. What follows from the Cohenian thesis is that ultimate principles cannot be justified by facts. They can be justified in another way:

> For my argumentative purposes, fact-free principles might be self-evidently true, or they might for some other reason require no grounds or they might need grounds and have grounds of some non-factual sort [...], or they might need grounds but lack them, or, [...] they might be judged outside the space of grounds, [...] they might not be objects of belief at all (RJE: 238).

However, one could also start with a different fact F that would support the principle P, so that other fact-free principles would be reached. The principle P could be, otherwise, grounded in fact F that breaking promises is wrong because it is a violation of trust. In this case, the ultimate principle is that one should not transgress trust. "And that more ultimate principle is either itself fact-insensitive, or, if it is indeed fact-sensitive, you will know by now how I would press beyond it to a fact-insensitive one" (RJE: 236).

So, the relationship between a fact and a principle exists because this principle is related to another principle, which is not related to the fact. Without their tight relation with ultimate principles, (normative) principles cannot be reflected in facts. Cohen consolidates his thesis with an argument based on three premises, each of which is presented, argued and defended.

2.2 The Argument

The first premise is that there is always an explanation why a fact F constitutes one of the grounds for affirming the principle P: "an explanation of how, that is,

F represents a reason to endorse *P*" (ibid.). Cohen affirms this premise in the light of another more general "self-evidently true" claim that says that "there is always an explanation why any ground grounds what it grounds" (ibid.). Cohen thinks that this claim seems self evidently-true, and he therefore does not need to defend it. At this level of the argument, the explanation for why a ground grounds what it grounds that Cohen is searching for is not defined yet.

This explanatory form is determined by a second premise that presupposes a more ultimate principle P1, which survives the denial of fact F and explains why fact F confers support on the principle P. In order to support his second premise, Cohen "challenges anyone who disagrees to provide an example in which a credible and satisfying explanation of why some *F* supports some *P* invokes or implies no such more ultimate principle" (ibid.). Here Cohen has not yet affirmed that the more ultimate principle should be fact-free as opposed to insensitive to particular facts and sensitive to others.

Cohen proceeds in the analysis of the principles from the more ultimate principle, which is on the second level of the argument, to an even more ultimate one. And, "once that more ultimate principle has been stated, whether *it*, in turn, is based on any fact, and so on, reiteratively, as many times as may be required, until she comes to rest with a principle, which reflects no fact, unless the sequence of interrogation proceeds indefinitely" (RJE: 237). In order to defend this premise, Cohen tries to deny it, by affirming that the sequence of interrogation can continue indefinitely. However, he finds this implausible, even impossible since it would violate the self-understanding stipulation. The self-understanding stipulation or the clarity of mind requirement affirms that the person, who affirms the principles, should be able to know what their principles are and the grounds for holding them. "The thesis applies to anyone's principles, be they correct or not, *so long as she has a clear grasp both of what her principles are and of why she holds them*" (RJE: 233). It is implausible and impossible, because it is very difficult for persons with finite capacities to construct a sequence of indefinite numbers of principles. Besides, "we can surely say that a person, who cannot complete the indicated sequence, because she has to go on forever, does not know why she holds the principles she does" (RJE: 237). An unending sequence of justifications violates the self-understanding requirement, indicated earlier, for any person who wants to affirm normative principles.

> It follows from the stated premises that, as I claimed, every fact-sensitive principle reflects a fact-insensitive principle: that is true both within the structure of the principled beliefs of a given person, as long as she is clear about what she believes and why she believes it,

> and, [...] within the structure of the objective truth about principles, if there is an objective truth about principles (ibid.).[5]

2.3 The Defenses

As to the first premise, it does not say that every principle should be grounded in something, but rather whenever a principle is grounded in a fact, there is always an explanation that explains that grounding relation. Cohen insists on the term "explanation", which is different from justification. A principle is justified by the fact it reflects, but this justification needs to be explained by analyzing the sequence of principles in order to answer why the fact (a ground) grounds the principle (what) it grounds. Cohen claims that the answer implies a further principle, and the sequence reaches its end, i.e. a fact-insensitive principle, to which Cohen's question (why does this fact support this principle?) does not apply.

Yet the defense of the second premise is indeed a defense of the role and the status of fact-insensitive principles, in explaining the grounding relation between facts and fact-sensitive principles. Following Cohen, there is no other alternative that fulfills the explanatory role of fact-insensitive principles. He anticipates possible objections, which might accept the first premise that there must be an explanation why a fact F supports a principle P, but deny the second premise, which says "that the only type of explanation cites a further normative principle" (RJE: 239). According to Cohen, Rawls, who chooses the original position device for generating the principles of justice, or any other constructivists, would cite a methodological principle to explain why the principle P is supported by the fact F. A methodological principle is not a normative principle telling the agents what they ought or ought not to do, but rather gives them a methodology for choosing the normative principles. So, the constructivists explain why the facts support the normative principles chosen in the constructivist procedure, such as the original position[6] procedure, by a further principle. This further principle, incorporated in the procedure is not normative, but methodological.

---

5 Following Cohen, his thesis holds even if there is no objective truth about principles. In this case, beliefs about principles are "expressions of endorsement, or universal commands" (ibid.).

6 For a further presentation of the original position, see chapter 1.

> The objector says: yes, something more general than the principle supported by a fact explains why that fact supports that principle, but the required more general principle can be something other than a normative principle itself (RJE: 240).

Cohen offers two replies to the objection by referring to the original position machine, and thereby defending the second premise of the argument. One must remember that the original position procedure is a hypothetical situation imagined by Rawls to justify his choice of the principles of justice. According to Rawls, representatives of social classes would stand in the original position, under the same conditions of knowledge and ignorance in order to choose the most suitable principles for the regulation of their social cooperation. The Cohenian reply entails, on the one hand, the suspension of the facts available to the persons in the original position. If these facts are suspended, the persons in the original position would choose a normative principle insensitive to facts. "[I]t will not be possible for those who endorse the original position methodology and, therefore, the *P* that it selects in the light of the facts, to deny *P1*, or its justificatory role" (ibid.).

On the other hand, Cohen considers that the procedure, which is Rawls's original position, is not itself justified. Therefore, not only the selected principles should be justified but also the principles that justify the selection of the procedure itself. Yet, Cohen stresses what he considers to be a contradiction in the Rawlsian theory: Whereas Rawls affirms that fundamental principles of justice should depend on facts about human nature and condition, he, also affirms that "not everything is constructed" (*Political Liberalism*: 103). Moreover, according to Cohen, Rawls justifies the original position device for the selection of the principles of justice because it reflects a fact-insensitive principle, which says that persons are free and equal.

Concerning the third premise, Cohen replies to a possible holistic objection, which supports every statement by a subset of statements. "On a holistic view, justifications lie not on a line with a beginning and an end, but on a finite beginningless and endless network of (now branching, now converging) lines of justification that runs through a body of belief and along which one may travel for as long as one likes" (RJE: 241). So, the holistic objection says that a person knowing what their principles are and the grounds for holding them could continue indefinitely justifying their principles, with their finite beliefs. Cohen affirms against this objection that the statements and their impacts on one another should not be considered in a holistic way. In fact, some statements are sensitive to certain facts and insensitive to other facts. For example, facts about human psychology are insensitive to facts of astronomy. Therefore, the statements about human psychology do not affect in anyway the substance of the statements about astronomy.

> It would require exposition of an enormous network to connect [those facts]. [...] It is always a legitimate question, even for a holist, whether there is any substantial influence of one sort of statement on another, for selected statements, and sometimes the answer is: no (RJE: 242).

Cohen does not agree on the holistic view that affirms fact-insensitive principles and facts belonging to a whole, because it is extremely difficult to prove that "a change in one's view of a principle can alter one's belief about the sort of fact that they think supports principles" (RJE: 243).

In order to consolidate his defense of the thesis, Cohen highlights it in two further examples, which show how he reaches, at the end of the sequence of normative principles, a normative affirmation that is not grounded in any facts.

In the first example, Cohen supposes the factual statement that religion is important in some people's lives. Upon this fact, the normative principle which announces the freedom of religion is affirmed. Cohen's thesis says that if a person believes that this fact supports this principle, it is because they believe a more general principle, independent from this fact. This ultimate principle could state that people should be free to pursue what they believe to be important in their lives. The sequence of principles does not reach its end at this level. Cohen suggests, through an analysis of the principled beliefs, proceeding from one normative principle to a more ultimate one, until the last normative principle is arrived at, which is not grounded in any facts at all.

The second illustration considers the principle that affirms that human bodies should be treated with caution upon the factual statement that says that human beings have nervous systems. Following Cohen, the followers of this principle based on this fact, believe another fact, namely that organisms with nervous systems are liable to pain. However, the latter fact – that Cohen calls G – (beings with nervous systems are liable to pain) makes the first fact (human beings have nervous systems) a reason for affirming the normative principle (human bodies should be treated with caution). "But the question remains, what confers that potency on *G*? And the answer, manifestly, is a further principle, *P1*, which says that, absent other considerations, *one should avoid causing pain*. And *P1* is probably the relevant end-of-line fact-independent principle here" (RJE: 245).Cohen goes on to present further explanations of the character of his thesis such as the clarity of mind required of persons who affirm the normative principles, using the Cohenian method. Every person is expected to apply this method, if they want to reach fact-free principles. In order to achieve this aim, the person must exhibit a certain clarity of mind but should also realize and respect the conditional character of the Cohenian thesis. What does the conditional character of the thesis imply? Is it feasible, to demand that all the followers of the principles on the Cohenian conceptual analysis methodology, meet the prerequisite of having the same clarity of mind?

2.4 The Requirements

The condition of clarity of mind is a requirement to be satisfied by those who affirm the principles. As indicated earlier, the person, who believes certain principles, should have a reflective self-understanding of the affirmed principles. This means that the person should know what their principles are and why they believe them. What are the grounds that support these principles? Cohen observes that "the clarity of mind requirement is by no means universally satisfied by affirmers of principles: people display contrasting degrees of certainty with respect to why they affirm the principles that they affirm" (ibid.). For example, two persons could affirm the same normative principle that says that beings should be protected against suffering. They both know what their principle is. But the status and the nature of this normative principle and the way they reach it could be different. Whereas the first person considers this principle as an ultimate normative affirmation independent from any facts, a second affirmer could consider it fact-sensitive if they ground it on other factual statements and thereby affirm it for other reasons. Moreover, Cohen imagines two cases presented in the following, where it is very difficult to "understand why we believe the principles that we affirm" (RJE: 246) and, therefore, difficult to explain the normative significance of these principles. Hence, he stresses the reflective and enlightening role of philosophy, which should specify what one ought to know. But, even in those difficult cases, his thesis remains applicable: "[W]here a principle P is affirmed in the light of certain facts, we can ask for a fact-free principle which explains why P is affirmed in the light of those facts" (ibid.).

The first example imagines someone who lives for only twenty-four hours. Cohen asks what principles could be affirmed for this person. Would freedom matter more than welfare? The answer is difficult because "we don't know what it is about decades that makes their normative significance different from that of twenty-four hours" (ibid.). In the second example Cohen imagines that a foetus, instead of becoming humanoid, regresses and becomes less human-like until one day before being born when it miraculously becomes a human. He then poses the normative question whether in such a case an abortion is legitimate two days before birth when the foetus in this hypothetical situation would still not be a human. “Our norms are formed under the factual constraint that fetus-age goes with foetus-level-of-development, but since our norms are indeed so informed, we don’t know what to say when asked what their ultimate warrant is” (RJE: 247). It follows from the Cohenian thesis that the fact-insensitive principles, which Cohen calls fundamental principles, enjoy a certain logical priority over fact-dependent principles. This logical priority means that the affirmations of fact-insensitive principles are logically prior to affirmations of principles grounded in facts. The fact-insensitive principles are logically prior to the fact-sensitive principles insofar as they justify the relationship between fact-sensitive principles and certain facts. This relationship is grounded in a more ultimate principle logically prior to the fact and the principle supported by the fact, without which this connection would not have existed.

“The priority of fact-insensitive principles is a matter of what utterances of principle *commit* one to, not of how one comes to believe or know what one says in uttering them” (ibid.). Hence, if someone wants to know what their principles are, they should consider the facts present in their mind and determine the normative principles which respond to these facts. The commitment to the principles related to these facts, does not imply the commitment to fact-insensitive principles because of the logical priority and independence of utterances of fact-independent principles. As aforementioned, Cohen insists on the conditional character of his meta-ethical thesis, which is to be neutral to central questions in meta-ethics. He thereby rejects the causal and the psychological features that could be wrongly attributed to his thesis. The Cohenian thesis is conditional in the sense that *if* any facts support any principles, then fact-independent principles, which are the grounding of the relation of support between facts and principles, reflect these facts. The thesis does not question whether facts ground principles, but rather assumes that facts ground principles and aims at finding the reason for that grounding relationship. Cohen says that all principles which reflect facts reflect them only because they also reflect principles that do not reflect facts. So, the ultimate principles that do not reflect facts are the ultimate grounding of all principles including the fact-dependent principles.

> [M]y thesis concerns what happens if and when facts ground principles, not whether actions can be justified by facts only through principles. Most people think, as I indeed do, that facts do ground principles, and my thesis claims that they are thereby committed to acknowledging the existence of fact-insensitive principles (RJE: 248).

On the one hand, Cohen's thesis is not causal, because it does not explain why people hold their principles, but rather how their principles are structured and interconnected. The Cohenian method does not conclude with why certain normative principles are selected, but with the structure of belief in all normative principles and the ultimate grounding of these principles. Cohen assumes that principles are substantially selected as a result of experiences in life, which is a reflection of the experience of facts. His thesis does not concern the substance or the genesis of the selected principles, but the structure of these normative beliefs. How should persons appraise their normative beliefs, no matter how they arrived at affirming them? His claim is that the normative principles people believe in, depend on beliefs in principles that are independent of anything they consider as facts. It is, for example, an arithmetical truth that six and three equals nine no matter what objects are counted. The experiment that proves this truth does not disprove the arithmetical principle. So, "it is, typically, in and through experience that people form and adjust their principles, but facts of experience are nevertheless immaterial to their ultimate principles" (RJE: 255).

On the other hand, the meta-ethical thesis is not a psychological one. The Cohenian thesis starts with the "if" clause, which makes the thesis non-psychological. If a person knows what their principles are and the grounds for holding them, then they proceed from one principle to another until the fact-free principle is reached. If one assumes that a person affirming the principles does not come to a fact-free principle because of an inaccurate analysis of the structure of their principles, the fundamental, original fact-insensitive principle remains the ultimate, though not achieved, grounding of all principles of this affirmer. This incapacity to reach the fact-free principle, for whatever reasons, does not affect the Cohenian thesis, which is meta-ethical, and therefore, does not depend on psychological facts related to experiences in life. Likewise, the incapacity of reaching the ultimate foundation of all principles is a result of the Cohenian thesis that questions what the fundamental, original grounding of normative affirmations is a priori.

> The question how many people can state ultimate fact-free principles that ground all of their principles is […] *a posteriori*. But mine is the *a priori* thesis that, if facts ground principles, then fact-free principles are at the foundation of the structure of belief of anyone who is clear about what they believe and why they believe it (RJE: 257).

But what if persons, who use the Cohenian analysis method to reach fundamental principles, find them unfeasible, due to facts about their human situation? Do these facts constitute a ground for rejecting fact-free principles? If, as Cohen says, facts cannot be grounds for affirming fundamental normative principles which should be fact-free, could they be grounds for rejecting them? This objection is based on the idea that "ought" implies "can", according to which facts disqualify the ultimate fact-free principle as impracticable and are the grounds for rejecting it. This objection and Cohen's reply are presented in the following.

2.5 Challenges, Critiques and Replies

In order to understand the above-mentioned objection to Cohen's thesis, it is important to explain the traditional meta-ethical ideas[7] of going from an "ought" to a "can", and going from an "is" to an "ought".

Some philosophers think that one can go from an "is", which is a factual statement to an "ought", which is a normative affirmation. For example, "the statement that Harry is in pain entails that Harry ought to be assisted" (RJE: 248). However, other philosophers do not agree that a normative principle logically follows from a fact. But Cohen insists that his thesis is neutral to that question and presupposes neither a denial of this idea nor an endorsement of it. His theory stipulates that all fact-sensitive principles suppose fact-insensitive principles and can be affirmed and applied without bias in this meta-ethical dispute. But he affirms that almost all philosophers agree that a "can" follows the normative affirmation "ought". "Yet, while there is no doubt some truth in the "ought" implies "can" thesis, the truth in question lacks the significant implications for the nature of normativity that is typically claimed for" (RJE: 250). Therefore facts would make the principle either feasible or not, and would constitute grounds for rejection, even if it were not possible for people to put the principle into practice. Cohen argues that this objection does not challenge his thesis that facts ground principles because of further fact-insensitive principles. In fact, excluding a principle because a "can" does not result from an "ought" is different from grounding any principle. If a fundamental normative principle is excluded because it cannot be observed, "we may then ask what we should say about the putatively excluded principle on the counterfactual hypothesis that it *could* be obeyed" (RJE: 251). If a principle is excluded because it is unfeasible, this exclusion principle would imply endorsing it, if proved feasible. Hence, the ultimate normative fact-insensitive principle in this case is reached which says that one ought to execute a principle if it is possible to do so. But, "if I am right,

7 In this case, the adjective "meta-ethical" refers to the philosophical discipline called "meta-ethics" and not to the Cohenian meta-ethical thesis, which is neutral to questions of meta-ethics.

the dictum that "ought" implies "can" is misused when it forms part of an attempt to show that feasibility constrains the content of ultimate normative judgment" (ibid.).

Applied to the virtue of justice, the rules that result from the "ought" implies "can" do not cover the nature of justice itself. Cohen affirms that the doctrine of feasibility is misapplied to the content of fundamental, fact-free principles of justice,[8] which are independent from any facts. Facts could affect and disqualify normative rules, but not fundamental principles as Rawls and the Rawlsians think.[9]

> Facts about agent incapacity are (usually) the end of the matter with respect to rules of regulation, but not with respect to ultimate principles. It's futile to adopt a rule that no one can follow, but to say it's futile to subscribe to a certain fundamental principle is a category mistake: unlike instituting a rule, subscribing to a principle is not an action, but the having of a belief or an attitude (RJE: 253-254).

In fact, Rawls thinks that fundamental principles of justice, which he calls "first principles", are a response to the facts of the human condition, which is why the representative persons in the original position receive the general facts of economics and psychology. If fundamental principles of justice are responses to facts, it follows that Cohen's thesis that fundamental principles are fact-insensitive is rejected by Rawls. Cohen aims to prove that, even in the Rawlsian theory, the selected principles are chosen according to fact-insensitive principles. Indeed, Rawls affirms that if he appraised the facts in a different way, he would reject the difference principle, which permits too much inequality. Cohen argues that this premise implies a further fact-insensitive principle, which might demand less inequality. The phrase "excessive inequalities" used by Rawls, confirms the second premise of the Cohenian argument, which invokes an ultimate fact-insensitive principle, "since it fuses reference to a fact with a reference to a principle that renders that fact relevant: excess qualifies as *excess* only in the light of a principle which says how much is *too* much" (RJE: 259-260).

Moreover, Cohen argues that the Rawlsian principles of justice do not really express Rawls's thoughts on justice, which involves a trade-off between two fact-free principles. On the one hand, Rawls wants to advance the situation of the underprivileged, and on the other hand, his theory seeks to promote equality. Rawls believes that those who affirm that fundamental principles of justice

8 See the strong thesis in chapter 3.
9 This point is presented and discussed in details in chapter 3.

should be independent of facts are committed to legislate, not only principles but also facts: How would the persons in the original position choose the suitable principles for regulating their social cooperation if they did not know the facts about the human condition? If principles are chosen based on facts, but these facts are ignored, then they should be legislated and regulated, as in the original position, in order to make them ground the principles. Cohen replies to the Rawlsian viewpoint by saying that the original position machine is justified by the "free and equal standing of members of society, but that standing reflects fact-free principles about the proper treatment of beings of the sort that they are" (RJE: 263). The Rawlsian mistake is not the mistake of calling the selected principles first principles. He is mistaken insofar as he does not consider the importance of fact-free principles which should be identified with fundamental principles of justice. He is mistaken in the sense that he endorses the procedure of using facts about the human condition to identify a fundamental principle. But what if Rawls means by "first principles of justice" rules of regulation?

According to Cohen, "Rawls fails to distinguish between rules of regulation that we decide whether or not to adopt and (his expression) "first principles" that are not in that way optional" (RJE: 265). Rawls's fundamental error is that he mistakes rules of regulation with fundamental principles of justice.[10] The question about the principles should be the question about the rules of regulation and not about the fundamental convictions on justice. An answer to the first question is not possible without an answer to the second question, as people only adopt or put into practice certain principles (rules) in light of their ultimate beliefs and convictions. But, why are the basic principles or fundamental principles so important, if the rules of regulation also tell people what they ought or ought not to do?

> The response is unsustainable because we necessarily have recourse to basic principles to justify the rules of regulation that we adopt: facts cast normative light only by reflecting the light that fact-free first principles shine on them (RJE: 267).

Cohen explains that fundamental principles of justice, for example, do not only guide in practice and thus determine just actions, but also constitute what justice is. They serve practical purposes if they are related to facts about the world, but "their standing, too, lies upstream from their serving practical purposes" (ibid.). Fundamental principles express the virtue of justice, and, justify the relation between facts of the world and fact-sensitive principles. Thus Cohen's

10 For a further discussion, see chapter 3.

meta-ethical thesis that answers an a priori question different from the "ought/is" question identifies and clarifies the fact-free principles, which are at the grounding of all other principles. Cohen's method of analyzing the structure of principles and beliefs is the conceptual approach for reaching the fundamental principles of justice. His thesis shows the difference between fact-free principles of justice or ultimate convictions about justice and adopted rules of regulation, mistakenly identified by constructivism in general.

However, in his article, "Cohen to the Rescue" (CTR), Pogge questions the Cohenian method of analyzing the relation between principles and facts. "Why should it be true that anyone committed to at least one fact-sensitive principle must therefore also be committed to at least one fact-insensitive principle?" (CTR: 90).

2.6 Pogge's Critique of the Cohenian Meta-Ethical Method

In CTR, Pogge focuses on Cohen's rescue of the concept of justice and on his distinction between fact-sensitive and fact-insensitive principles. According to Cohen, philosophers are divided into two camps. In the first camp, philosophers think that all moral principles are fact-sensitive, whereas those in the second believe that some of these principles are fact-insensitive. On the one hand, Cohen reasserts that philosophers of the first camp think "that our beliefs about matters of normative principle, should reflect, or respond to, truths about matters of fact" (RJE: 231). On the other hand, "he proposes that only such fact-insensitive principles can be accepted as ultimate and thus deserving the title of principles of justice" (CTR: 89). Cohen denies what most philosophers affirm, namely that normative principles are grounded in the facts of human nature and of the human condition. He argues that a principle responds to a fact, only because it responds to a more ultimate principle, which stands the denial of that fact. Here Pogge explores and refutes Cohen's argument differentiating between two definitions of fact-sensitivity.

Pogge envisages Cohen's interlocutor, whom he questions about the structure of principles and beliefs, accepting the principle "that we ought to express our respect for people" (ibid.), but resisting Cohen's "conclusion that they must therefore be committed to some fact-insensitive principle" (ibid.). In other words, Pogge affirms that the interlocutor accepts a narrow, conditional ought: "For all X, if X has the relevant characteristics, then it ought to be the case that I respect X" (ibid.). Pogge describes Cohen's argument as assigning a universal and unconditional ought: "It ought to be the case that, for all X, if X has the relevant characteristics, then I respect X" (ibid.).

Moreover, Pogge distinguishes between two senses of fact-sensitivity. Firstly a principle can be fact-sensitive in its content, when the instruction it gives depends on one or more facts. For example, a person ought to act in a certain manner whenever certain facts incur. But Pogge does not mean that the directive of the principle is invalid if these facts do not occur. He calls this principle, an internally fact-sensitive principle.

"I call a principle internally fact-sensitive when it so conditionalizes its directive upon facts. A principle is internally fact-insensitive, then, when its directive is not conditionalized upon facts" (CTR: 93). Then again, the range of a principle can be fact-sensitive when it is in a context where certain facts incur. Pogge calls this principle externally fact-sensitive. He explains that the endorsement of such a principle is conditional in the sense that whenever certain facts occur, the principle is valid. But, he does not mean that if these facts do not incur, the principle is not valid.

> I call a principle externally fact-sensitive when its endorsement is conditional on certain facts. A principle is externally fact-insensitive, then, when it is endorsed for any and all factual contexts (ibid.).

Pogge views Cohen's principles as externally fact-sensitive, which "shows that he thinks of principles as attached to particular persons: as normative beliefs rather than as detached normative propositions" (ibid.). Therefore, a principle in the Cohenian sense may be externally fact-sensitive for those who endorse it for certain facts and externally fact-insensitive for those who hold it for all contexts.

However, a principle can be internally and externally fact-sensitive, and its fact-sensitivity can be externalized and internalized. Pogge gives the example of the following principle:

> *rational beings are permitted to choose childlessness when by doing so they would violate no promise*' specifically for contexts where such rational beings belong to a species that is not under threat of imminent extinction (CTR: 93-94).

The internal fact-sensitivity of this principle is shown through the permission granted to remain childless unless a promise is violated. This condition is understood, according to Pogge, as a sufficient condition and not as a necessary condition. However, the external fact-sensitivity of this example is that the principle is endorsed for factual contexts when the agent's species is not under threat of extinction. Moreover, the fact-sensitivity of this example is wholly internalized, in the principle "'*rational beings are permitted to remain childless when doing so would violate no promise and they belong to a species that is not under threat of extinction*'" (CTR: 94). Yet the fact-sensitivity would be wholly externalized in the principle saying that "'*rational beings are permitted to remain childless*"' (ibid.).

Pogge affirms that philosophers from the first camp do not see that the same principle can be internally fact-sensitive and reformulated into an externally fact-sensitive principle. He takes the Cohenian example, "'*treat any person with respect*'" (ibid.), which is an externally fact-sensitive principle. Then he shows how Cohen transforms it into an externally fact-insensitive but internally fact-sensitive principle: "'*treat with respect anyone who has the relevant (respect-meriting) characteristics*'" (ibid.).

Nevertheless, Pogge argues that Cohen's victory is a Pyrrhic victory because he does not succeed in rescuing justice. It is true that Cohen's method attains externally fact-insensitive principles, but he does manage to rescue the concept of justice. "All they [Cohen's imagined interlocutors] need do is reformulate their principles so that any external fact-sensitivities are internalized" (CTR: 95). Facing this challenge, Pogge argues, Cohen could define principles of justice as both externally and internally fact-insensitive but does not do so. On the contrary, Cohen's endorsement of the principle, one ought to respect beings who have the relevant respect characteristics, proves, according to Pogge, that he accepts certain facts, namely whether the beings possess the respect characteristics or not. Moreover, Cohen's endorsement of the egalitarian distribution of wealth is undertaken after a comparison of the socioeconomic situation of members of society.

"In these ways, reference to facts is once more built in and – unless Cohen wants to rescue the concept of justice also from himself – such internal fact-sensitivity cannot then be for him incompatible with the status of a genuine principle of justice" (CTR: 96). Likewise, Cohen states that the regulatory rules or the Rawlsian principles of justice only cover one context (the Rawlsian basic structure), while genuine principles of justice should hold "whatever the facts may be, in all possible worlds and contexts" (CTR: 97). Pogge illustrates this idea with the Cohenian discussion of utilitarianism and slavery. The defense of utilitarianism is based on facts about this world, in which slavery cannot maximize happiness. Therefore, Pogge concludes that unreal circumstances cannot be used to determine moral principles.

However, analyzing the different verbs[11] used by Cohen to describe the relation between facts and principles, Pogge recognizes an ambiguity concerning

11 The Cohenian expressions are enumerated by Pogge, such as that the facts give reason to affirm a principle, or the principle reflects the fact, or responds to the fact, or depends on the

the fact-sensitivity. Therefore he deduces two understandings of it. "On a broad understanding, a fact-sensitive principle is one that is taken to hold *whenever* certain facts obtain: the facts are a sufficient condition for the principle's holding" (CTR: 99). For example, the commitment of utilitarianism's defenders must be understood in this broad meaning, because the principle is only valid in a specified context (the real world). Yet, "on a narrow understanding, a fact-sensitive principle is one that is taken to hold *just in case* certain facts obtain: the facts are a necessary and sufficient condition for the principle's holding" (ibid.).

Pogge continues his argumentation by saying that in a narrow understanding, "fact-insensitive" and "fact-sensitive" are contraries and not contradictories. He explains that two predicates are contraries: when one is true, then the other must be false, unless both are false. He gives the example of "bachelor" and "unmarried" "because it is impossible to be both but possible to be neither (namely an unmarried woman)" (ibid.). However, two predicates are contradictories: when one is true then the other must be false and inversely. For example, "married" and "unmarried" "because it is impossible to be both and impossible to be neither" (ibid.). Therefore he concludes three possible commitments to a moral principle. The first commitment is fact-insensitive, which means that the principle is true regardless of any facts. The second possible commitment is narrowly fact-sensitive, which means that the principle is true whenever certain facts incur and is not true when the facts do not incur. In the third commitment, even if the facts incur, it is left open whether the moral principle is valid; "the commitment is neither fact-insensitive nor narrowly fact-sensitive" (CTR: 100). Thus, on the broad understanding, the second and the third possible cases are combined into one case, so that fact-insensitive commitments and fact-sensitive commitments are contradictories. "Since Cohen clearly wants his distinction to be exhaustive in the realm of principles, we must ascribe to him the broad understanding of fact-sensitive" (ibid.).

Pogge considers the case of a fact-sensitive commitment to a principle P, grounded in facts of our world, but not committed to P's holding or not in other worlds. He imagines himself answering Cohen on the fact-sensitivity of the principle without any reference to a more ultimate fact-insensitive principle.

> I can say that the meaning and significance of the terms in which *P* is couched is interwoven with the basic standing features of this world and that it makes no sense, therefore, to

---

fact, or is grounded in the fact or is supported by the fact or based on the fact or justified by the fact, or fact-bound, or fact-infested or fact-reflecting, or fact-supported.

> extend *P* to *F* worlds. I can say that I find it absurd, and morally offensive, to extend my moral principles to beings and life contexts that I have not experienced do not really understand (CTR: 101).

Pogge deduces that a commitment to a fact-sensitive principle does not imply a commitment to a more ultimate fact-insensitive principle "deeply alien to the [world] we live in" (ibid.). Pogge presents Cohen's example about foetuses that were initially more babylike and become less baby-like as they proceed toward birth until the day before birth, when they become humans. Following Pogge, Cohen claims that our morality should cover all possible worlds and contexts, although he affirms, that "until we unearth the fact-free principle that governs our fact-loaded particular judgments about justice, we don't know why we think what we think just is just" (RJE: 291). This means that we should explore the essential nature of morality, which will reveal moral principles.

Pogge concludes that Cohen shares Kant's belief in the objectivity of our morality, even though he does not agree with him on the moral principles. Kant affirms that propositions are true or false in virtue of humans' limited mental faculties. "[T]here might exist beings whose sensibility differs from ours. If we could encounter them, such beings, would appear three-dimensional to us. But neither they nor we would appear three-dimensional to them" (CTR: 104-105).

From this argumentation, Pogge affirms two points: Firstly, Cohen fails to consider the fact-sensitivity that we are all beings endowed with reason, according to which we hold our judgements and principles, and which we cannot transcend. Secondly, it is possible to extend this fact-sensitivity to all possible worlds and contexts.

> But does it make sense? Does it make sense to apply our moral principles to beings whose mental life is profoundly different from ours so that the basic structure of our moral thinking is incomprehensible to them and the basic structure of their decision-making incomprehensible to us? One can plausibly answer this question in the negative (CTR: 105).

Pogge's main idea is to prove that a commitment to fact-sensitive principles does not involve a commitment to fact-insensitive principles. However, by applying the Cohenian analysis method of principles and beliefs, Cohen questions the nature of fundamental principles of justice. He starts analyzing principles endorsed by facts and attains principles, which are not related to facts. He reveals that the principles of justice chosen by Rawls do not represent justice, but a mixture of justice and other considerations. Pogge tries to refute the Cohenian conclusion that at the summit of our normative principles, there are principles of justice that are not related to facts. But he does not succeed in refuting the Cohenian analysis method of the principles' structure, which reaches the ultimate principles. These principles represent all our virtues and not only the virtue of justice. Yet Cohen is not allergic to facts. He affirms that facts determine our capacity to achieve justice and questions the virtue of justice independently of this capacity. The argument used by Pogge against this Cohenian project is: "What for?", "Does it make sense?" and tries to show that Cohen's project aims at covering other planets. In fact it makes sense to know what the ideal principles of justice are independently of our human condition and situation, according to which the practical fact-sensitive principles of justice are chosen for humans and not for aliens.

3 A Meta-Ethical Theory: Cohen's Rescue of Justice

The meta-ethical part of RJE, in which Cohen attempts to rescue the concept of justice consists of two complementary rescues. The first is a rescue of the concept of justice from facts, while the second is a rescue of the concept of justice from the constructivist approach. For the purposes of the first rescue, Cohen develops the meta-ethical thesis about the relationship between facts and principles.[1] Normative principles reflect facts in virtue of reflecting ultimate principles, which do not reflect facts. At the end of the analysis of principles and beliefs, persons reach their fundamental principles, which are not grounded in any principles and which do not reflect any facts at all. Cohen also pursues his rescue of justice in chapter 7 of RJE by criticizing the constructivist methodology. The rescue of the concept of justice is completed by its rescue from the constructivist method, which allegedly provides the fundamental principles of justice. Cohen criticizes constructivism, which mistakenly identifies fundamental principles of justice with the optimal rules for the regulation of social cooperation. According to Cohen this mistake has different expressions of which he depicts four, from which he separates justice. The rescue from the facts, presented in the previous chapter, detaches the concept of justice from facts. The other three separations disconnect justice from the Pareto principle, from considerations of publicity and considerations of stability. In the following, the Cohenian argument against the constructivist approach to social justice and its manifestations are presented, and the relationship between justice on the one hand, and the Pareto principle, and considerations of publicity and stability on the other hand are explored. Some matters arising from the Cohenian argument and the Cohenian reply concerning the "circumstances of justice" as constraints on justice are presented at the end of this chapter, together with Cohen's affirmation about justice that follows from his argument, namely that justice is not the first virtue of social institutions.

3.1 Rescue of Justice from Constructivism

In its general definition, "constructivism is the view that a principle gains its normative credentials through being the product of a sound selection proce-

1 For a further discussion, see chapter 2.

dure" (RJE: 274). However, Cohen's examination of constructivism only concerns the constructivist approach to social justice, which views the normative credentials of fundamental principles of justice as the product of a selection procedure. This procedure aims at answering the question: "What rules of governance are to be adopted for our common social life?" (RJE: 275). In fact, Cohen's criticism of constructivism applies in general to all constructivist approaches, such as the Scanlonian contractarianism or to Gauthier's contractarianism, where a procedure is required to identify the nature of justice. Cohen focuses on Rawlsian constructivism,[2] as a prime example of the constructivist procedures using the original position to determine what justice is.

According to Cohen, the constructivist approach to social justice mischaracterizes justice due to two main errors. It considers justice as sensitive to facts about human nature and human condition, but fails to distinguish between the virtue of justice and other virtues. These errors show that constructivism is misguided as it confuses fundamental principles of justice with the most suitable and effective set of principles for the regulation of real social cooperation.

> My objection to that identification is that, simply because they *are* the *all*-things considered best principles to live by, optimal all-things-considered principles are therefore not necessarily the best principles considered from the point of view of justice alone (ibid.).

Cohen explains that constructivism's misidentification of principles of justice with optimal principles of regulation results from the question put to those selecting the principles in the constructivist procedure, such as the original position in the Rawlsian case. For example, representative members in the original position are not asked to define what justice is, but rather to choose the best principles for their social collaboration. These are two different questions, which should receive two different answers. Therefore, Cohen criticizes the constructivist approach,[3] which answers the question posed in the constructiv-

---

2 Rejecting Rawlsian constructivism strengthens Cohen's rescue of the egalitarian distributive justice from the Rawlsian difference principle, presented in the first five chapters of RJE. Both rescues of equality and justice are interdependent, and since Cohen has already rescued the egalitarian thesis from the Rawlsian treatment of it, in the first part of his book, the rescue of justice from Rawls's constructivist approach strengthens both rescues and makes the book more interesting insofar as it focuses on the Rawlsian definition of the substance (first part of RJE) and the concept (second part of RJE) of justice.

3 Cohen makes an important philosophical distinction concerning the validity of the principles, which is at the heart of meta-ethics, but has no bearing on his own argument. He distinguishes between the view that principles are valid because they are the product of a constructivist procedure and the view that the constructivist procedure makes the principles valid. Is it

ist device with the answer to the question of what justice is. However, in this device this is not the question. The answer to the question on the nature of justice cannot be the same as the answer to the question what the best principles to live by are.

As indicated earlier, the Cohenian critique, which highlights two errors in constructivism, is grounded in two central distinctions. The first distinction is between fundamental principles and mere principles of regulation, which Cohen calls rules of regulation. Fundamental principles are normative principles, which are not derived from other normative principles and which are not grounded in any facts. Rules of regulation are created and adopted in order to regulate social cooperation between members of society in the light of the human condition and the facts of the world. These rules can be dictated by the state, such as income tax rules, or beyond the realm of the state, such as rules that regulate gender issues. However, rules are adopted "in the light of what we expect the *effect* of adopting them to be. But we do not in the same sense adopt our fundamental principles, any more that we adopt our beliefs about matters of fact" (RJE: 276-277; my italics). Whereas fundamental principles are objects of substantial deontological convictions and beliefs, the adoption of feasible rules of regulation represent and serve a practical task. They are adopted in virtue of their likely beneficial effects and consequences for the task at hand. Human social behaviour is justified by the principled convictions, objects of belief, which also justifies the choice of the rules of regulation. Rules of regulation are thereby created and adopted in the light of fundamental principles, which represent the central convictions which they serve or express.

Hence, Cohen distinguishes between three questions. The first question, which is a sociological question, asks: What are the rules that regulate society? The second question, which is a question in political theory, asks: What rules should regulate society? And the third question, which is the philosophical question, asks: What is justice? These three different questions show that the nature of justice "transcends rules of regulation" (ibid.).

The second distinction is a distinction between justice and other virtues, which constructivism fails to respect. The distinction is actually between the principles that serve the virtue of justice and the principles that express other values, such as human welfare. According to Cohen, representative persons in the original position standing behind the veil of ignorance are asked to choose

the procedure that endows the principle with its validity or is the principle itself valid? However, Cohen does not discuss these views. He simply asks if the principles, produced in the constructivist procedure, are therefore principles of justice.

the most suitable principles for their social life. Their answer is supposed to confirm what the fundamental principles of justice are and what the virtue of justice is. But the question they deliberate in the original position is different from the question about the nature of justice: What is justice? Therefore, by identifying fundamental principles of justice with the best rules of regulation, Rawls and the Rawlsians violate both distinctions sketched by Cohen.

> They are not asked to say what justice is: it is we who ask that question, and the constructivist doctrine is that the answer to our question is the answer to the different question that is put to constructivism's specially designed selectors, which is, what are the optimal rules of social regulation? My generative criticism of constructivism is that the answer to that question need not, and could not, be the same as the answer to the question: what is justice? (RJE: 275).

It is, however, of great importance to stress that the Cohenian criticism is not a criticism of the original position as a methodological device for answering the question about the right rules of regulation, and whose answers might be correct. In fact Cohen criticizes the Rawlsian misidentification of the results of the original position with what justice is. The identification is doubly mistaken as fundamental principles of justice are confused with rules of regulation that serve values other than justice. On the one hand, the result of the original position device misidentifies fundamental principles of justice with rules of regulation that are supposed to serve justice. On the other hand, it misidentifies fundamental principles that serve other values and rules of regulation that are supposed to serve those values. So, Cohen does not affirm that the selectors of the principles answer the question in a wrong way, but he argues that the question they are asked is the wrong question if the aim is to define the fundamental principles of justice. One must remember that according to Cohen, there is a strong relationship between justice and equality. A just distribution of benefits is an equal distribution as long as inequality is not warranted by a choice or fault or merit. Therefore justice favours or even implies equality. Yet, the misidentification of fundamental principles of justice with rules of regulation serving values other than justice, strengthens the relationship between the rescue of equality, which constitutes distributive justice, and the meta-ethical rescue of the concept of justice. "The two rescues are connected because each of the two errors in the Rawlsian identification of principles of justice with optimal rules of regulation induces us to disidentify justice and equality" (RJE: 279). The first error consists of identifying justice with a feasible and efficient social scheme, because equality is unfeasible. Hence, Cohen attempts the rescue of equality, which advances equality as an essential element of distributive justice. The second error consists of introducing principles of values other than justice which compete with equality. For this reason, Cohen attempts to rescue the concept of justice from these values. "Accordingly, the rescue of the concept of justice serves the end of rescuing the egalitarian thesis about distributive justice" (ibid.).

3.2 Weak and Strong Defenses

In chapter 6 of RJE Cohen establishes that fundamental principles are principles which are not derived from or are not grounded in other normative principles, and do not reflect any facts at all. It is Cohen's firm conviction that facts about human nature and condition, and thereby about the feasibility of the selected principles, do not control fundamental principles of justice, which constructivists fail to properly identify and expose. However Cohen's weaker conviction, based on the thesis presented in chapter 6 of RJE, is that facts do not affect fundamental principles in any way because they are fact-insensitive. Both views, which consolidate Cohen's criticism of constructivism, are presented in the following.

According to Cohen, a fundamental principle[4] is not an applied principle, which has the characteristic of being derived from another principle together with something else. For example, an applied principle of justice is derived or affirmed on the basis of another principle of justice and something other, such as empirical facts, or a value or a principle that does not serve justice, but some other value. Consequently, whereas applied principles of justice reflect a certain mixture of judicial considerations and other considerations, fundamental principles of justice do not reflect any mixtures and are in this sense "pure". They reflect pure justice or pure thoughts which are not thoughts on justice.[5] An applied principle of justice applies justice on the basis of factual information or a principle or a value that do not express the virtue of justice alone.

> To put the matter more crudely, but perhaps more accessibly, applied principles of justice come from justice *and* something else, whereas fundamental principles of justice, *so far as*

4 According to the clarity of mind required by Cohen from the affirmers of normative principles, the same normative principle could be fundamental in the structure of beliefs of a given person and derived in the structure of beliefs of another person.

5 If fundamental principles are affirmed on the basis of something other than justice, they are, as a matter of fact, derived from what they are affirmed. But, Cohen argues, that "since it is not then justice from which they derive, they are, nevertheless, fundamental *as* principles of justice" (RJE: 280).

> *the mere definition of what they are is concerned*, come from nothing but justice or from nothing but something other than justice (RJE: 280).

According to constructivism, fundamental principles of justice are derived from judgements about the right procedure for selecting the principles of justice, and facts about human nature and the human condition. Here is the disagreement with Cohen, who believes that fundamental principles of justice cannot be grounded in facts and cannot reflect virtues other than justice. "I thereby affirm that constructivists miscast applied principles of justice in the role of fundamental ones. […] My claim is that constructivists are mistaken about the structure of their *own* belief" (RJE: 281). In fact, constructivists commit this error because they assign a wrong role to fundamental principles in constructivist procedures such as the original position. Fundamental principles of justice are not expected to regulate social cooperation; they are given the wrong task in the constructivist legislative procedures. This role is determined by the question that the legislators are asked to answer, namely, what are the best principles to regulate social life? Moreover, the legislators are also given a wrong task, insofar as they are provided with facts about their nature and society, in order to define what justice is. Cohen argues that the selected rules are, indeed, rules of regulation and not fundamental principles of justice. On the one hand, rules of regulation are not fundamental principles because they do not merely reflect the contents of justice, but also factual contingencies and other values "that determine how justice is to be applied, or that make justice infeasible, *and* values and principles that call for a compromise with justice" (RJE: 283). However, as demonstrated earlier, fundamental principles cannot be grounded in facts. So, the constructivist procedures, which select the right set of principles for social cooperation, fail to identify the fundamental principles of justice, because they take other considerations into account. "The influence of other values means that the principles in the output of the procedure are not principles of *justice*, and the influence of the factual contingencies means that they are not *fundamental* principles of anything" (ibid.). On the other hand, Cohen regards the factual information given to the selectors of the principles, about their nature and society, as irrelevant for determining fundamental principles of justice. The information needed for selecting the rules of regulation, should be feasible in order to be accepted and put into practice. Rules of regulation cannot be feasible, unless they reflect facts about the persons, who will apply them.

> I am here arguing, facts are irrelevant in the determination of fundamental principles of justice. Facts of human nature and human society of course (1) make a difference to what justice tells us to do in specific terms; they also (2) tell us how much justice we can get,

> and they (3) bear on how much we should compromise with justice, but, so I believe, they make no difference to the very nature of justice itself (RJE: 285).

The selection of rules of regulation is influenced by three principles, which are presented later in this chapter: the Pareto principle, the principle of publicity and the principle of stability. Thus, rules of regulation do not only serve the value of justice, but also the aforementioned principles, which call for a compromise with justice. The strong thesis[6] affirmed by Cohen states that fundamental principles of justice are fact-insensitive principles of justice, which are, however, implicitly affirmed by constructivists as well when they select the optimal rules of regulation. "It will be those principles which endow the constructively selected principles with whatever amount of justice that they have" (RJE: 287). However, constructivists fail to identify and separate these principles, because they fail to analyze and expose fact-insensitive principles, and thereby fail to affirm Cohen's weaker thesis, which claims that all normative principles which reflect facts reflect these facts, because they also reflect fact-independent principles.

Beyond the disagreement with the constructivists, Cohen belongs to the Socrato-Platonic tradition in various ways. Cohen agrees with Socrates that the fact-free principle that is at the grounding of all judgements and convictions about justice is still unexposed. "We don't know why we think what we think just is just. And we have to retreat to (what we consider to be) justice in its purity to figure out how to institute as much justice as possible" (RJE: 291). Moreover, Cohen agrees with Plato in the book V of *Republic*, where Plato affirms that, in order to recognize a principle as reflecting a fact, when this fact is true, an analysis of what is justice must precede. "That is how justice transcends the facts of the world" (ibid.). Furthermore, Cohen agrees with Plato "that justice is the self-same thing, across, and independently of, history [the facts]. [...] Justice is, ultimately, facts-free, within anyone's belief structure" (ibid.).

3.3 Illustrations

Cohen provides two illustrations to support his strong thesis which claims that fact-sensitive principles of justice presuppose fact-insensitive principles of justice, which are the foundation for all principles of justice.

6 Cohen presents two illustrations of the strong thesis, but does not prove it, like he does with the weak thesis. For a further presentation of the weak thesis, see chapter 2.

The first illustration is about differential care signifying that people tend to reduce the care they apply to things or persons for different reasons, especially "when they know that (some of) the slack induced will be picked up by others, such as government, or insurance companies" (RJE: 308). This fact must be taken into account when optimal rules of regulation are selected, because it influences the practicability of the rules. In fact, it is extremely difficult to determine exactly the differential care, namely, the lesser care. Therefore facts about this lesser care are relevant for the selection of rules of regulation. But, Cohen argues that there is a contradiction between justice and the principles selected by the constructivist procedure, when facts about the differential care, for example, are included. This contradiction presupposes a conception of what justice is. "Principles reflecting those facts are not fundamental principles of justice, precisely because their selection reflects, in part, the stated facts" (ibid.). But, Cohen affirms that these principles, which are not fundamental, are sometimes principles for minimizing injustice and, sometimes, principles that trade justice off against other considerations. In fact, it is impossible to minimize justice, in the light of facts of differential care,

> unless you have a conception of what justice itself is, or, at any rate, a view of what would be more and less just, independently of such facts. Nor can you, under the pressure of the facts, trade justice off against other desiderata, unless again, you have a conception, which constructivism, *ex hypothesi*, cannot supply, of what justice, independently of such facts, is (RJE: 309).

The example of damage done to dwellings by bad weather and not covered by insurance demonstrates that every person is likely to protect their dwellings. Cohen examines three hypothetical states of affairs, S1, S2 and S3. S1 is the state scheme where all persons should be compensated equally for similar damages. However, some people might benefit from other people's pain, or they might slacken their care, so that this scheme would benefit some people at the expense of others. Hence, the second state scheme S2 is proposed, under which every person has to pay the first £ 100 of all weather damage. This measure reduces how much some people benefit at the expense of others. From a philosophical point of view the second scheme reflects justice as well as other considerations such as facts about the differential care. It would be therefore wrong to affirm that these facts alone make the scheme just. S2 is the best feasible strategy which produces a maximum of justice. But,

> in instituting *S2*, we are seeking to fix the excess at a level that minimizes injustice, but we cannot set about doing that unless we have some prior conception of what justice itself is

> (in the present case, so I am supposing, it is a certain equality in the distribution of burdens across similarly insured people (RJE: 311-312).

If differential levels of care are detected, a just scheme, S3, which compensates relatively to inputs of care, would be feasible. S2 would still be retained "because the great cost of securing the justice that *S3* provides might make it reasonable to sacrifice justice in favour of an unjust scheme under which, so we can assume, everyone would fare better" (RJE: 312). If S2 is chosen, justice is not maximized, but traded off against considerations of efficiency. Cohen states that the fact-insensitive principle here is that people should bear the costs their lack of care imposes on others. This principle is latently affirmed, which reflects an underlying conception of justice, according to which the schemes are selected and traded off.

The second illustration is about "council tax", a British property tax, which divides properties in seven bands, according to a certain progressive tax principle. For example, Mr. 90.000 pays the same amount of taxes as Mr. 99.999, because they belong to the same band. Cohen affirms that this rule of regulation, according to which taxes are determined, is not a principle of justice. Would it be just that the person who earns 90.000 pays considerably more than the person who, at 89.999 has nearly the same income? Now, if a computer could calculate precisely all property values, "who could deny that the distribution of tax burden would then be *more* just than the distribution that we are actually able to achieve?" (RJE: 315). As mentioned in both illustrations there is indeed a misidentification between rules of regulation and fundamental principles of justice which sometimes hides certain contradictions between them. As indicated earlier, Cohen attempts to separate fundamental principles of justice not only from rules of regulation, but also from other values. He detaches justice from other values albeit with compromises, such as the Pareto principle, considerations about publicity, and considerations about stability. These values cannot alter the pure nature of justice because they reflect something other than justice, and can therefore not participate in determining the contents of fundamental principles of justice, which do not reflect any mixtures. They do no more than influence the choice of the best rules for mutual social life.

3.4 What is not Justice?

Rawls initial argument affirms that justice requires equal distributions of benefits. However an unequal but efficient strategy, under which everyone is better-off, is preferable to an equal distribution. This constitutes a Pareto improvement[7] that Rawls endorses as just. Cohen objects: "I think, that it is not a reason of *justice* to make that change, while others will think that it is indeed a reason of justice" (RJE: 315). Cohen explores the relationship of justice to the Pareto principle, by considering an egalitarian distribution and an unequalizing Pareto-improvement on it. He imagines persons A and B, with similar powers and preferences, and among whom distributive justice prevails through an equal distribution of manna-bundles. Each person receives five units of manna, but three extra manna fall from heaven. The question is whether to distribute all manna-bundles unevenly or none at all.[8] What would be the feasible set? What would be a just set? Whereas in the first distribution, both persons would have five units of manna, in the second distribution person A would have seven units of manna and person B would have six. The second unequal distribution is a Pareto-improvement situation, since both persons are better off than under the first equal distribution. While Rawls adopts the second distribution warranting it as a just distribution, which advances everyone's situation, Cohen considers it a policy, which does not level out and thus does not promote justice.

Cohen imagines a state of nature, where manna falls from heaven and is shared equally, because "the sharers think that's the right way to deal with manna from heaven" (RJE: 317). Then an extra, undividable piece of manna falls onto Jane's share. Jane believes it unfair to have more than the others for no choice or merit or fault of her own and suggests making a big bonfire, to which everyone is invited and the manna is shared equally.

> If you think Jane is being *merely* foolish, then you can reject the claim that justice favours equality in this elementary case. But I for one would not think that Jane is being foolish. I would think that she is simply a remarkably just person, and I think we should commend her for being one (RJE: 317-318).

Cohen argues that Rawls would justify the unequal distribution, which improves the situation of everyone, in the original position. Representative persons "have no reason to oppose the occurrence of accidental inequalities that make everybody better off" (RJE: 318). But, Cohen disagrees that this distribution, which might be reasonable, reflects the virtue of pure justice. If justice

---

7 The Pareto principle is presented and discussed in chapter 4. However, Cohen argues that the Pareto argument for inequality fails because the "grounds upon which that argument recommends an unequalizing Pareto improvement are inconsistent with the grounds upon which it recommends the initial equality which the Pareto-improving inequality upsets" (RJE: 315).

8 There is no way of distributing the extra manna-bundles equally.

requires equality, the unequal distribution is unjust. But, unequal distribution might nevertheless be chosen for human prosperity, albeit that it does not reflect what justice is, but a mixture of justice and other values.

> Suppose that Sam has 3 and Saul has 9. If we give Saul the widget, he goes up to 15. If we give it to Sam, he goes up to 3.1. Can anyone believe that it's simply more just to give the widget to Saul? I can't (RJE: 323).

Furthermore, Cohen, in criticizing the constructivists' viewpoint about publicity, disconnects justice from considerations of publicity. He argues that while publicity influences the choice of the best rules of regulation, it is not a requirement of justice itself. The old slogan that justice must be seen to be done is taken as an explanation for the publicity requirement. Applied on distributive justice, it does not suffice that the right distribution takes place, but everyone must see and be assured that it is the right type of distribution. "Now, Rawlsians, […] at least for certain contexts, they could not agree that justice, and injustice, might be done where it is not possible to be assured that it has been done" (RJE: 324). Constructivists, who confuse rules of regulation with fundamental principles of justice, insist on the publicity requirement, as it allegedly influences the choice of the best rules for social regulation. Hence, constructivists affirm that the publicity requirement belongs to the nature of justice, since they mistake justice for rules of regulation. But Cohen argues that the selected and accepted rules put into practice and complied with, should be shaped on the grounds of sociological facts about compliance, which do not affect the content of justice. "Constructivism promotes the extraneous (to justice) considerations that properly figure in the justification of rules of regulation to the status of constraints of what justice *is*" (RJE: 327). Cohen considers the requirement of stability, in order to separate justice from it. Something is stable, when it has the propensity to last. The requirement of stability implies that the chosen principles last over generations. In fact, constructivists want to elect principles binding for all members of society and stable and durable from one generation to another. "Now, since well-formed constructors must seek stability, Rawlsians, who believe that justice is what well-formed constructors choose, must claim that stability is a requirement that justice satisfies" (ibid.). Cohen uses this argument for rejecting the constructivist view of justice and the stability requirement.

"For to treat the evident desideratum of stability as a constraint on what justice might be thought to be, to judge that principles qualify as principles of justice only if, once instituted, their rule has a propensity to last, is absurd" (ibid.). He argues that if stability is used as one of the criteria to select the principles of justice, these principles would certainly be stable. According to Cohen the fear behind the stability requirement is the fear of rejecting or putting the principles of justice at risk. But it is this fear that shows that stability is not a feature of justice, because it cannot tell what justice is. Rules of regulation, chosen upon facts that reflect the stability condition cannot be expected to determine what justice is. Representatives in the original position, who want to choose rules of regulation that last from one generation to the next, thereby put a constraint on the rules, which justice does not imply.

> It seems to me evident both that selectors of rules of regulation must have regard to stability and that just principles might be [...] fragile: accordingly, justice is not what those selectors select. [...] What matters is the contrast between two desiderata, namely justice and stability (RJE: 330).

However, the Cohenian rescue of justice, which has been widely challenged, affirms that justice is not the first virtue of institutions. This Cohenian affirmation, which rejects the Rawlsian definition of justice, and Cohen's replies to various objections are explored in the following.

3.5 Objections and Replies

First, Cohen replies to five questions that result from his meta-ethical thesis. The first question is: What facts ground the choice of principles in the original position, and what fact-free principles explain why these facts do so?

Cohen argues that fact-free principles are implicit in the choices made in the original position. The original position is justified by a fact-free principle, which says that persons are free and equal. But then there is a fact-free principle, that lies behind the difference principle, and which might demand that too much inequality is intolerable. Furthermore, the order of the two principles of justice is determined by the absence of severe scarcity. "The general conception generates no lexical priority for liberty or fair equality of opportunity under severe scarcity, but it does generate such priorities under limited scarcity" (RJE: 293). However, the general conception depends on the fact that there is a list of primary goods, which people need in order to pursue their life plans. This conception rests on the fact-insensitive principle that one ought to promote fulfilling lives. Moreover, an important fact is that society is marked by a conflict of interests, where every person pursues their interests and holds their own conception of the good. Cohen affirms that "fact-insensitive principles that are stated endow each of those facts with normative relevance" (RJE: 294).

The second question, to which Cohen replies, is: How do the claims of the Cohenian thesis bear on non-Rawlsian constructivisms? Cohen affirms that the procedure of *any* constructivism is misguided because it cannot support fundamental principles of justice. These are not the product of certain procedures, which take other values into account. In principle, every person is encouraged to reach and uncover their fundamental principles by analyzing their own structure of beliefs and principles.

The third question, urged on Cohen by his American namesake Joshua Cohen, concerns the Rawlsian overlapping consensus,[9] which is the justification in the real world of the principles selected in the original position. J. Cohen asks: Does the Rawlsian overlapping consensus justify the claim that justice depends on facts?

> Judgments about what ought to be done, all things considered, must, of course, be sensitive to all sorts of practical matters, since issues of practicality plainly are among the things to be considered. The question is what sorts of constraints on realizability are constitutive of ideal justice ("Moral Pluralism and Political Consensus": 271).

Cohen answers that "there is no reason to think that it is in the nature of an overlapping consensus that (all) the principles that it favours qualify as principles of justice in particular" (RJE: 297). If the overlapping consensus imposes principles that are just (reasonable) to impose, they are not necessarily principles of justice.

However, what happens if facts are suspended in the constructivist approach to social justice? Either it would make a difference in the choice of the principles, which would reflect more equality, because the facts call for a compromise with equality, but, Cohen affirms that Rawls would not accept removing the facts, since fundamental principles should be responses to facts about human nature and condition. Or, even if these facts were suspended, a constructivism about justice would mistake justice for other values, such as the stability or the publicity considerations.

The fifth question is: How is the Cohenian critique of Rawls related to Cohen's endorsement of luck egalitarianism? Cohen affirms that there is a divergence between the Rawlsian project and the project pursued by luck egalitarians, who say that "inequalities are just if and only if certain facts about responsibility obtain with respect to those inequalities" (RJE: 300). Even though Rawls condemns morally arbitrary contingencies, his endorsement of the differ-

---

9 See chapter 1 for a further presentation.

ence principle justifies inequalities, whose causes are morally arbitrary. Whereas luck egalitarians are interested in the nature of justice, Rawls is interested in the identification of the most suitable principles to best regulate social life. Further objections leveled against Cohen assert that the circumstances of justice, as defined by Rawls, namely limited altruism and limited scarcity, constitute facts which "bear on the question of what the fundamental principles are" (RJE: 331). Cohen separates the objection into different questions: 1) Under what circumstances is justice possible? 2) Under what circumstances do questions of justice arise? 3) What is justice? He concludes that the answer to the last question does not depend on the answer to the first questions. If the Rawlsian conception of justice does not apply in extreme circumstances of justice, this "could therefore have no bearing on the determination of what justice is" (RJE: 335). If facts determine the feasibility of principles, they do not determine the content of the principle. They remain external to the principle in question. Beliefs about the content of principles of distributive justice are independent of the "beliefs about the (perhaps) restricted conditions under which conformity to those principles might be observed, or under which they might be thought to apply" (ibid.).

3.6 Justice Is Not the First Virtue of Social Institutions

It could be criticized that Cohen claims that "justice" is the name of the set of principles produced by an ideal procedure, the original position, in order to regulate social life. "Accordingly, so it might be objected, the gap that I have sought to expose, between those regulating principles and justice, cannot open, in virtue of the Rawlsian definition of 'justice'" (RJE: 302). However, Cohen rejects this Rawlsian use of the term "justice" and argues that constructivism is mistaken in the sense that it defines rules of regulation by justice and other considerations. Therefore, whatever the content of justice is, it should be the only value, according to which rules of regulation are determined. Rawls defines justice as "the first virtue of social institutions, as truth is of system of thought" (TJ: 3), by which Cohen takes "him to have meant the following: a system of thought may display virtues other than truth, such as economy and coherence, but if it lacks the virtue of truth, then its other virtues do not save the system from unqualified condemnation" (RJE: 303). Cohen recognizes a certain analogy between justice and truth, but like the system of thought, which might display virtues other than truth, social institutions display values other than justice. Therefore, justice is not the first virtue of social institutions as Rawls allegedly claims; in any case it is not their sole virtue, and if it is not their sole virtue, it is then sometimes justifiable for social institutions to deviate from justice. Cohen stresses the difference between determining the right rules for just social institutions and questioning the idea of justice.

> Determining what the right rules of regulation are is undoubtedly a reasonable project, but what's in the name of 'justice', what that name denotes, is an elusive virtue discussed for a few thousand years by philosophers who did not conceive themselves to be (primarily) legislators and who consequently had a different project (RJE: 304).

3.7 The Justification of the Two Principles Is Not Contractarian

Rawls describes the original position, which is the justification of the two principles of justice as contractarian. Cohen rejects this definition by suggesting a plausible, necessary condition for the application of the term "contractarian", which he states lacks a canonical definition within moral and political philosophy.

> A justification of an obligation, whether to obey the sovereign, or to comply with a principle, is contractarian only if it grounds that obligation for each individual either in an undertaking that the individual has made or in one that she would make under specific circumstances (RJE: 338).

Cohen gives three examples of contractarians, who support his understanding of the term, Locke, Hobbes and Gauthier. In Locke's contractarianism, civil obligation is grounded in an act of consent to comply with the civil order. In Hobbes's contractarianism, Cohen recognizes elements that indicate a submission to the sovereign, which is the ground of the obligation to obey. And he also recognizes elements "that point to the idea that it is because you *would* agree to the authority of a sovereign in any situation in which there isn't one, that is, in any state of nature, that you are bound to obey the sovereign" (ibid.). Gauthier's contractarianism justifies compliance with selected, in their form hypothetical, moral principles, which persons are obligated to observe. The Cohenian understanding of contractarianism implies an individual obligation to obey or to comply with the principles, grounded in an individual actual or hypothetical undertaking.

However, Rawls does not propose such a theory of political obligation. According to him, people are under a moral obligation to obey the state because the state implements justice, and not because they agree with its authority. "There is no actual or hypothetical choice in favor of the state–its existence is assumed, and it is owed obligation if and because it is (sufficiently) just" (RJE:

339). Moreover, Cohen rejects the idea that Rawls might be a contractarian, because he demands members of society live in full agreement with the principles of justice. "But I do not think his use of the original position, on its best interpretation, is contractarian in character" (ibid.).[10] In the Rawlsian case, persons should respect the principles, not as a personal undertaking but rather because all persons agreed to comply with them in the original position. The fact that all persons agreed to the principles, establishes that they are principles of justice, which should be followed.

> So I am bound by them not because I (in particular) would have agreed to them, but because we would all have agreed to them. And we are obliged not (directly) because we would have agreed to the principles, but because the fact that we would all have agreed to them in this position of supposed impartiality makes them principles of justice (ibid.).

Cohen also discusses the "anti-contractarian objection", which uses his same understanding of the term contractarian in order to reject the original position justification of the principles. The anti-contractarian argument says that hypothetical contracts are not binding, and the original position is a hypothetical contractarian device. Quoting Hobbes, who says that none of us had the opportunity to be born in a state of nature, and still we would have agreed to obey a coercive state, Cohen rejects the major premise. "It strikes me as plausible, that, in general, if I would have agreed to X in *any* circumstances lacking X, then I am bound to accept X" (RJE: 341). Members of society should accept state sovereignty if in its absence they would have agreed to create it. In the Rawlsian case, the agreement made between members of society, in the original position and behind the veil of ignorance, cannot be made under different circumstances, "there is nothing self-evident in the claim that any principles chosen under the veil of ignorance qualify as principles of justice" (RJE: 343). Principles are just only because the special circumstances under which they are made are defined as just. So, according to Rawls, everyone would agree to the principles, because of a reasonable decision under the veil of ignorance, and they are therefore the right principles to choose and everyone should comply with them.

---

10 Cohen explains that the "best interpretation" of the use of the original position is not to be taken from Rawls, who following Cohen, provides different and ambiguous interpretations at different times. The best interpretation would be the one that represents the Rawlsian theory, which says that principles of justice should be respected because of the fact that they are principles of justice and nothing else.

> Hobbes, Locke, and Gauthier are true contractarians, because it is my actual or hypothetical agreement that obliges me to obey Hobbes's sovereign, Locke's rules of civil society, and Gauthier's moral principles. But Scanlon's 'reasonable rejection' test is not contractarian in the present sense: What obliges me to observe the principles that his device generates is not that I could not reasonably reject them but that no one could (ibid.).

In conclusion, this chapter presents the second part of the Cohenian rescue of the concept of justice. Cohen attempts to rescue justice from constructivism, which misidentifies fundamental principles of justice with optimal rules for regulating social cooperation. He concludes that constructivism is mistaken, in the task, question, and definition of the concept and the content of justice. The constructivist approach to social justice asks a factual question without providing an answer that shows the singular virtue of justice. Cohen does not only prove that the Rawlsian principles of justice are not fundamental principles of justice, but are rules of regulation, he also rejects the original position device as a contractarian device, thus weakening the Rawlsian theory, Rawls's methodology and his principles.

4 The Difference Principle

4.1 The Rawlsian General Conception of Justice

As we saw in chapter 1, Rawls develops a theory of justice informed by the idea of a social contract for liberal democratic societies marked by a reasonable pluralism. Free and equal citizens agree on principles, which establish a fair system of cooperation between each other securing the advantage of each and to be applied to the main institutions of society. The two principles of justice chosen in the original position assign equal basic rights and liberties to all citizens as well as a fair share of income and wealth. These principles are part of Rawls's conception of justice as fairness, which allows inequalities of income and wealth and regards them just, if they are to the advantage of the least favoured members of society. This Rawlsian treatment of social and economic inequalities has been criticized extensively by many political philosophers and plays a central role in Cohen's critique. The content and the Rawlsian interpretation of the second principle of justice as well as the argument for it from the original position are explored in this chapter.

Both principles of justice that Rawls suggests as the result of the choices made in the original position[1] apply to institutions of society and express the same general idea of justice. The Rawlsian general conception of justice is based on equal distributions of primary goods, such as liberty and opportunity, as well as income and wealth, unless an unequal distribution of one or all of them is to everyone's advantage. But, "it imposes no restrictions on what sort of inequalities are permissible; it only requires that everyone's position be improved" (TJ: 62). Justice as fairness with its two principles of justice in the order put forward by Rawls is a general conception of justice. Whereas the first principle of justice refers to an equal distribution of liberty such as the right to vote or the liberty of conscience and freedom of thought, the second principle of justice, explored in this chapter, focuses on distributions of income and wealth obtained by holding positions and offices open to all members of society, and by arranging social and economic inequalities so that they benefit everyone.

"While the basic liberties of citizens are all required to be equal, the distribution of income and wealth need not be equal, it must be to everyone's ad-

---

1 Recall from chapter 1 that this is a thought experiment that Rawls conducts to justify the choice of the two principles of justice. In this hypothetical situation, representative individuals of all social classes stand equally behind a veil of ignorance to choose the most reasonable principles of justice for their society.

vantage, and at the same time, positions of authority and offices of command must be accessible to all" (TJ: 61). Certain inequalities of wealth Rawls considers permissible are allowed within the Rawlsian conception of justice if they improve the condition of the least advantaged members of society. Equality is not an actual and necessary precondition in the Rawlsian theory for the realization of justice. In fact Rawls uses it as a theoretical benchmark of justice for judging the possible improvements of the social and economic situations of different social classes within a liberal democratic society. He envisages an equal starting point characterized by equal distributions of all the social primary goods: Citizens have the same rights and liberties and even the same shares of income and wealth. He then assumes a later stage of development characterized by certain inequalities of wealth but not of liberty. His question is: Why not tolerate inequalities if they make everyone better-off than in the initial hypothetical starting point of equal liberty and wealth?

To illustrate the idea that certain unequal distributions of income and wealth could benefit all members of society more than an equal distribution, two economic situations are compared in the following. The first case is characterized by an unequal distribution of wealth by maintaining a specific tax system that allows high levels of income for the most advantaged social classes. The second economic situation is characterized by an equal distribution of income and wealth by providing the same shares of income to all social classes. Rawls argues, an unequal distribution would benefit everyone – including the least advantaged members of society – more than an equal distribution. Rawls believes that higher incomes for the most advantaged, who can generate business, would motivate them to increase production. As a consequence more opportunities and financial gains would accrue which could be redistributed among all social classes. The financial inequalities would function as incentives to motivate the most productive and advantaged social classes to enhance their productivity. Rawls thus opts for an unequal distribution of income, which is articulated in the second principle of justice.

4.2 Justice as Fairness: The Second Principle of Justice

The revised version of the two principles is given by Rawls as follows:

> Each person is to have an equal right to the most extensive total system of equal liberties compatible with a similar system of liberty for all.
> Social and economic inequalities are to be arranged so that they are both:
> a) to the greatest benefit of the least advantaged [...]; and

b) attached to offices and positions open to all under conditions of fair equality of opportunity (TJ: 302).

The first principle of justice, examined in the first chapter, requires all members of society to possess maximum equal rights and liberties. Institutions should apply this principle equally to every citizen.

Within Rawls's conception of justice, the equality of liberty expressed by the first principle of justice is more important than the equality of income and wealth articulated in the second principle of justice. This priority is reflected in the order of the two principles of justice. This order means that the equality of liberty is to be applied fully as a precondition for the application of the second principle. Moreover, equal rights and liberties "cannot be, justified by, or compensated for, by greater social and economic advantages" (TJ: 61). Exchanges between basic liberties and economic and social gains are thus not allowed. The priority of the first principle over the second "expresses an underlying preference among primary social goods" (TJ: 63). Besides, the priority or the importance of the first principle is obvious within the Rawlsian society, characterized as *liberal* democratic, where free and equal members have the same rights and liberties and aim to achieve greater social and economic advantages.

4.3 Fair Equality of Opportunity

The second part of the second principle of justice is the idea of fair equality of opportunity. According to Rawls, within a fair conception of justice, social positions should be open to all. If positions are not open to all, the construct that applies to the basic structure of society is not fair towards all individuals of society. This would oppose the idea of a social cooperation[2], in which citizens of the same society live together in a fair social system that preserves the collective rewards. It is unfair and unjust if "some places were not open on a basis fair to all, [and] those kept out would be right in feeling unjustly treated even though they benefited from the greater efforts of those who were allowed to hold them" (TJ: 84).

The system of cooperation should be organized in a way that profits are shared among all members of society. Rawls suggests treating "the question of

2 The idea of cooperation refers to the rational commitment of members of society to assist each other to realize the welfare of all. Citizens have to agree on rules and procedures that respect the equality of liberties and rights as well as shares of income and wealth for all members of society.

distributive shares as a matter of pure procedural justice" (TJ: 85). He illustrates the notions of perfect, imperfect and pure procedural justice with the simple example of fair division of a cake among a given number of people. The question is: What procedure will assure a fair division of the cake if – as in this case – a fair division is an equal one? The procedure, according to which the fair outcome would be given, should be determined before the division takes place. In a perfect procedural justice,[3] the person who divides the cake should have the last piece, so that he divides equally and assures for him and for all others the biggest possible shares. "The essential thing is that there is an independent standard for deciding which outcome is just and a procedure guaranteed to lead to it" (ibid.). In an imperfect procedural justice, the procedure to reach a just outcome depends on the circumstances, and is impossible to capture in a general procedural rule. "[W]hile there is an independent criterion for the correct outcome, there is no feasible procedure which is sure to lead to it" (TJ: 86). However, in the case of pure procedural justice, there is no independent criterion "by reference to which a definite outcome can be known to be just" (ibid.), but a fair procedure that leads, when adopted, to a fair outcome. Rawls illustrates the situation with the example of gambling, where a number of persons engage in a series of fair bets.[4] The distribution of money after the last bet, no matter what it is, is not unfair because the procedure of betting is fair even without reference to a specific just distribution.

> What makes the final outcome of betting fair, or not unfair, is that it is the one which has arisen after a series of fair gambles. A fair procedure translates its fairness to the outcome only when it is actually carried out (ibid.).

Similarly, the idea of pure procedural justice should be applied to distributive shares within the Rawlsian conception of justice, without reference to a definite evidently just conclusion. A just arrangement of social and economic institutions as the result of applying the two principles of justice would secure a fair distribution of rights, liberties, wealth, and equal opportunities. In a competitive market determined by a liberal democratic system, citizens enjoy equal rights and liberties. Wealth should be distributed through a system of taxation,

---

3 Following Rawls, "pretty clearly, perfect procedural justice is rare, if not impossible, in cases of much practical interest" (TJ: 85).

4 Rawls assumes that the betting procedure is fair and fair bets are made voluntarily, without any expectation of gain.

according to a procedure that guarantees a "reasonable social minimum".[5] Fair equality of opportunity should be secured by holding positions open to all and by making these positions accessible to all. This includes providing equal educational training opportunities for all members of society. Persons who have similar talents and skills would thus have similar opportunities for developing their talents no matter to which social class they belong.

> [I]t would appear that the resulting distribution of income and the pattern of expectations will tend to satisfy the difference principle. In this complex of institutions, which we think of as establishing social justice in the modern state, the advantages of the better situated improve the condition of the least favored. Or when they do not, they can be adjusted to do so, for example, by setting the social minimum at the appropriate level (TJ: 87).

4.4 The Interpretation of the Second Principle of Justice

Rawls's second principle of justice refers to the expectations of representative individuals in a liberal democratic society. It aims at maximizing the expectations of members of all social classes. This principle, divided into two parts, reflects two ideas. On the one hand, it stresses the idea that the existing inequalities should improve the social and economic situation of the lower social classes. On the other hand, the principle implies that social positions and offices should not only be *equally open* to all members of society, but also equally *accessible* to all members. Under this condition, the principle legitimizes and tolerates existing inequalities used for the improvement of everyone's situation in society. Rawls argues that the most disadvantaged members of society, who agreed to this principle in the original position, would view their situation with the existing inequalities more favourable to their chances without these inequalities.

Rawls holds that there are four possible interpretations of the two principles of justice. In fact, the first principle of justice can only be understood in one way. However the ambiguities of two crucial phrases in the statement of the second principle – "to everyone's advantage" and "equally open to all" – has led to four interpretations of the two principles or four different political systems: natural aristocracy, a system of natural liberty, liberal equality and a

5 Note that Rawls does not precise the economic system that should be applied. His aim is to give the normative principles for a just distribution of income and wealth, which determine how the distribution should be done. The choice of the suitable economic system does not belong to the sphere of political philosophy.

democratic equality. These are explained in the following as well as the democratic equality preferred by Rawls as best matching the intentions of his theory and both principles of justice.

4.4.1 The System of Natural Aristocracy

In all types of societies, differences in natural and social contingencies are reflected in the different social classes[6]. The system of natural aristocracy is characterized by the existence of social classes within the same society. It is characterized by equality of liberty and the idea of equal opportunities. Yet, the equality of opportunity remains formal because natural and social contingencies are not regulated. Since prospects in life are determined to a large degree by social and natural endowments influenced by social circumstances or contingencies, Rawls calls for a conception of justice that regulates the effects of natural endowment and the contingencies of social circumstance. However, in the system of natural aristocracy, no serious effort is made to mitigate the effects of natural and social contingencies. For example, socially and naturally better endowed persons would be those who could afford a good education that enables them to develop their skills and reach the relevant social positions. Those who cannot afford a good education would not have the same chances to attain such positions. Even though positions are formally open to all, no attempt is undertaken to make them truly accessible to all members of society.

Thus, a system of natural aristocracy might fulfill the difference principle insofar as it strives to limit the gains of the rich in order to improve the situation of the poor. The "advantages of persons with greater natural endowments are to be limited to those that further the good of the poorer sectors of society" (TJ: 74). So, it would be just if the better endowed social classes gained less, if more were gained by the less endowed. Although social and economic inequalities are regulated to benefit the least favoured members of society, the system of natural aristocracy does not fully reflect the Rawlsian principles of justice, since social positions are not equally accessible for the underprivileged.

6 For example, the least advantaged social classes are those with the lowest expectations of social goods, in opposition to the most advantaged social classes, which have the highest expectations.

4.4.2 The System of Natural Liberty

The second possible interpretation of the two principles of justice is as a system of natural liberty. As in all other possible systems, the first principle of justice is satisfied. Rights and liberties are equally assigned to all members of society. However, the other part of the second principle of justice – that positions are open and accessible to all – is put into practice by opening careers to talents. Reaching certain social positions or offices of command depends on the natural and social skills of the candidates and the way they developed them. So those who are naturally and socially better endowed would have better chances to reach the positions theoretically open to all. Those who are less endowed would not have the same chances to attain these positions due to their "bad" endowment. The first part of the second principle of justice stipulates that a distribution is just if it is to everyone's advantage (the difference principle). The system of natural liberty attempts to apply both principles of justice to the basic structure of society in the form of the principle of efficiency and the principle of careers open to talents.

The principle of Pareto efficiency, also called the principle of Pareto optimality, and the Pareto principle are named after the Italian economist Vilfredo Pareto, and should not be confused. On the one hand, Pareto assumes that everyone enjoys the consumption of goods or services and wants to have more rather than less of any utility. It is true that if a person has five bottles of wine and one slice of cheese, in this distribution cheese is more valuable than wine. But, the person would be indifferent towards the distribution of wine and cheese if cheese and wine was apportioned equally. So, any distribution of wine and cheese would make the person equally happy, unless the value is accrued by an increase of wine and cheese.

On the other hand, Pareto assumes that humans are fundamentally the same; They all want the same things. Therefore, comparisons of utility across individuals are not allowed in his theory. He takes persons A and B; person A has wine and person B has cheese, so that they both have something to exchange with the other, thus increasing the utility. They decide to exchange wine and cheese voluntarily in a way that makes them happier, until the utility improvement of one of them diminishes the utility of the other. The distribution is then called Pareto optimal or Pareto efficient, insofar as no more Pareto improvements can be made, because what is wanted by person A is rejected by person B.

The principle of Pareto efficiency was developed out of a concern for the distribution of income and wealth. It was meant to apply to "distributions of goods among consumers" (TJ: 67). This principle states that a distribution of goods or "a configuration is efficient whenever it is impossible to change it so as to make some persons (at least one) better off without at the same time making other persons (at least one) worse off" (TJ: 68). For example, if two persons – A and B – exchange goods, such as apples and bananas, a distribution of these goods is efficient when person A profits without person B being disadvantaged. "Indeed, an efficient distribution is one in which it is not possible to find further profitable exchanges" (TJ: 70).

In the system of natural liberty, Pareto's principle of efficiency together with the principle of careers open to talents should apply to the basic structure of society. A just distribution of the social goods is achieved through the application of these two principles. "Assigning rights and duties in this way is thought to give a scheme which allocates wealth and income, authority and responsibility, in a fair way whatever this allocation turns out to be" (TJ: 66). Rawls argues that the Pareto efficiency should be applied to the basic structure of society since it would be chosen by representative individuals in the original position. He asserts that the set of rights and liberties selected in the original position is Pareto efficient because there is no better arrangement to maximize the expectations of some representative individuals without lowering the expectations of others.

Thus, if political liberty is equally assigned according to the first principle of justice, there are many efficient arrangements for distributing income and wealth. According to the system of natural liberty, all efficient distributions that benefit some social classes without lowering the expectations of other social classes are just. Rawls disagrees on this point: Efficiency is not justice. Not all efficient distributions are equally just. "The problem [says Rawls] is to choose between them, to find a conception of justice that singles out one of these efficient distributions as also just [...]. The principle of efficiency cannot serve alone as a conception of justice" (TJ: 71). In a competitive market economy, where income and wealth are to be efficiently distributed, efficient distributions might be influenced by prior distributions of natural talents and skills determined by natural and social contingencies. "Intuitively, the most obvious injustice of the system of natural liberty is that it permits distributive shares to be improperly influenced by these factors so arbitrary from a moral point of view" (TJ: 72).

This shows that the criterion of efficiency is not sufficient to realize a just distribution of goods. Efficient distributions are also based on arbitrary natural and social contingencies such as natural talents and skills. The Rawlsian problem is the identification of an efficient distribution of goods that is also just. Within the Rawlsian conception of justice, the idea of justice has priority over the idea of efficiency. An efficient distribution based on natural talents proves arbitrary and unjust. Therefore, it is rejected by Rawls as it is not in line with the difference principle. Hence, Rawls searches for an interpretation, which proves just and efficient, with the idea of justice prior to the idea of efficiency.

4.4.3 The Liberal Interpretation

The third possible interpretation of the two principles of justice is the liberal interpretation. It corrects the injustice of careers open to talents by applying the principle of fair equality of opportunity. Citizens born into different social classes endowed with equal skills and talents should have the same chance to develop them in order to reach social positions accessible to all. "[W]e might say that those with similar abilities and skills should have similar life chances" (TJ: 73). So, the least advantaged members of society would have realistic opportunities to attain relevant positions. But, if the liberal interpretation succeeds in mitigating the injustice resulting from the arbitrariness of *social* contingencies, such as the class of origin, it still fails to reduce the injustice caused by *natural* circumstances. Hence, it allows the distribution of income and wealth to be arbitrarily and unjustly influenced by natural contingencies, such as abilities and talents:

> [D]istributive shares are decided by the outcome of the natural lottery; and this outcome is arbitrary from a moral perspective [...]. It is impossible in practice to secure equal chances of achievement and culture for those similarly endowed, and therefore we may want to adopt a principle which recognizes this fact and also mitigates the arbitrary effects of the natural lottery itself. That the liberal conception fails to do this encourages one to look for another interpretation of the two principles of justice (TJ: 74).

4.4.4 The Difference Principle within the Democratic Interpretation

The democratic interpretation of the Rawlsian principles of justice applies the equality of opportunity and the difference principle, which combines the ideas of efficiency and justice. In the interpretation preferred by Rawls, efficient distributions are not all equally just. We have seen that the criterion of efficiency alone is not sufficient to make the distribution just. Rawls argues that both efficiency and justice are reflected in the difference principle. This principle determines the justice of every efficient distribution by "singling out a particular position from which the social and economic inequalities of the basic structure are to be judged" (TJ: 75). The greater advantages of the privileged members of society are just if they improve the expectations of the underprivileged members of society. So a just distribution is a distribution that benefits all members of society including the least advantaged. Hence, any distribution of goods that is merely efficient but does not benefit the least advantaged citizens, is unjust and should be rejected according to the difference principle.

Rawls illustrates the interpretation of the difference principle and the inequalities it permits with the example of entrepreneurs and unskilled workers. Entrepreneurs will always have better prospects than unskilled workers because of their better starting positions. Yet according to the difference principle, these inequalities are to be allowed only if they are to the advantage of the unskilled workers. If inequalities fail to improve the situation of the least advantaged members of society, they should not be permitted. According to Rawls, "the greater expectations allowed to entrepreneurs encourages them to do things which raise the long-term prospects of the laboring class. Their better prospects act as incentives so that the economic process is more efficient" (TJ: 78).

Rawls is aware of the danger of unjust arrangements and their effects on the least advantaged members of society. Indeed, the difference principle is a principle of maximizing the minimum prospects of an intersection society. It allows inequalities as long as they benefit the least advantaged members of society. If the rich have excessive expectations, the resultant gross inequalities should not be considered just. The situation of the least favoured citizens would improve, only if extravagant expectations of the most advantaged members decreased. Rawls tries to delimit the expectations of the privileged above which inequalities are no longer tolerable. He argues that large differences would violate the principle of mutual advantage as well the principle of democratic equality:

> How unjust an arrangement is depends on how excessive the higher expectations are and to what extent they depend upon the violation of the other principles of justice [...]. [A] society should try to avoid the region where the marginal contributions of those better off are negative [...]. The even larger difference between rich and poor makes the latter even worse off, and this violates the principle of mutual advantage as well as democratic equality (TJ: 79).

Through the application of the difference principle, the effects of social and natural contingencies would be minimized. Citizens have equal rights and are capable of attaining social positions and of improving their economic situations even if they were born into a lower social class. The difference principle proposes fair means to deal with the effects of arbitrary and undeserved social and natural circumstances. These contingencies are important facts in everyone's lives insofar as they represent the undeserved natural and social advantages everyone acquired at birth and which partly determine expectations and plans for life. These advantages or endowments differ from person to person. Additionally the morally arbitrary means and possibilities a person owns for developing and improving them, increases the differences and inequalities among the persons holding these endowments. What are the options for dealing with these facts? Is the difference principle a principle of redress?

A principle of redress states "that undeserved inequalities call for redress; and since inequalities of birth and natural endowment are undeserved, these inequalities are to be somehow compensated for" (TJ: 100). The idea is to level or equalize the arbitrariness of natural and social contingencies by compensating the least favoured members of society. This compensation implies, for example, an effective equality of opportunity, where

> society must give more attention to those with fewer native assets and to those born into the less favorable social positions [...]. In pursuit of this principle greater resources might be spent on the education of the less rather than the more intelligent, at least over a certain time of life, say the earlier years of school (TJ: 100-101).

Rawls affirms that even though the difference principle realizes some points of the principle of redress, it *is not* a principle of redress. Although the difference principle prevents the unfair use of social and economic inequalities, it does not strive to remove them. In fact, social and economic inequalities result from facts, which are neither just nor unjust, neither bad nor good. Why should they be removed? Facts, which are neither just nor unjust, are not determined by persons, but rather by nature. Principles, however, according to which institutions should work and deal with these natural facts, are determined by persons. Therefore principles can be just or unjust. In the Rawlsian conception of justice, a society would be just because people agree to principles of justice that secure the mutual advantage of everyone. Contrariwise, "[a]ristocratic and caste societies are unjust because they make these contingencies the ascriptive basis for belonging to a more or less enclosed and privileged social class" (TJ: 102). And so the difference principle aims at improving the expectations of the least advantaged members of society. This can be achieved, for example, by assigning a higher share of resources in education[7] to them, or by securing a minimum level

---

7 The role of the education is very important according to Rawls, but it is not only related to the social welfare of the citizens or the advantages and the chances they have because of their education. It is mainly the only way to enable "a person to enjoy the culture of his society and to take part in its affairs, and in this way to provide for each individual a secure sense of his worth" (TJ: 101).

of income for all as well as by effectively[8] applying fair and equal opportunities. The central idea of the difference principle is that "no one gains or loses from his arbitrary place in the distribution of natural assets or his initial position in society without giving or receiving compensating advantages in return" (ibid.). In this way, Rawls not only allows social and economic inequalities but encourages their use, for the benefit of all members of society, unless they do not improve the situation of the least advantaged members:

> Those who have been favored by nature, whoever they are, may gain from their good fortune only on terms that improve the situation of those who have lost out [...]. No one deserves his greater natural capacity nor merits a more favorable starting place in society. But it does not follow that one should eliminate these distinctions. There is another way to deal with them (TJ: 101-102).

Furthermore, the difference principle is a principle of mutual benefit, articulated by the ideas of reciprocity and fraternity. According to Rawls, the difference principle expresses a conception of reciprocity because all representative members benefit from it mutually and would therefore, he hopes, agree to it. Consequently, the main institutions of a society's basic structure are organized according to the principles of justice in order to advance the interests of all members of society. Rawls believes that the least advantaged members would accept the idea of greater benefits for the most advantaged members without which the economic situation of the disadvantaged would not improve.[9] From their point of view, the most advantaged members should be convinced that their well-being cannot be enhanced without a fair system of social cooperation, in which the members of society cooperate fairly with one another under fair terms and conditions.

"The difference principle, then, seems to be a fair basis on which those better endowed, or more fortunate in their social circumstances, could expect others to collaborate with them when some workable arrangement is a necessary condition of the good of all" (TJ: 103). It has been depicted that the difference principle reflects the idea of fraternity (or solidarity, as it is called nowadays)

---

8 An effective application of fair equality of opportunity could be realized by holding social positions open to all members of society and making them accessible to all.

9 A common critique of the Rawlsian theory is that it neglects to treat the real problem of envy between members of society. This problem does not seem to threat the Rawlsian theory in the sense that Rawls thinks that representative members, who stand in the original position are "envy-free". The least advantaged members of society would accept the idea of greater benefits to the most advantaged members because of the values of fraternity, mutuality and reciprocity, which are also dictated by the difference principle. This Rawlsian idea seems to be unrealistic.

insofar as the most advantaged members do not receive greater benefits unless they are to the benefit of others (the least advantaged members). Rawls presents the example of the ideal family to illustrate the idea of fraternity which exemplifies the difference principle. "Members of a family commonly do not wish to gain unless they can do so in ways that furthers the interests of the rest" (TJ: 105). Likewise, according to the difference principle, the better endowed should strive for more benefits within a scheme that improves the social and economic situation of the less fortunate members of a social group.

> [L]iberty corresponds to the first principle, equality to the idea of equality in the first principle together with equality of fair opportunity, and fraternity to the difference principle. In this way we have found a place for the conception of fraternity in the democratic interpretation of the two principles (TJ: 106).

4.5 The Argument for the Second Principle of Justice

The first chapter describes the original position as a heuristic device of representation that models the fair conditions under which free and equal citizens would agree – from a given list of principles – on the most reasonable principles of justice for their society. It also models the ways of reasoning or the common basis of reason, according to which the parties would choose certain principles and reject others. Rawls supposes that the representatives in the original position "reason by comparing alternatives two at a time" (JF: 95). Yet if the Rawlsian principles of justice were compared with the principle of average utility[10],

> the first comparison, which gives the reasoning for the first principle, is I think, quite conclusive; the second comparison, which gives the reasoning for the difference principle, is less conclusive. [...] Nevertheless, despite the limited scope of this two-part argument, it is instructive in suggesting how we can proceed in other comparisons to bring out the merits of the two principles (ibid.).

The principle of average utility states that the "institutions of the basic structure are to be arranged so as to maximize the average welfare of the mem-

10 This principle represents the utilitarianism, which principle of justice applies to society as a as a social system organized to produce the most good summed over all its members. Rawls chooses this principle in his comparison because, together with the idea of society as fair system of cooperation between free and equal citizens, those principles represent the prominent contrasting ideas in the history of democratic thought.

bers of society, beginning now and extending into the foreseeable future" (JF: 96).

So, after agreeing to the principles of equal rights and liberties and equal opportunities in the first conclusive comparison, the main divergence within the second comparison is about the way social and economic inequalities should be regulated. Using the maximin rule, which instructs individuals to compare the worst outcome of each alternative and to choose the best one of these worst outcomes, citizens would opt for the two principles of justice. In fact, for the sake of greater advantages, the principle of average utility may require, for example, that restrictions are imposed on rights and liberties. But such limitations, Rawls argues, would not be acceptable: "[T]hose persons would never put their basic rights and liberties in jeopardy as long as there was a readily available and satisfactory alternative" (JF: 102). Thus, to guarantee that the basic interests of citizens as free and equal persons are secured, representatives would select the Rawlsian principles of justice. Moreover, these principles would "encourage the spirit of cooperation between citizens, on a footing of mutual respect, and allows within itself sufficient social space for (permissible) ways of life fully worthy of citizens' allegiance" (JF: 118). Rawls takes the arguments presented so far to prove the superiority of both principles of justice over the principle of average utility. This principle, "combined with a suitable social minimum" (JF: 102) is compared with the difference principle in the original position. Rawls argues that both, the most and the least advantaged members of society would opt for the difference principle, against the indeterminacy of the other principle. This choice reflects the difficulty of determining the ideal of a social minimum. "This concept of the minimum is vague in that the guidelines it suggests do not specify a very definite minimum, which will in any case depend in part on society's level of wealth" (JF: 129). As a result, the life-prospects could be minimized if the social minimum did not suffice to cover the needs required for a decent life. The difference principle, Rawls conceives, would thus be selected because it is thought to maximize the minimal expectations for life. It expresses the idea of reciprocity that the principle of average utility ignores. The Rawlsian principle applies the idea of reciprocity to the basic structure insofar as "social institutions are not to take advantage of contingencies of native endowment, or of initial social position, or of good or bad luck over the course of life, except in ways that benefit everyone, including the least favoured" (JF: 124). The most advantaged, already blessed by nature, would accept the difference principle, which allows them to increase their benefits, "provided that they do so in ways that improve the situation of others" (JF:

126). The least advantaged would select the difference principle because it guarantees an improvement of their unfortunate social and economic situation.

In sum, both principles of justice stated within the Rawlsian conception of justice, justice as fairness, would be reasonable principles for a liberal democratic society. An equal assignment of basic rights and liberties together with equal opportunities reflects the idea of equality that the main institutions apply to all citizens of a society. The difference principle reflects the idea that unequal incomes and riches are permissible and therefore just if they are to the advantage of the least advantaged members of society. It does not aim at removing social and economic inequalities, but tries to regulate and mitigate them under fair conditions for all. These conditions are realized if everyone benefits from the resulting inequalities. Besides, Rawls argues, the representative individuals would have selected the difference principle in the original position, because it guarantees the mutual advantage of everyone in society within the ideas of reciprocity and fraternity which it endorses.

But, if the difference principle secures a fair distribution of income and wealth for the rich and the poor members of society, why does it remain the target and subject of so many philosophical critiques?

5 The Rescue of Equality from the Rawlsian Theory of Justice

5.1 Cohen's Critique of the Difference Principle

In the example, featuring the distribution of manna bundles, discussed in chapter 3, Cohen and Rawls opt for the *same* distribution of manna. Cohen discusses, from different philosophical viewpoints, whether an unequal distribution of manna is fair. He concludes that those who think that justice requires equality would choose the division (5/5) that keeps the extra manna undistributed. Cohen ultimately selects, like Rawls, the second, unequal distribution of manna (6/7), which favours one person over another for no fault or merit or choice of their own. Whereas the Rawlsian choice is justified and endorsed as just within the difference principle (that allows inequalities of such a kind), the unequal distribution of manna is preferable according to Cohen so that humans might prosper but is per se unjust. The Cohenian-Rawlsian choice hides a sharp disagreement concerning the relationship between equality and justice that motivates Cohen to rescue both concepts from the misleading Rawlsian treatment.

The first part of RJE attempts to rescue the concept of equality from the Rawlsian argument, which promotes inequality and thereby injustice, with the two principles of justice. As already mentioned the first principle of justice requires equality of basic rights and liberties and the second principle of justice requires fair equality of opportunity together with the difference principle. This principle allows social and economic inequalities based on the fact that greater benefits and advantages are unequally redistributed according to the Pareto principle, which implies a collective improvement of the situation for all members of society. Consequently, the difference principle does not express the value of justice because it approves inequalities. Therefore Cohen attempts to rescue the concept of equality from the difference principle, which, he argues, violates its nature. The Cohenian rescue is achieved through the critique of the difference principle and the Rawlsian arguments for it: the incentives argument and the Pareto argument.[1] These elements as well as the Cohenian viewpoint about equality and its relationship to justice are explored in the following. What

1 Chapters 5 and 6 of this work will expose the arguments of the first chapter of RJE, which has been published in 1992 as "Incentives, Inequality, and Community", in: Grethe Peterson, ed., *The Tanner Lectures on Human Values*. Salt Lake City: Utah University Press. Vol. 13, pp. 263-329.

would be the Cohenian alternative for regulating social and economic inequalities? How could the difference principle be corrected in order to coincide with Cohen's understanding of justice?

5.2 Rescue of Equality from the Incentives Argument

Rawls's incentives argument stipulates that if affluent people are impelled to boost the economy, all members of a society will benefit. According to Rawls, the talented or the most advantaged persons would not increase their productivity, unless they received greater profits, which in turn would augment social and economic inequalities. The rewards would be the incentives to motivate them to boost their production.

Cohen thinks that the incentives argument endorsed within the difference principle does not articulate the virtue of justice. He starts his critique with a small conversation taken from Jan Narveson's article "Rawls on Equal Distribution of Wealth". This imaginary conversation takes place between a rich and a poor citizen and shows that the moneyed cannot uphold the view that they can only generate more business if they receive more benefits. The incentive argument to that effect fails:

> Well-off: Look here, fellow citizen, I'll work hard and make both you and me better off, provided I get a bigger share than you.
> Worse-off: Well, that's rather good; but I thought you were agreeing that justice requires equality?
> Well-off: Yes, but that's only as a benchmark, you see. To do still better, both of us, you understand, may require differential incentive payments to people like me.
> Worse-off: Oh. Well, what makes them necessary?
> Well-off: What makes them necessary is that I won't work as hard if I don't get more than you.
> Worse-off: Well, why not?
> Well-off: I dunno... I guess that's just the way I'm built.
> Worse-off: Meaning, you don't really care all that much about justice, eh?
> Well-off: Er, no I guess not (RJE: 27).

To begin his critique of the difference principle, which relies on the soundness of the incentives argument, Cohen compares its effects to the consequences that followed Nigel Lawson's[2] tax cut in Britain in 1988, when the top rate of income tax was brought down from 60 to 40 percent. As a matter of fact, "that cut en-

2 Nigel Lawson was at that time (March 1988) Her Majesty's Chancellor of the exchequeur.

larged the net incomes of those whose incomes were already large, in comparison with the British average, and, of course, in comparison with the income of Britain's poor" (ibid.). To the political right, rich people are entitled to their wealth, whether they produced it or others. According to the utilitarians, this inequality would motivate well-off persons to increase their productivity and thereby the "sum of human happiness". However, the Rawlsians – who refuse the principles of entitlement and desert[3] and the idea of the sum of human happiness[4] – reject this inequality, unless it improves the social and economic situation of the least advantaged members of society.

> [T]heir high levels of income cause unusually productive people to produce more than they otherwise would; and, as a result of the incentives enjoyed by those at the top, the people who end up near the bottom are better off than they would be in a more equal society. [...] For Rawls, some people are [...] capable of producing more than others are, and it is right for them to be richer than others if the less fortunate are caused to be better off as a result (RJE: 29).[5]

Yet Cohen, who accepts the difference principle in its general form, questions "its application in defense of special money incentives to talented people", by highlighting the contradiction that it embodies. On the one hand, Rawls refuses to justify social and economic inequalities on the grounds of entitlement or merit. He believes that the difference principle justifies inequalities related to extra money incentives. He argues that inequalities are justified and thereby allowed as long as the lower classes gain from them. Now, the justification of incentives and the associated inequalities seems problematic to Cohen, because it violates the spirit of the difference principle, which is designed for a community, or a group of persons living together in a system of social cooperation. According to Cohen, if talented persons were committed to the difference principle, they would *not need* special money incentives to enhance their productivity. "Accordingly, they must be thought of as outside the community upholding

3 No one merits the natural and social advantages or disadvantages of no fault or choice or merit of their own that is why social and economic inequalities cannot be justified by merit or desert.

4 Rawls criticizes the utilitarian principle of happiness, which implies the realization of the happiness of the greatest number of citizens.

5 Cohen stresses the ambiguity of the inequality endorsed by the difference principle. It is not clear, according to him, whether the difference principle allows inequalities that either do not improve the situation of the worst-off or do not make their situation worse. In its generous form, the difference principle allows, inequalities "that do not help but also do not hurt the worst off" (RJE: 29).

the principle when it is used to justify incentive payments to them" (RJE: 32). Why do citizens living together under the values of fraternity and community represented by the difference principle, need to be motivated to increase their productiveness? Cohen concludes that this principle either embodies a fundamental contradiction – between the idea of community and the justification of inequalities due to money incentives – or inequalities resulting from these incentives are not justified by the difference principle.

> I want to record here my doubt that the difference principle justifies *any* significant inequality, in an unqualified way. [...] The worst off benefit from incentive inequality in particular only because the better off would, in effect, go on strike if unequalizing incentives were withdrawn (RJE: 33).

To explain the incentives argument endorsed by the difference principle, Cohen concentrates on the justification formulated by the talented persons for Lawson's tax cut. In this critique, Cohen focuses on the persons who "produce a lot by exercising skill and talent, rather than by investing capital" (RJE: 34) and he challenges the incentives "conferring high rewards on people of talent who would otherwise not perform as those rewards induce them to do" (RJE: 35).

The central idea is: *If* the talented persons do not receive greater rewards, they will produce less and as a result poor people would be even more worse-off than they are. In the following, the three premises of the argument are discussed:

1) Economic inequalities are justified if they improve the material situation of the poor (major, normative premise)
2) When the top tax rate is 40 percent (minor, factual premise):
   a) the talented produce more than when the top tax rate is 60 percent, and
   b) the situation of the worst off citizens is materially improved[6] as a result.
3) Therefore, the top tax should not be raised from 40 to 60 percent.

Cohen examines the validity of the incentives argument by applying the interpersonal test. "This tests shows how robust a policy argument is by subjecting it to variation with respect to who is speaking and/or who is listening when the argument is presented" (RJE: 42). Cohen imagines a conversation between a prosperous person and a destitute person, where the former personally enunciates the argument to the latter. "[A]lthough the argument may sound reasona-

6 Talented persons would produce more when the top tax is at 40 percent, so that more income and work opportunities would be produced and redistributed among the different social classes within the society.

ble when it is presented in blandly impersonal form, [...] it does not sound so good when we fix on a presentation of it in which a talented rich person pronounces it to a badly off person" (RJE: 35). Does the incentives argument pass the interpersonal test?

5.3 The Interpersonal Test

Cohen believes that for a policy to be accepted in a community, it should pass the interpersonal test. The idea of community refers in the Cohenian understanding to a justificatory community, "which is a set of people among whom there prevails a norm [...] of comprehensive justification" (RJE: 43). This means that for a norm to prevail, it should be accepted and justified within the community. Thus, it is justified only if it passes the interpersonal test. "Now an argument fails the interpersonal test, and is therefore inconsistent with community, if relevant agents [such as talented rich persons] *could* not justify the behavior the argument ascribes to them" (RJE: 44).

Hence, Cohen asks the talented persons, who formulate the incentives argument, to give an acceptable justification for their premise of refusing to produce more when the top tax rate is at 60 percent. If they cannot justify this argument within the interpersonal test, they consequently make its minor factual premise true.

In order to explain how a premise could be vindicated, Cohen introduces the argument of the kidnapper who refuses to release the children, unless he is paid ransom money. The kidnapper would present the following argument: "Children should be with their parents. Unless you pay me, I shall not return your child. So you should pay me" (RJE: 39). This argument owes its force to the decision of the kidnapper, who refuses to release the children unless he is paid by the parents.

If the talented rich are unable to justify their behaviour of not being able to work more and enhance their production when the top tax is 60 percent – within the interpersonal test, then their argument would fail in a justificatory community.

> If lack of community is displayed when the rich present the incentives argument, then the argument itself (irrespective of who affirms it) represents relations between rich and poor as at variance with community. It follows [...] that the incentives argument can justify inequality only in a society where interpersonal relations lack a communal character (RJE: 46-47).

Cohen aims to prove that talented rich people make the minor premise of the incentives argument true and thereby fail the interpersonal test. "I have to show that the minor premise of the incentives argument owes its truth to their [of the talented persons] decisions and intentions" (RJE: 48). Why is the factual premise of the argument true? Are the rich unable to work (inability) or unwilling to work (decision) hard at a 60 percent top tax rate?

After considering the possible reasons that might push the talented persons to work hard only at a 40 percent top tax rate, Cohen concludes that they do not *want* to work as much otherwise. If they were, for example, physically unable to work hard at a 60 percent tax rate, they would not make the factual premise true. They are not unable, but rather *unwilling* to be as productive at a 60 percent tax rate, because they need to be motivated by higher rewards. "As a result of that choice, the badly off will be worse off than they were before [...], and, a fortiori, worse off than they would be if the talented rich maintained at 60 percent tax the effort they put in at 40 percent" (RJE: 55). Yet, Cohen asks whether the choice, which does not improve the situation of the least advantaged citizens, is justified within the interpersonal test. "Given that you would still be much better off than we are if you worked as you do now at the 60 percent tax, what justifies your intention to work less if the tax rises to that level?" (RJE: 60).

The rich, according to Cohen, cannot justify making the factual premise of the incentives argument true. They cannot say why the special money incentives are necessary, "since it is they who make it necessary" (ibid.), by a decision of their own. There is no other reason other than the fact that they are unwilling to work hard without receiving extra money incentives. "Finding it difficult to provide a convincing reply, the rich may represent their own optional attitudes and decisions as given facts" (RJE: 66), which they are unable to justify and which the poor are requested to accept. As the rich are unable to justify their behaviour, the incentives argument fails the interpersonal test; and as such it is not consented to within the justificatory community. Consequently, rich people live outside the community. But if all citizens of different social classes live together, the incentives argument is incompatible with the communal character of society. Moreover, Cohen argues that if there is no justification for the strategy proposed by the most advantaged citizens, it would seem reasonable for the least advantaged to reject the choice. Yet, would it be sensible for the same reasons to reject the Rawlsian difference principle, which endorses the incentives argument?

> But it would not necessarily be irrational for the poor to reject what the rich suggest [...]. It is not necessarily irrational (and it is sometimes felt to be morally imperative) to refuse to deal with a person who wields power unjustifiably (RJE: 64).

Cohen is aware of the differences between Rawls's ideas on social and economic inequalities and those of the Lawson's tax cut defenders. But he justifies his analogical comparison by highlighting the similarities of their arguments, which both defend inequalities.

5.4 Two Readings of the Difference Principle: Rawls's Contradiction

As maintained above the difference principle states that inequalities are just if they are necessary to improve the situation of the impoverished members of society. Cohen examines the two possible meanings of the term "necessary", which gives the difference principle two possible readings. While the aim is to make the worst-off materially better-off, necessary inequalities could be either "apart from human choice" or dependent on "what some people's intentions are" (RJE: 68). Inequalities that express the intentions of the talented persons, such as the fact that they are unwilling to provide the same productivity at a 60 percent top tax rate, are endorsed by the lax reading of the difference principle. However, the strict reading of the difference principle, which for Cohen is "intention-independent", endorses the inequalities necessary to improve the material position of the poorest, regardless of the intentions of the rich.

Cohen argues that Rawls himself "has in effect two positions on the matter" (RJE: 69). When he talks about the spirit and the culture in which people should apply the difference principle – together with the ideas about dignity and fraternity – he points to the strict understanding of it. However,

> by endorsing incentives, Rawls treats inequalities whose necessity is relative to the intentions of talented people as acceptable to the difference principle: he proceeds as though he affirms the principle in its lax interpretation (ibid.).

According to Cohen, in order to ensure justice, Rawls should have adhered to the strict interpretation of the difference principle and should not have endorsed the incentives argument within the lax difference principle. Thus Cohen questions its description as a fundamental principle of justice. Does the lax interpretation honor the ideas of dignity and fraternity, which ground the principles of justice? One must remember that the idea of fraternity is realized when the privileged refuse greater economic benefits, unless this benefits the underprivileged. Yet, the lax interpretation of the difference principle implies that everyone within the society "gets what she can through self-seeking behavior in a market whose rewards are so structured by taxation and other regulation that the worst off are as well off as any scheme of taxed and regulated market rewards can make them" (RJE: 74). Rawls believes that if a certain economic strategy, which justifies the incentives argument, could improve the material situation of the poor, the ideas of fraternity and dignity would be honored within the lax difference principle. Cohen criticizes what he takes to be the Rawlsian contradiction: How can the wealthy, acting in accordance with the difference principle, seek greater benefits and at the same time only accept these benefits if they benefit the situation of the other citizens?

> Rawls must give up either his approval of incentives to the exercise of talent or his ideals of dignity and fraternity, and the full realization of persons' moral natures. I think the ideals are worth keeping (RJE: 80).

However, in a society where the strict difference principle is applied, citizens living together in social cooperation would share the same understanding of the idea of justice. This common interpretation of the idea of justice would motivate them to put it into practice in their daily lives and so ensure that their decisions and actions are just. There would be no big difference between the private and the public choice, because "citizens want their own economic behavior to satisfy the principle, and they help to sustain a moral climate in which others want the same" (RJE: 70). As a consequence just people must put into practice the strict difference principle. Yet,

> for the strict difference principle to prevail, there needs to be an ethos informed by the principle in society at large. Therefore, a society [...] does not qualify as committed to the difference principle unless it is indeed informed by a certain ethos or culture of justice. [...] Talented persons would not expect the high salaries whose level reflects high demand for their talent (RJE: 73).

Cohen introduces the strict interpretation of the difference principle to emphasize the Rawlsian contradiction between the socialist values of fraternity and dignity and the incentives argument. The incentives argument conflicts with the strict reading of the difference principle. According to Cohen, citizens in a well-ordered Rawlsian society would live in a fair system of cooperation and would comply fully with the principles of justice. All citizens would know exactly the same as the others and would be committed to the same principles. Rawls states that members of society should use these principles as a guideline for their daily lives. Cohen also quotes the Rawlsian viewpoint on the exploitation of the morally arbitrary contingencies, which causes social and economic inequalities; Rawls opposes this exploitation which contradicts the communal character within which citizens should live: "by abstaining from the exploitation of the contingencies of nature and social circumstances within a framework of equal liberty, persons express their respect for one another in the very constitution of their society" (RJE: 76). How can Rawls, accept the unequalizing incentives argument but refuse the idea of exploiting morally arbitrary contingencies, which leads to greater undeserved and random inequalities, and base this approach on the same philosophical perspective?

However, Cohen explains that in some cases, "it would be a mistake not to concede incentives inequalities" (RJE: 82), if they are needed to support effective productivity and performance. But, "it does not follow that having them is a requirement of basic justice, where a basic principle of justice is one that has application in a society where, as in Rawls's, everyone always acts justly" (ibid.). Accordingly, the incentives argument cannot be justified by a fundamental principle of justice. The difference principle in its lax interpretation is not a fundamental principle of justice "but a principle for handling people's injustice. [...] We might call it a principle of damage limitation in the field of justice" (RJE: 84). So, although there might be contexts in which it is right to put the difference principle in its lax reading into practice, this does not mean that it is a basic principle of justice. We may then search for other candidate principles.

5.5 Rescue of Equality from the Pareto Argument

To rescue the concept of equality from the Pareto argument endorsed by the difference principle, Cohen endeavours a critique of this argument as it is reformulated by Brian Barry in his *Theories of Justice*. He establishes that the sort of inequality Rawls tolerates "requires for its defense the very notions of desert and entitlement that he wants to reject" (RJE: 91). The difference principle allows inequalities if they are to the benefit of the most disadvantaged members of society. Cohen questions neither the difference principle nor the Pareto principle, but rather the Pareto (two-stage) argument, upon which inequalities are said to be just. Of course, the argument Cohen contends is not the actual Rawlsian argument, but "it manifestly serves to advance the Rawlsian purpose, which is, here, to reconcile certain inequalities with justice, and many like Barry, have found the argument convincing. So it is worth scrutinizing" (RJE: 88). According to Cohen, the starting point of the argument's first stage is the principle of equality of opportunity. This principle is in fact realized, when all morally arbitrary causes[7] of inequalities are removed and, by the same fact, equality of outcome is realized. Indeed, all inequalities result directly or indirectly from morally arbitrary contingencies. Therefore, equality of opportunity is the benchmark because morally arbitrary contingencies cannot be eliminated. Besides, "it might yet be true that an inequality could be just in virtue of its consequences" (RJE: 89). As a consequence, the second stage of the argument is formulated; inequalities are just if they cause (as a result) everyone to be better-off, including the most disadvantaged members of society. Why – as Rawls asks – should we insist on equality if inequality makes everyone better-off?

Hence, Cohen questions the move from an equal distribution determined by the equality of opportunity that implies an equality of outcome to an unequal distribution endorsed *solely* by the difference principle. "I claim that the particular type of Pareto improvement picked by Rawls contradicts the rationale of the original move from equality of opportunity to equality" (RJE: 90). The Pareto improvement chosen by Rawls abandons equality and supports the justice of inequality, because this benefits everyone's material position. The unequal distribution favoured by Rawls is according to him a Pareto-superior scheme, in which everyone would be better-off. Cohen argues that the two parts of the argument are inconsistent with each other. Equality is affirmed at the first stage in order to limit inequalities resulting from morally arbitrary contingencies, because they are undeserved and thereby unjust. However, inequality is endorsed instead of equality, which Rawls believes to be a Pareto-inferior improvement, in comparison to inequality which benefits everyone.

According to Cohen, Rawls could have defended the choice of inequality in another way in order to avoid the inconsistency of both parts of the argument. He should not have picked equality as a starting point, by favouring it over inequality; "[T]he best feasible equal distribution is Pareto-inferior to some feasible unequal distribution. An unequal distribution is, therefore, always to be preferred" (ibid.). In order to challenge the argument, Cohen proposes a state of affairs D1, in which social primary goods are equal but natural primary goods such as talents are unequal. He moves then from D1 to D2, which is a Pareto-superior alternative. In D2, talented rich persons are more advantaged than in D1. In fact, next to their natural advantages, they enjoy even greater social goods.

7 Those are divided into social advantages, such as the social class of birth and natural advantages, such as the skills and talents, the physical force. All those circumstances are causes of underserved and thereby unjust social and economic inequalities.

> We might find it surprising that the talented in particular should end up with more, since a principal insistence of the first part of the argument, which took us to D1, was that the circumstance of their greater talent justifies no distributive effect. And egalitarians might regret this "giving more to those who have than to those who have not (RJE: 98).

He presumes that talented and untalented persons work the same number of hours in D1 but that the talented are more productive due to their talents. However, both groups receive the same wage rate W. In D2, the talented [Wt] and untalented [Wu] do not receive the same wages. For their extra productivity the talented obtain more goods than in D1, which results in an increase in income of the less talented.

Furthermore, Cohen imagines a third distribution D3, "in which the same amount is produced as in D2 but which differs from D2 in that in D3 [We] wages are equal" (RJE: 100). So, the untalented would be better-off in D3 than in D2 in contrast to the talented who would be less well-off in D3 than in D2. But both would be better-off in D3 than in D1 because the productivity in D3 is superior to that in D1. Cohen considers this distribution a better alternative to the Rawlsian one, in which those already favoured receive even more benefits.

> If D3 is feasible and talented people are willing to produce at We what they do at Wt, then Rawls's claim about the irrationality of insisting on equality in the face of the possibility of a Pareto-superior inequality would lose its force, since a Pareto-improving equality-preserving move, in which no one is as badly off as some are in D2, would now also be available (RJE: 101).

Cohen criticizes the move from equality to inequality justified by the Pareto argument. This move hides the Rawlsian discrepancy on the matter. The causes of almost all inequalities are morally arbitrary, which is why Rawls chooses to start with equality which compensates undeserved inequalities. Moreover he abandons it for inequalities which would benefit the worst-off people, even though the causes of these inequalities are still morally arbitrary. Therefore, the difference principle permits through the Pareto argument, inequalities whose causes are morally arbitrary. This Cohen criticizes. What would be the Rawlsian treatment of morally arbitrary contingencies? What is the Cohenian "conception of justice"?

5.6 Rescue of Equality from the Contradiction of the Difference Principle

Let one assume that the talented persons are truly unable – due to an insurmountable inability – to increase their production without receiving unequalizing incentives, "then there would be no consequent stain of injustice on the resultant society" (RJE: 153). But, even if inequalities were needed[8] to augment productivity, they would remain unjust, because they result in one way or the other from morally arbitrary contingencies. Therefore, "the impossibility of justice, whether or not it is due to a flaw in human nature, is insufficient for the justice of the possible" (RJE: 155).

On the one hand, Cohen argues that the moral arbitrariness of social and economic inequalities and thereby their injustice contradicts the content of the difference principle, which endorses the justice of these inequalities. He explains furthermore that there are two versions of the difference principle which express different rationales. Whereas on the canonical view, "there is nothing especially privileged about equality" (RJE: 157), acting within the non-canonical difference principle implies "not wanting to have greater advantages unless this is to the benefit of others who are less well off" (ibid.). On the other hand, the inequality that the canonical difference principle tolerates does not compensate for undeserved and thereby unjust morally arbitrary contingencies. This inequality increases the social and economic differences among the social classes.

> The unfairness of arbitrarily caused inequality is the starting point of a chain of reasoning that ends in affirmation of the [canonical] difference principle, but that principle shows no trace of commitment to fairness that justifies that starting point (RJE: 158).

Thus differences in talent do not justify social and economic inequalities and that is why, Cohen argues, Rawls starts with equality and then justifies inequality (within the Pareto argument), which is based on morally arbitrary causes. Therefore, "fairness fanatics will then eliminate the inequality, and sensible folk, like me, will tolerate it, while judging it to be unfair" (RJE: 168). Cohen highlights another contradiction between the Pareto argument and the moral arbitrariness that the difference principle embodies.

---

8 In the case of an insurmountable inability, Cohen does not blame the talented persons for the inequalities that result from the special money incentives.

> The reason we begin with equality is the moral arbitrariness of the standard causes of inequality. We are then told that, if everyone can be made better off, there is no reason to stay with equality. But there is a (nonconclusive) reason to stay with it, to wit, the reason we had to begin with it (ibid.).

5.7 The Cohenian Conception of Justice

In this section, Cohen argues that principles of justice within the main social institutions should not only apply to the basic structure of society, but also to the choices members of society make in their daily lives. Cohen doubts the difference principle, which tolerates more advantages to those already more advantaged. He focuses on the privilege which gives talented persons the choice whether they work more or less. "[T]hey are so positioned that, happily, for them, they do command a high salary and they can vary their productivity according to exactly how high it is" (RJE: 120). This privilege is morally arbitrary because the position of the gifted, which allows them to enjoy this advantage, is undeserved as it is due to accidental circumstances. If they chose to opt for the incentives argument, Rawls would justify their choice, as it implies more productivity and thereby more goods to be distributed. Cohen tries to prove that the "incentives argument for inequality represents a distorted application of the difference principle" (RJE: 121). He assumes that a talented person would affirm the difference principle, unless they do not live in a just society, committed to the principles of justice. Moreover, in the Rawlsian understanding of the concept of justice, members of a just society should observe the principles of justice in their daily lives. This enables them to exercise their two moral powers and thereby achieve their sense of justice. Cohen asks the talented persons, living in accordance with the difference principle, "whether the extra [money] they get is necessary to enhance the position of the worst off, which is the only thing, according to the difference principle, that could justify it" (RJE: 122).[9]

Indeed, the unwillingness of talented persons[10] to work without receiving financial incentives shows that they are not committed to the difference principle. "[T]he difference principle can justify inequality only in a society where not

---

9 Recall that Cohen defines the two meanings of the term necessary, which leads to two different questions. "Is it necessary tout court, that is, independently of human will [...]? Or is it necessary only insofar as the talented would decide to produce less than they do now? (RJE: 122).

10 Their unwillingness implies that the untalented persons are less advantaged than they would be without the high rewards provided to the talented.

everyone accepts that very principle. It therefore cannot justify inequality in the appropriate Rawlsian way" (RJE: 123). Consequently, a society's justice depends not only on the applied principles but also on the choices made by members of this society in their daily lives. Their choices must be informed by an ethos of justice, which induces them to make just decisions.

> A society that it is just within the terms of the difference principle, so we may conclude, requires not simply just coercive rules, but also an ethos of justice that informs individual choices. [...] [T]he required ethos promotes a distribution more just than what the rules of the economic game by themselves can secure (ibid.).

Yet, the objection to the basic structure[11] doubts the Cohenian affirmation that principles of justice should apply to individual choices and not only to society's main institutions. Cohen justifies his affirmation through three main Rawlsian ideas, which highlight the role of that ethos; the ideas of fraternity, dignity and the realization of a sense of justice. Fraternity is not realized through applying the principles to the basic structure of society, but when members of society refuse to gain more economic advantages, unless the others also benefit from them. "If justice relates to structure alone, since it might then be necessary for the worst off to occupy their relatively low place only because the choices of the better off tend strongly against equality" (RJE: 130). According to Rawls, people in a just society, who exercise their moral powers, act from the principles of justice in order to include their sense of justice in their daily lives and thereby in their individual decisions.

Cohen provides a more fundamental reply to the basic structure objection, and consolidates his thesis that justice requires an ethos which informs daily choices and decisions. He starts by arguing that the definition of the basic structure is not precise within the Rawlsian theory. It is unclear, which social institutions the basic structure refers to. In its first reading, the basic structure represents the "coercive outline of society" (RJE: 133)[12], which determines people's actions in the light of law. Yet in its second reading, "institutions belong to the

---

11 For a further elaboration of the basic structure objection, see chapter 7.

12 Following Cohen, the coercive power functions insofar as it prevents members of society "from doing things by erecting insurmountable barriers [...] and it deters people from doing things by ensuring that certain forms of unprevented behavior carry an (appreciable risk of) penalty" (RJE: 144). Moreover, the knowledge of what would happen if the forbidden behaviour is done would influence the individual choices. In opposition to the coercive structure, the noncoercive structure would manifest through sanctions such as criticism, disapproval, and refusal of cooperation.

basic structure whose structuring can depend far less on law than on convention, usage, and expectation: a signal example is the family" (RJE: 134). How can principles which apply to the family structure not apply to daily choices and decisions? Whereas, citizens conform to the principles of justice, members of a family conform to the values that inform their conduct. Therefore, principles of justice should not only apply to the basic structure of society, but also to individual daily choices and decisions.

> If the values that govern the basic political framework of social life thereby govern the very groundwork of our existence, so too do the values that govern our nurture and conduct in the family (RJE: 136).

Accordingly, everyday economic choices should be made on the basis of the applicable principles of justice. Citizens should not only apply the rules, upon which social institutions are built but should also reconsider their selection of the incentives argument and the inequalities it tolerates. The principles of justice should therefore not only govern the basic structure of a just society but should inform people's daily lives through an ethos of justice. A just society is achieved through just social institutions together with just personal choices.

In sum, this chapter presents the Cohenian rescue of the concept of equality from the Rawlsian misguiding treatment of it. According to Cohen, the difference principle, which endorses the justice of social and economic inequalities, contains various contradictions. The first contradiction is voiced by the gifted members of society who call for financial incentives in line with the incentives argument. The Cohenian critique shows that citizens living under the auspices of the principles of justice cannot realize the values of dignity and fraternity while seeking to gain greater benefits. The second contradiction is the Pareto argument, which justifies the move from an equal distribution of goods to an unequal one: The morally arbitrary inequalities, which initially impelled Rawls to take an equal distribution as a corrective for the natural inequalities, are endorsed as just, as long as they benefit the least advantaged members of society. However the same inequality judged unfair because of its undeserved character, remains unjust even though it is needed to boost productivity. In the course of his critique of the difference principle, Cohen presents his own philosophical alternative, which focuses on the ethos of justice that should determine our daily actions and decisions. To ensure a relatively just society, principles of justice should not only apply to the basic structure of society but also to individual daily choices.

But would Cohen have criticized the Rawlsian principles of justice if Rawls had maintained the elements of the strict difference principle? Is the Cohenian rescue of equality from the difference principle justified?

6 Scrutinizing the Cohenian Rescue of Equality

Cohen attempts to rescue the virtue of justice from the facts, which "pollute" it, and endeavors to rescue equality from the difference principle, which he thinks misleading in questions of justice and equality. In his attempt to rescue equality from the difference principle, Cohen analyzes inequalities the principle allows in accordance with the Pareto principle. He starts by accepting the difference principle in its general form, preferring its strict interpretation over the lax reading but ultimately he does not accept it as one of the principles of justice. According to Cohen, a principle of justice should not – cannot! – condone the incentives argument proposed by the upper classes in order to justify their social and economic privileges. Moreover a principle of distributive justice should not consider inequalities caused by morally arbitrary contingencies fair. In the following section Cohen's arguments for the rescue of the value of equality from Rawls's mistreatment of it are explored and discussed. Can a liberal democratic society (like the Rawlsian one) be informed by egalitarian principles of justice?

6.1 The Cohenian Critique of the Incentives Argument

Chapter 5 outlined how Cohen accepts the difference principle in its general form, but questions its application that justifies financial incentives for talented individuals.[1] "I believe that the idea that an inequality is justified if, through the familiar incentive mechanism, it benefits the badly off is more problematic than Rawlsians suppose" (RJE: 32). The justification of inequality is thus difficult without any reference to entitlement or desert.[2] Cohen believes that if talented persons were committed to the difference principle and its values of fraternity and community, they would not need incentives to increase their productivity. "Accordingly, they [well-off persons] must be thought of as outside the commu-

1 "Talented persons" refers to well-off persons; the word "talented" means "gifted" or "endowed". This could be a social (social class) or an economic (money) or a natural endowment (physical force).

2 Rawls refuses to justify social and economic inequalities with reference to the ideas of desert or entitlement. No one deserves or is entitled to his/her social and economic endowments because those depend on socially and naturally arbitrary contingencies that could be to the advantage or disadvantage of the persons. Good or bad luck should not justify social and economic inequalities.

nity upholding the principle when it is used to justify incentive payments to them" (ibid.).

Moreover, rightly understood, the difference principle does not only fail to justify inequalities resulting from money incentives, but "any significant inequality, in an unqualified way" (RJE: 33).[3] In fact, poor people would benefit from these inequalities, which could be obliterated, if rich people accepted their obliteration. But the affluent reject any social arrangement which does not preserve these inequalities. On this condition the impoverished have to consent to any "suitable" strategy, which might improve their socioeconomic situation.

> This inequality benefits the badly off only within the constraint set by the inegalitarian attitude, and the consequent behavior, of the well off, a constraint that they could remove [...]. The unequal medical provision helps poor people, but only against the background of a prior income inequality (which no doubt itself reflects further structural inequality and inegalitarian attitude) that has not [...] been shown to benefit them (ibid.).

To Cohen, it is difficult to determine which inequalities either do not harm or are even beneficial for the underprivileged. "[I]n the construction of the feasible set [of principles of justice], the more one encounters open possibilities that were closed by human choice, [...] the harder it is to identify inequalities that do not harm the badly off" (ibid.). However the two expressions ("do not harm" and "are to the greatest benefit of") do not have the same meaning.[4] The first expression "do not harm", which Cohen introduces, excludes the Rawlsian idea of the difference principle, according to which economic inequalities must benefit the least favoured members of society. Cohen also recognizes the difference between his expression and the different implications Rawls's formulation "to be to the greatest benefit of the least-advantaged members of society" (JF: 43) could have. He criticizes this ambiguous Rawlsian expression and argues that inequalities that "do not harm" might aid the least advantaged persons, without necessarily improving their social situation. Although Rawls's alternative essentially[5] seeks to improve the social and economic situation of the underprivileged, the Cohenian term (chosen by Cohen to refer to the Rawlsian idea) which

3 Recall that Cohen does not criticize all incentives, but only incentives that produce inequalities, which "are said to be justified because they make badly off people better off" (RJE: 35).

4 This is related to the canonical and familiar articulations of the difference principle, both suggested by Cohen and elaborated below.

5 According to the difference principle, inequalities are permitted only if they are to the advantage of the least advantaged members of society.

does not dictate financial improvement veils its importance within the Rawlsian conception of justice.

Moreover, Cohen confirms that the incentives argument proposed by privileged, talented, and rich persons fails to prove successful and convincing. The interpersonal test[6], which confronts a rich with a poor citizen, shows that the rich cannot justify their incentives argument which states that they need financial incentives to be able to increase their productiveness. "Given that you would still be much better off than we are if you worked as you do now at the 60 percent tax, what justifies your intention to work less if the tax rises to that level?" (RJE: 60). The Cohenian test shows that rich people are not unable to work harder at low(er) money returns, but rather unwilling.[7] So, "they cannot respond by saying that the money inequality that they defend is necessary to make the poor better off, since it is they who make it necessary" (ibid.). Consequently, the poor are not provided with "a reason to accept" (ibid.) the inequality recommended by the difference principle, and the wealthy presenting their own choices and attitudes as given facts, are thus not in a position to answer the questions posed by the impoverished.

> The talented rich cannot justify the fact that the minor premise of the (naked) incentives argument is true. If they cannot justify the truth of its minor premise, then they cannot use the argument as a justification of inequality (RJE: 47).

Cohen concludes that the only way to justify the incentives argument is to imagine the rich people as not living in the same community[8] as the poor people. If the incentives argument were disregarded, rich people would work hard and would pay 60 percent tax, for example, in the case of the British society. Cohen argues that even at this level of taxation, wealthy people would be able to buy the goods they want.

> The extra money that executives (and so forth) get at 40 percent can hardly be required to finance whatever luxuries we might imagine they strictly need to perform at a high level: they could afford those necessary luxuries with what they have left even when they pay a 60 percent tax (RJE: 49).

---

6 For an elaborate presentation, see chapter 5.

7 Cohen illustrates his critique of the Rawlsian incentives argument through the critique of Nigel Lawson's tax cut in Britain (March 1988), when the top rate of income tax was brought down from 60 to 40 percent. Cohen compares the argument for the tax cut in Britain with the kidnapper's argument. For a further discussion, see chapter 5.

8 The very important idea of community in Cohen's theory is explored in details in chapter 10.

But is it not true that high rewards are requisite in order to encourage motivation and thereby expectations of obtaining certain goods? Are the financial incentives not indispensable for boosting the motivation[9] to raise people's productiveness?

According to Cohen, the motivation argument is not conditional. It does not state that talented individuals would only work as hard at a 60 percent tax rate as at a 40 percent tax rate as long as they are generously compensated. The argument rather states that "the rich cannot get themselves to work as hard when they expect to be taxed at 60 percent as they can get themselves to work when they expect to be taxed at 40 percent" (ibid.). Focusing on the motivation challenge, Cohen recognizes that low rewards can disappoint expectations insofar as "too low rewards can cause, at least somewhat independently of the will, a morose reluctance that operates as a drag on performance" (RJE: 50). But he affirms this contention represents talented persons as being very feeble. They "find it harder to raise up enthusiasm for choices that now promise smaller rewards. It does not follow that they cannot make, and effectively pursue, those choices" (ibid.). If talented individuals affirmed that social and economic inequalities are caused by socially arbitrary contingencies and are thus undeserved, their utterance would be inconsistent with their justification of more inequality in the incentives argument. The single argument left for them is the "habituation factor", which implies that they are used to obtaining high rewards. To this point, Cohen simply answers that habits can change, not only on the personal level, but also and certainly on a social level, by reforming educational structures.

6.2 Challenges to Cohen's Critique of the Incentives Argument

6.2.1 Need for a Psychology of Egalitarianism

Samuel Scheffler does not reject the Cohenian conclusion that the rich do not have the right not to work as hard at 60 percent tax as they do at 40 percent, but he claims that Cohen does not prove this conclusion. According to Scheffler, incentives might be important in eliciting motives, which enable individuals to perform better. He gives the example of the runner who needs competition to

9 Cohen illustrates the motivation idea as following: "You eventually give the biscuit to the performing dog so that the same procedure will work again next time, and not because the dog needs the calories it gets from the biscuit to enable it to go on performing" (RJE: 49).

achieve his best, or people, who work best under pressure; the ability of doing something depends, according to Scheffler, on the reasons and motives people have for doing it. He concludes that an egalitarian social arrangement should consider man's motivational resources, which need to be examined in depth to see whether they correspond to the egalitarian scheme. Hence, an adequate egalitarian conception of justice must be complemented by a psychology of egalitarianism, which should display how egalitarian rules support the reactive attitudes and emotions of individuals, and show how the psychological procedures by which egalitarian social structures uphold individuals' self-respect as being free and equal citizens.

Independently from the results of Scheffler's program[10] in the search for possible equality-supporting human motivational resources, Cohen replies that all the cases considered by Scheffler in his examples

> involve a drive to perform well [...]. The motivation in question contrasts with the search for gains that [...] are quite external to the performance itself. [...] [I]n estimating what it would be like for a person to accept a salary that is much lower than what full exercise of market power would provide, the strain to think about is the one he would feel when, ex hypothesi, people like him are accepting similarly modest salaries. We are talking about an egalitarian society, not about a population of talented people each of whom is a unique moral hero (RJE: 53).

The next section elaborates on the first challenge which also deals with the legitimacy of applying the interpersonal test.

6.2.2 Legitimacy of Applying the Interpersonal Test

The interpersonal test exemplifies that a rich man cannot defend the financial returns received for a rich man's work to a poor man on the grounds that without financial incentives the rich are unwilling to increase their productiveness. The test itself hypothetically confronts the two representatives of the two social classes. The test leads to negative results, as the rich person does not provide

---

10 The program of work is supposed to show whether a society, whose citizens believe in equality and act accordingly is reproducible. The point is to explore what psychological features in human nature make the regeneration of an egalitarian society difficult or even impossible. "As a practical purpose, normative egalitarianism indeed requires a corresponding psychology" (RJE: 52).

satisfactory reasons for only working with appropriate rewards. According to these results, Cohen concludes that the incentives argument is not valid.

However, the use of the interpersonal test is not suitable for examining the Rawlsian difference principle, insofar as the test confronts two specific citizens and judges the justice of the argument from their personal viewpoints and the way it affects their concrete economic situation. Whereas Cohen personalizes the Rawlsian theory, Rawls warns of such comparisons and essentially frames his theory for institutions.

> There is no reason to suppose ahead of time that the principles satisfactory for the basic structure hold for all cases. These principles may not work for the rules and practices of private associations or for those of less comprehensive social groups. They may be irrelevant for the various informal conventions and customs of everyday life (TJ: 8).

As defined by Rawls, the principles of justice apply to society's basic institutions. They do not apply to individual persons or to their personal choices or daily decisions. The interpersonal test envisages two particular citizens who represent two different social classes. Cohen expects that they decide about the legitimacy of the incentives argument. Rawls, however, constructs the original position with persons who do not know the social class to which they belong.[11] So the test, which intends to check the validity of the principles of justice – especially the difference principle, applies to persons in contrast to the principles themselves, which apply to institutions. Is the inspection that examines the just functioning of basic institutions (original position) not more suitable to check the validity of the principles, since they do not apply to particular persons?

> [N]either principle applies to distributions of particular goods to particular individuals who may be identified by their proper names. The situation where some is considering how to allocate certain commodities to needy persons who are known to him is not within the scope of the principles (TJ: 64).

It follows that the discussion between both rich and poor chosen by Cohen is not suitable and therefore illegitimate to give the right answer about the argument for the difference principle; a principle that does not apply to particular persons, but to institutions, and which requires further examination.

---

11 Whereas Cohen faces a poor citizen with a rich citizen, unable to justify his demand of greater inequality, Rawls's representatives in the original position decide that the more citizens work, the more they could achieve social and economic benefits.

6.3 Removing Inequalities: Just or Unjust?

As presented above, Cohen argues that it is more difficult than liberals suppose to justify inequality on the grounds that the obliteration of inequality would not benefit the lower classes. He describes the situation of the deprived as living within "the constraint set by the inegalitarian attitude", affected by the "consequent behavior" of the affluent. These, however, could choose to act differently and remove this constraint, which would benefit the least advantaged citizens to a much greater extent than the justification of inequalities would. However, removing this constraint would abolish social and economic inequalities or at least render them undue. Ergo the difference principle would not be considered a principle of justice, because, according to Cohen, inequalities cannot be justified in an egalitarian arrangement.

We expect from Cohen's socialist-egalitarian viewpoint that he criticizes the inequalities granted by the difference principle and rejects them in order to reinforce justice. But would it be just to remove social and economic inequalities caused by morally arbitrary contingencies? Although these inequalities are originally undeserved, people's merits to make good or bad use of their natural and social endowments, should be considered as they can improve or regress a person's socioeconomic situation. The merits depend on many social and natural factors, such as education, or the development of natural accomplishments. It would be very difficult to accurately distinguish the "pure" merit of a person and thereby judge whether they deserve their social and economic advantages. What if individuals deserve their social status because of their efforts? Should these inequalities associated with their socioeconomic situation be removed within an egalitarian social scheme? Would justice be achieved, if these inequalities were removed? In this difficult undertaking, Cohen's demand for egalitarianism could lead to injustice.

In his critique of the incentives argument, Cohen uses a concrete example from British politics. He questions its application and the consequences on the British social classes. However, the incentives argument works differently in Cohen's British illustration than Rawls's argumentation for the difference principle. Even if there are similarities between both arguments, Cohen exaggerates by comparing both arguments. What applies to one (Lawson's tax cut) argument does not necessarily apply to the other (the difference principle).

6.4 The Cohenian Critique of the Difference Principle

In suggesting two readings of the difference principle, Cohen criticizes on the one hand the inherent contradiction that it entails and on the other hand prefers the strict interpretation. "It is usually supposed, and it is evidently supposed by Rawls himself, that his affirmation of the difference principle is consistent with his endorsement of the inequalities that come with special incentives to people of talent" (RJE: 68). But Cohen argues that the Rawlsian conception of justice, which endorses incentives, also condemns them. It therefore contradicts itself. "[N]o society whose members are themselves unambivalently committed to the difference principle need use special incentives to motivate talented producers" (ibid.). The contradiction implies that there are two interpretations of the difference principle. Is this Cohenian interpretation a rescue of the Rawlsian understanding of justice?

Both readings depend on two different understandings of inequality, defended by the difference principle. Whereas the strict reading of the difference principle counts inequalities as necessary, independently from human choices and intentions, the lax interpretation tolerates intention-relative necessities.[12] "So, for example, if an inequality is needed to make the badly off better off but only given that talented producers operate as self-interested market maximizers, then that inequality is endorsed by the lax, but not by the strict, reading of the difference principle" (RJE: 69). So, inequalities cannot be endorsed within both readings of the difference principle; they are either approved by the lax or the strict interpretation. Cohen argues that the two incompatible readings are defended by Rawls, which reveals an essential inconsistency in his theory of justice, or that he has in fact two irreconcilable positions on the matter.

> His comments on the spirit in which people in a just society affirm the difference principle point to the strict, 'intention-independent' reading of it: that reading goes with his remarks about 'full compliance', the dignity of the badly off, and fraternity. Yet, by endorsing incentives, Rawls treats inequalities whose necessity is relative to the intentions of talented people as acceptable to the difference principle: he proceeds as though he affirms the principle in its lax interpretation (ibid.).

According to Cohen, if members of society were committed to the idea of justice in their daily lives and to the principles it mandates, they would undoubtedly choose to apply the strict reading of the difference principle. "[They] want their own economic behavior to satisfy the principle, and they help to sustain a moral

12 For an elaborate presentation of both readings, see chapter 5.

climate in which others want the same" (RJE: 70). In order to prevail, there must be an ethos that corresponds to the strict reading of the difference principle and the values it entails. This ethos should inform all daily choices and decisions. "Therefore, a society (as opposed to its government) does not qualify as committed to the difference principle unless it is indeed informed by a certain ethos or culture of justice" (RJE: 73). In this case, talented persons would not expect to obtain higher rewards for their talent.

Cohen rejects the lax reading of the difference principle as a principle of justice and not as a principle of public policy. To consolidate his thesis, he illustrates his rejection through the example of a doctor, who knows he could earn £100,000 annually in a hospital position. The doctor also believes that if he took half of the amount for doing the same job, "then any difference between my reward and what the less-well-paid get would be justified by what I strictly need to do the job, and/or by its special burdens, and/or by my legitimate personal prerogative" (RJE: 70). He might also take the whole sum and donate half to charity. The last possibility reflects the lax interpretation of the difference principle, in the sense that the doctor is allowed to achieve greater returns, if the destitute benefit from that. Justice would then be, according to Cohen, a compromise or balance between self-interest and the value of equality.

> [T]he lax difference principle is at best an imperfect proxy for a just balance and not, what it is supposed to be, a fundamental principle of justice. The compromise idea is, simply, different from the idea that inequalities are justified if they are necessary to benefit the badly off, given that agents are (or might be) self-regarding maximizers on the market (RJE: 72).

Consequently, the Rawlsian contradiction within the difference principle shows the inconsistency of his thesis. He affirms on the one hand that citizens are free and equal persons, who respect the dignity of each other, recognize the value of fraternity, are committed to the principles of justice and act in accordance with them in their daily lives. On the other hand, Rawls affirms that privileged citizens are allowed to seek greater benefits. Whereas Rawls rejects the exploitation of morally arbitrary contingencies to achieve social and economic inequalities, he allows talented persons to maximize their benefits. "For wanting 'not to gain unless they can do so in ways that further the interests of the rest' is incompatible with the drive for enrichment motivating market maximizers" (RJE: 78). This means Rawls must either give up his defense of money incentives for the development of talent, or his belief in the values of dignity, fraternity, the full compliance to the principles of justice, and the full realization of persons' moral powers.

> A society of market-maximizers with taxation and regulation dictated by the lax difference principle is necessarily preferable from the point of view of the worst off to a laissez-faire society, but in neither society is the conduct of high fliers consistent with the essentially socialist value of fraternity or with motivation informed by the difference principle (RJE: 80).

Cohen believes the ideals are worth keeping. Should Rawls obey the strict reading of the difference principle and abandon the lax reading to rescue his thesis from inconsistency?

6.5 Analysis of the Cohenian Critique of the Difference Principle

6.5.1 Two Complementary Levels

The argument in this part completes and consolidates the thesis in chapter 5 which suggests two levels of the principles of justice.[13] In order to understand the consistency of any conception of justice, it is necessary to distinguish between theoretical and practical levels. In the Rawlsian case, the theoretical level describes the choice of the principles of justice, with equality considered a benchmark and where the values of fraternity, dignity, self-respect and full compliance to the principles of justice are included. The practical level refers to the application of the principles of justice in the real world. No doubt,[14] disagreements or inconsistencies might arise in the real world, when the principles as they were theoretically articulated find their practical employment. Cohen is aware of these levels, since he recognizes an "applied difference principle". He affirms that "[o]n a Rawlsian view, there is no reason of basic principle why the talented should earn more than the untalented. It is merely that things (supposedly) fall out that way when the difference principle is applied" (RJE: 76).

In fact, Cohen considers both levels separately, but does not recognize that the circumstances of applying a principle at the practical level may require pro-

13 The same argument is reproduced here. In chapter 5, it was used to affirm that the Rawlsian principles of justice are not, at the theoretical level, grounded in facts, but rather in the fundamental principles of equality and fairness. The selected principles should be associated to facts about human nature at the practical level, where they need to be accepted and applied by members of society.

14 The application of the principles implies that they confront with the real world. One should, therefore, expect their adjustment to it.

found modifications and adaptations of the principle conceived in theory. Whereas the Rawlsians think that the theoretical level reflects what Cohen calls the strict reading of the difference principle, the lax interpretation reveals the same principle in its applied form; Cohen recognizes a profound opposition between both levels, which he believes to be incompatible. It is not simply that the practical level is the theoretical level in its applied form because the profound incompatibilities between both levels do not only reproduce (expected) defects or imperfections due to the confrontation with the real world, but show basic contradictions behind the difference principle.

In order to understand the Cohenian critique, the relationship between all levels of the Rawlsian conception of justice and the corresponding understanding of equality in each level are illustrated in the following.[15]

6.5.2 Justificatory Level: Equality 1

This level consists of justifying the choice of distributive justice. It refers to the original position, where equality is taken as a baseline together with the Pareto principle[16], according to which the expectations of members of society should be maximized. This level, which could be called "Equality 1", where equality implies the idea of distributive justice, is the justificatory level of the Rawlsian conception of justice as a whole. This level implies the next level, on which certain rules of distribution are chosen to regulate the redistribution of goods.

6.5.3 Rule of Distribution: Equality 2

This second level corresponds to the choice of both principles of justice. In order to regulate the distribution of rights, liberties, and social and economic inequalities, certain rules of distribution should inform society's basic structure. The second level reflects the second understanding of equality, "Equality 2", which implies an equal distribution of rights, liberties, and opportunities as well as a fair distribution of social and economic benefits (difference principle). Both levels are theoretical, insofar as they represent the choice of the principles of

15 The different levels were sketched by Wilfried Hinsch in a discussion about the alleged contradictions in the Rawlsian theory.

16 For an elaborate discussion, see chapter 4.

justice and their basis of justification. In opposition to these theoretical levels, the third level entails particular distributions.

6.5.4 Particular Distributions: Equality 3

This level corresponds to the application of the principles of justice in the real world. It represents any particular distribution that maximizes the benefits of the least advantaged members of society. The value of equality has a further meaning on this level. Equality, which is taken as a baseline on the first level is substituted by fairness on the second level to justify certain necessary inequalities on the third level.

Thus, the contradictions within the difference principle, highlighted by Cohen (such as the incentives argument for achieving great benefits or the exploitation of morally arbitrary contingencies) appear on the third level. For example, whereas the difference principle on the second level is not morally arbitrary, it could justify morally arbitrary inequalities on the third level, depending on the particular distribution in question. Cohen believes that the incompatibilities between taking values such as fraternity, mutuality, and equality as a reference for a just distribution and justification for unequal distributions, as a result of the application of the Pareto principle, in the name of justice itself, occur at the justificatory level. He therefore affirms the inconsistency of the Rawlsian conception of justice. The contradiction in the Rawlsian theory of justice is profound because it occurs before the confrontation with the real world.

6.6 The Cohenian Rejection of the Difference Principle

Cohen believes that his arguments "provide reasons for denying that unequalizing incentives are justified by the difference principle, [but] not, explicitly, reasons for denying the difference principle itself" (RJE: 153). Even if the inequalities produced by the incentives mechanism are justified by the difference principle, they remain unjust, because they were originally based on morally arbitrary contingencies. "The incapacity of the talented would explain, but not supply a morally nonarbitrary justification of, incentives inequality. [...] [T]he difference principle permits inequalities that are morally arbitrary" (RJE: 154).

The Cohenian critique of the difference principle rejects not only the lax interpretation, but also the principle itself. Cohen focuses on the moral arbitrariness claim to dismiss the difference principle as a principle of justice. He describes the Rawlsian treatment of inequalities caused by morally arbitrary contingencies. According to Cohen, Rawls starts affirming that "none should fare worse than others through no fault of their own" (RJE: 156) and refuses to justify inequalities caused by morally arbitrary circumstances.[17] But Rawls feels the force of the Pareto principle, which welcomes inequality which benefits everyone, even if this inequality is caused by morally arbitrary contingencies.

Consequently, Cohen criticizes the Rawlsian move from equality as a standard to inequality. Thus, he proposes two articulations of the difference principle, the canonical or lexical form and the non-canonical or familiar form, which have "two different rationales".

> The thought behind the insistence in the familiar form of the principle that inequality must positively benefit the worst off is that inequality is (at least prima facie) unfair, specifically to those at the bottom of the inequality, but that it would be absurd to let a concern for those people dictate a prohibition on an inequality from which they benefit (RJE: 158).

The inequalities that the lexical difference principle allows are "justified on the basis that, if something is good for some and bad for none, then it is to be endorsed" (ibid.). This version of the difference principle does not imply a compensation for injustice.

> The unfairness of arbitrarily caused inequality is the starting point of a chain of reasoning that ends in affirmation of the lexical difference principle, but that principle shows no trace of commitment to fairness that justifies that starting point (ibid.).

Moreover, Cohen focuses on the status of equality in both articulations of the principle. Whereas in the non-canonical form, the difference principle "is silent about equalities"[18], in the canonical form, the difference principle implies, that "equalities are unjust unless they render the worst off better off" (ibid.). However, this conclusion is never mentioned by Rawls.

> If Rawls happily says that inequality is unjust unless it does not harm the badly off, but doesn't happily say that equality is unjust it does not harm them, despite the fact that the latter statement is also implied by the lexical difference principle, then that can only be because inequality faces a case to answer that equality does not face. And that is inconsistent with the theory of distributive justice that identifies distributive justice with the lexical difference principle (RJE: 158-159)

---

17 Morally arbitrary contingencies are elaborated in chapter 1.

18 Cohen explains this silence by the Rawlsian belief that inequalities are inevitable.

Cohen concludes that Rawls should have proved that inequalities are unfair and thereby unjust and any weak Pareto improvement on them always preferable from the point of view of justice. "But no such position is consistent with Rawls's unnuanced endorsement of the lexical difference principle. The stated position notices the persisting unfairness in the inequality: the lexical difference principle, conceived as the whole simple truth about distributive justice, does not" (RJE: 159). Conclusively, the Cohenian critique, which rejects the difference principle, shows that Rawls, who starts by condemning inequality caused by talent differences, ends up justifying their arbitrariness and the inequality they produce. What should be the suitable treatment of inequalities caused by morally arbitrary contingencies? What if Rawls did not move from equality to inequality?

> What really happens is that Pareto is suspended when we focus on moral arbitrariness and moral arbitrariness is suspended when we focus on Pareto. [...] The reason we begin with equality is the moral arbitrariness of the standard causes of inequality. We are then told that, if everyone can be made better off, there is no reason to stay with equality. But there is a (nonconclusive) reason to stay with it, to wit, the reason that we had to begin with it (RJE: 168).

6.7 Examination of the Cohenian Rejection of the Difference Principle

The difference principle, it seems, is not a principle of justice, as it represents the Rawlsian move from equality to inequality and also his justification of inequalities caused by morally arbitrary contingencies. However are not all social and economic inequalities originally produced by morally arbitrary contingencies?

Rawls does not justify all inequalities, but only those needed to improve the situation of the least favoured citizens. For this reason he rejects, for example, excessive inequalities, which would augment the differences between citizens of the same society. Yet if he did not justify certain inequalities within his principle of distributive justice, he should necessarily either eliminate their effects or compensate for them. But he can never nullify factual inequalities. In an egalitarian society, like the one imagined by Cohen, social and economic inequalities should be compensated for, so that their effects are more or less nullified. However, in a liberal democratic society[19], like the one established by

19 For a further discussion, see chapter 1.

Rawls, the effects of morally arbitrary contingencies are mitigated through an equal assignment of rights, liberties, and opportunities, in the sense that goods are distributed in proportion to labor. Otherwise, if no such social scheme is applied, it would be easy to renounce the liberal democracy and embrace another (more egalitarian) type of society.

"The intuitive idea is that since everyone's well-being depends upon a scheme of cooperation without which no one could have a satisfactory life, the division of advantages should be such as to draw forth the willing cooperation of everyone taking part in it, including those less well situated" (TJ: 15). In the Rawlsian move from equality to inequality through the Pareto principle, Rawls starts with two references reflecting two aims: How to maximize everyone's expectations? How to establish a just social system accepted by everyone? Both references, equality as a benchmark and the Pareto principle as an economic baseline, establish his principles of justice. If the Pareto principle does not represent the idea of justice and the principles of justice do not reflect the two Rawlsian references but only the idea of justice, the Cohenian critique should examine the role of the principles of justice and what values they reflect. What are the principles of justice in the Cohenian understanding?

6.8 The Legitimacy of the Move from Moral Arbitrariness to Equality

Before exploring the Cohenian alternative, it is important to examine Richard J. Arneson's article "Justice Is Not Equality" (JNE), which disputes Cohen's claim that the Rawlsian argument for the difference principle "involves an argument from moral arbitrariness to equality and then an illicit move away from equality" (JNE: 2). Arneson discusses the claim that the moral arbitrariness argument should establish equality as the reference for distributive justice.

In a Rawlsian just society, Arneson writes, there is a separation between public and private life. Justice is a norm for social institutions but also supported by individuals. Within this just society, citizens are given the liberty to advance their own projects. "This picture of the just society conjures up for Cohen the image of an economy in which selfish individuals try to do as well for themselves as they can within the just institutional rules. The image is defective says Cohen" (JNE: 5-6). Arneson affirms that Cohen attributes responsibility to members of society for achieving a just distribution. In everyone's daily life the idea of just distribution should be present, within the limits of an appropriate personal prerogative in order to contribute to the good of others. "The shape and structure of institutions must also satisfy principles of justice, but that's not enough" (JNE: 6). A just society depends on the just functioning of social institutions and on the dispositions and conduct of its members. Moreover, Arneson believes that a just distribution is an equal distribution of income and wealth in the Cohenian understanding.

> But to discover what is ideally fair one should abstract from any limits in people's willingness to comply with fairness constraints or to promote fairness goals. So if equality turns out to be ideally fair, it remains so even if we humans are so constituted that we are bound to act against this norm (JNE: 7).

Arneson concludes that, according to Cohen, the ideal of fairness is equality or equal access to advantage. It is indeed the aim of socialism to achieve an equality ideal in society. "Cohen is of the opinion that institutions and culture and individual will can shape motives, so socialist equality may also be feasible, but it would remain ideally fair even if it were motivationally out of reach" (ibid.). Arneson agrees with Cohen on the responsibility that should be attributed to members of a society in order to achieve social justice, but he disagrees with him on the status of equality in a theory of distributive justice. "Even if you thought equality were a big component of justice, why think it's everything?" (JNE: 8).

The starting point of the Cohenian criticism, according to Arneson, is the critique of the idea of an equality-versus-efficiency tradeoff, which is the foundation for the difference principle. The responsibility regarding equality and efficiency or productivity in a market economy should imply taxation, and transfer and redistribution of resources according to the best suitable tradeoff ratio. In this regard, Arneson finds Rawls egalitarian to the utmost because the difference principle is designated to maximize the situation of the least advantaged individuals. However, Cohen proposes another similarly productive possibility, where talented persons increase their productivity and relinquish their incentive payments.[20] This society imagined by Cohen would achieve even more justice than in the Rawlsian alternative.

> If all members of society are committed to egalitarian principles, and guide their economic choices by them, then no incentive inducements are needed to sustain productivity, and the equality-versus-efficiency tradeoff disappears, or rather, is no longer a binding constraint on the pursuit of equality (JNE: 9).

---

20 This is the Cohenian alternative that is discussed in chapter 7.

According to Arneson, Cohen accuses Rawls of abandoning equality in favour of inequality; Rawls starts by taking morally arbitrary contingencies which affect people's lives and affirms that equality is what distributive justice involves. He then abandons equality and chooses the Pareto norm, which affirms that an inequality which maximizes the situation of the worst-off is to be preferred to an equality that makes no one better off. According to Cohen, Rawls does not give any importance to equality of condition.

> An egalitarian argument leads to equality and then somehow incongruously lurches past it, pushed by some other value entirely, and the principle we then end up with is identified with distributive justice rather than a compromise with distributive justice or as a counterconsideration. So urges Cohen (JNE: 11).

Arneson confirms that the meaning of justice in the dictionary is "moral rightness, equity" (JNE: 12). This is similar to the Rawlsian understanding of justice, which is the first virtue of social institutions, just as truth is for systems of thought. In his review of different conceptions of justice, he considers John Stuart Mill's viewpoint on justice which accepts adjusting the ideal of justice from inexpedient equality to expedient inequalities. Arneson goes even further affirming that "when justice is identified with equality, it is equality of treatment that is in play, and the notion of equality here is formal, that people who are in relevant respects the same should be treated the same" (JNE: 13). However, in Cohen's view, a just distribution involves a comparison of individual earnings, which should be equal.

> I simply report that I don't find in my own convictions any trace of this supposed ideal of distributive justice; nor do I see that it is derivable from more basic common-sense convictions we should be loathe to relinquish (JNE: 13-14).

Focusing on the difference principle, Arneson says that this principle attributes no value to equality, but does so to the maximization of primary goods. Cohen finds incoherence in the Rawlsian argument. "From premises affirming the intrinsic moral value of equality, how can you validly reason to a conclusion that says inter alia that equality is not intrinsically morally valuable at all?" (JNE: 16). Arneson defends Rawls and finds incoherence in Cohen's argumentation, who assumes that equality of condition is the essence of distributive justice. Moreover, if it is true that Rawls moves from equality to "equality per se does not matter conclusions, this merely indicates that Rawls [is] a pioneer in the articulation of contemporary egalitarianism" (ibid.). Arneson concludes that even if Rawls starts with equality but ends with the difference principle, this is not a good reason to reject the final judgement.

> [A] presumption can be provisional, in the sense that its presence at the start of inquiry is compatible with its entire disappearance without remainder at the end of inquiry, or compatible with its thoroughgoing transformation into a doctrine of a quite different character during the course of normative inquiry. And a presumption can vary in strength, down to the vanishing point (JNE: 18).

Arneson asks however, whether the moral arbitrariness claim provides an argument for equality of condition. Equality of condition is a state in which members of society living under similar economic conditions have almost the same level of wealth. He affirms that the initial starting point in the moral arbitrariness objection is equality, but "nothing says this starting point has to be equality" (JNE: 19). It is true that, as Cohen conceives, it is bad, unjust and unfair if some are worse off than others by no fault of their own, but Arneson adds, it is bad, unjust and unfair if some are equally well off as others by no merit of their own. "[W]hat qualifies an individual as deserving or undeserving must not be a matter of sheer luck but must rather lie within her power to control" (JNE: 20).

In fact, according to Arneson, Cohen argues that the standard causes of inequality are morally arbitrary, unless the inequality has a non-arbitrary cause. So differences in people's lives are unjust, unless they involve differential merits. Therefore, incentive payments to talented individuals are unjust as they are based on differences caused by morally arbitrary factors. But Arneson replies that "equality of condition is unjust when it obtains among persons who are equally deserving and equality of condition is unjust when it obtains among persons who are unequally deserving" (JNE: 22). Yet if Arneson's claim that Rawls aims at achieving equality of condition he thinks it to be the essence of distributive justice, is correct, would this equality be obtained by choosing Cohen's alternative to the difference principle?

To conclude, this chapter discusses the Cohenian rejection of the difference principle as a fundamental principle of distributive justice. The Cohenian critique of the incentives argument for the difference principle, according to which inequalities are endorsed, uses the interpersonal test to check the validity of the argument. Yet, the interpersonal test itself seems not valid to check the difference principle, since the Rawlsian principle does not apply to specific persons. Moreover, the comparison between the kidnapper example and the tax cut in Britain, which should be an example of the Rawlsian conception of justice seems exaggerated. As a socialist-egalitarian, Cohen is not satisfied with the Rawlsian treatment of equality, which Rawls abandons in favor of inequality. The ideas of justice as equality and inequality as a feasible justice stated by the difference principle constitute profound contradictions lying behind this principle, as Cohen stresses. How would Cohen rescue justice from that feasibility constraint? What would be the Cohenian alternative to the difference principle?

7 The Cohenian Alternative

According to the Cohenian socialist-egalitarian philosophical viewpoint, the ideas of justice and equality are interdependent, so that the rescue of justice from the Rawlsian conception of justice remains incomplete without the rescue of equality. Cohen's rescue of the value of equality challenges the Rawlsian argument for the difference principle, which endorses social and economic inequalities as just:

1) "Inequalities are unjust unless they are necessary to make the worst off people better off, in which case they are just.
2) Unequalizing incentive payments to productive people are necessary to make the worst off people better off.
3) Therefore, unequalizing incentive payments are just" (RJE: 19).

As previously mentioned, Cohen argues against the second premise of the Rawlsian argument that "the unequalizing payments aren't strictly necessary, since they reflect the will of incentive seekers" (ibid.), who could decide to not require financial incentives in order to increase their productivity. This chapter, devoted to Cohen's objection to the first premise, questions the Rawlsian syllogism that starts from equality as a standard and easily "sacrifices" it on account of the Pareto argument[1], which affirms the justice of social and economic inequalities. Why is the rejection of the Pareto argument necessary for the rescue of justice and equality? What is the Cohenian alternative to the Pareto argument for the regulation of social and economic inequalities? What principles would the "Cohenian conception of justice" entail? How to apply such principles on the Rawlsian conception of justice?

> For if an inequality in which all are better off is feasible, then so, too, I claim, in the relevant cases, is equality at a higher level than that at which the initial equality was pitched, one that is not Pareto-dominated by the relevant inequality. And the said Pareto-incomparable equal state should clearly be preferred to the inequality that it rivals, on the premise that justified the initial preference for equality (RJE: 16).

1 The Pareto argument is another way to name the Rawlsian argument for the difference principle.

7.1 The Rawlsian Move

The Rawlsian move, which characterizes the argument for the difference principle, is a move from equality, taken as a reference to regulate undeserved social and economic inequalities, to inequality, endorsed as just within the Pareto argument. "The persuasive power of this defense of inequality has helped to drive authentic egalitarianism, of an old-fashioned, uncompromising kind, out of contemporary philosophy. The present essay is part of an attempt to bring it back" (RJE: 87).

Cohen argues through the scrutiny of Barry's[2] reconstruction of the Rawlsian conception of justice, that the two-stage argument[3] "does not establish the justice of the inequalities that Rawls thinks are just" (RJE: 88). The two-stage argument, which Cohen calls the Pareto argument is a product of Barry's representation of Rawls's argument for the difference principle. "But whatever role the argument is supposed to play, or does play, in Rawls's writings, it manifestly serves to advance the Rawlsian purpose, which is, here, to reconcile certain inequalities with justice, and many, like Barry, have found the argument convincing. So it is worth scrutinizing" (ibid.).

The two thoughts of the first stage of the argument as reformulated by Barry take equality of opportunity as a starting point. Whereas the first thought states that "true equality of opportunity is achieved only when all morally arbitrary causes of inequality are eliminated" (RJE: 89), the second thought states that all causes of inequalities are morally arbitrary. According to both thoughts, Barry affirms that true equality of opportunity implies an equality of outcome.[4] Hence, justice is achieved through applying a just social system that entails equality of opportunity (first stage). But, even if social justice was realized through the principle of equality of opportunity, inequalities could nevertheless be just in virtue of their consequences. This is the second stage of the argument, which states that inequality is indeed just when and because it causes everyone to be better-off.

> The two thoughts in the second stage of the argument are, first, that it is irrational to insist on equality when it is a Pareto-inferior state of affairs (why would anyone, and, in particu-

2 See Barry's reconstruction of the Rawlsian argument in *Theories of Justice*.

3 The two-stage argument, which Cohen calls the Pareto argument is a product of Barry's reconstruction of the Rawlsian theory of justice.

4 According to Barry, the radical interpretation of equal opportunity is "nothing other than equal prospects of success for all" (*Theories of Justice*: p. 224).

lar, the worst off, prefer equality to an inequality in which everyone is better off?); and, second, that sometimes, and indeed typically, equality is Pareto inferior (ibid.).[5]

7.2 The Cohenian Illustration of the Move

According to Cohen, the inequality justified by Rawls is an inequality of social primary goods. As already cited, primary goods are goods everyone needs to realize their rational scheme of life: rights, liberties, powers and opportunities, income and wealth, and self-respect. Inequality of primary goods is "justified when and because it represents a Pareto-superior alternative to an equal share-out" (RJE: 95).

Cohen examines three states of affairs and chooses one of them, which would at best represent his own "conception of justice". In the first one, D1, equality in social primary goods and inequality in talents or non social primary goods prevail. This state of affair represents the Rawlsian starting point, which takes equal distribution of primary goods as a baseline. Now, "we move to a Pareto-superior alternative state, D2, in which the talented enjoy not only their original advantage but the further one of a larger social primary goods bundle" (RJE: 98). In the move from D1 to D2, inequality of talent is reinforced by an inequality in social primary goods, which means that talented persons find themselves in D2 with more than what they obtained in D1. Even if, "we cannot say whether, and how, D2 improves on D1 until we know more than Rawls tells us about what D1 comprises" (ibid.); this move seems to contradict the Rawlsian egalitarian outset that refuses to justify greater benefits with greater talents. Cohen supposes that both talented and untalented people work the same number of hours at an equal wage rate W, but that the talented, taking advantage of their talents, produce more than the untalented. On the one hand, in D1, both talented and untalented workers would receive the same income because inequalities related to talents, which are caused by undeserved morally arbitrary contingencies, do not influence the distribution of social primary goods. Arbitrary circumstances "[are] among the factors whose effects are to be discounted in the argument for an initial equality" (ibid.). On the other hand, in D2, both talented and untalented citizens enjoy wage rates higher than W, but with Wt (W talented) higher than Wu (W untalented): "that it is the extra productivity (over what they supply at W) supplied by the talented when they receive Wt that enables the untalented to be paid Wu; and that the difference between Wu and

5 For an elaborate presentation of the Pareto principle, see chapter 4.

W is thought by Rawls to be necessary to justify the difference between Wt and Wu" (RJE: 100).[6]

7.3 A Pareto-Improving Equality-Preserving Move

To contest the Rawlsian argument about the irrational insistence on equality, since an inequality would make everyone better-off, Cohen considers a third state of affair, D3. In D3, which is not necessarily feasible, the same amount is produced as in D2, but with equal wages distributed to talented and untalented people alike. So D3, which is a Pareto-superior to D1, preserves equality, and makes untalented citizens better-off in D3 than in D2. Whereas the talented are less well-off in D3 than in D2, both talented and untalented people are better-off in D3 than in D1. Should D2 be replaced by D3 to ensure a Pareto-improving situation within an equality-preserving scheme? What would the consequences on the Rawlsian conception of justice be, if D2 was replaced by D3?

> We can suppose that if D3 is indeed feasible, then the additional product, vis-à-vis D1, is, once again, wholly due to the greater productivity of talented people. But, wage rates being equal in D3, the talented do not in D3 gain differentially from the increase in product, as they do in D2 (RJE: 101).

According to Cohen, there is an inconsistency in the Rawlsian argument, which would reject D3 for the same reasons[7] that drive him to endorse D1 as a baseline. Besides, the unfeasibility of D3 refers to the unwillingness of the untalented people to share an equal distribution of their product with other members of society. D3 would be objectively unfeasible, when its practicability does not depend on human will, but rather on certain economic circumstances or special burdens. In order to reply to the Rawlsian irrationality argument, the attitude of the talented, explored in the following, is examined by Cohen in three different cases. In the first case, called the "bad case", everyone receives equal wages, but the talented people refuse to increase their productivity, unless they obtain greater benefits than the untalented (Wt > We). Their refusal induces either less productivity or extra money incentives (Wt). In the good and the standard cases, the talented people "prefer, and are resolved, to produce less at We than at Wt, and that is why D3 is unfeasible" (RJE: 102).

---

6 Cohen supposes for simplicity that the talented produce the same in D1 and in D2.

7 Cohen argues that no one should benefit from undeserved morally arbitrary contingencies to achieve greater benefits at D1 as well as at D3.

The decision of the affluent people in the "good case", to work more and get more than the untalented members attests the special burdens they carry and for which they – from an egalitarian viewpoint – should be compensated.

> The egalitarian principle that greater burden justifies greater compensating reward operates in our context in favor of D2 and against D3 in the good case. [...] Accordingly, and because we are examining a supposed justification of an inequality, the good or special burden case poses no problem for us, for what we get when special burden is invoked is not a justification of an inequality, all things considered, but a denial that there is an inequality, all things considered (RJE: 103).

In the "standard case", wages are also not equal and the talented demand financial incentives (Wt) in order to increase their productivity although they do not carry special burdens for which they should be compensated. Cohen disagrees with Rawls on this (standard) case. "Then although talented people may, as in the bad case, successfully hold out for Wt as a condition of producing more than what they do in D1, and thereby make D3 impossible, it is hard to see why an egalitarian should be expected to regard what they then do as acceptable, even if nothing can be done about it" (ibid.).

Consequently, Cohen criticizes the Rawlsian inconsistency, which refuses to exploit morally arbitrary contingencies in order to prevent greater inequalities. But then defends special money incentives for talented people on the grounds that their extra productivity enhances the socioeconomic situation of everyone.

> If the talented had objected to the equality of D1 on the ground that they produce more than others do in D1, they would have been told that they were seeking to exploit morally arbitrary advantages. [...] We can ask: why was the original equality not pitched at D3, instead of at D1, when D3 is Pareto-superior to D1? (RJE: 104).

According to Cohen, if we had started with D3, which is, objectively, a feasible egalitarian scheme, D2 would be an unjustifiable scheme. If the talented carry special burdens in D2, they should be compensated for them, "in which case it is a mistake to represent movement from D1 to D2 as issuing in an inequality" (RJE: 105). But if talented people do not need surplus compensation for special burdens, then "there is no reason for an egalitarian to regard D2 as acceptable" (ibid.) and D3 should therefore be recommended. The Pareto argument either does not justify inequalities, when the talented workers deserve to be compensated, or it goes against the Rawlsian move from equality of opportunity to equality. If the distribution of social primary goods should not be influenced by the natural distribution of natural primary goods such as talents, "why is it (as Rawls says it is) a piece of fortune to be talented?" (RJE: 107). Why is the labor burden so relevant in D2 if the original equality in D1 is an equality of primary goods?

> In short, if we use a primary goods metric, then D2 indeed exhibits an inequality, but one that lacks justification: D3 being feasible, how can D2 be justified, with the assumptions that led to D1 still in place? If [...] we use a metric that includes labor burden, then it is unclear whether D2 exhibits an inequality, since it is specified in terms of primary goods alone. But if it does involve an inequality, then it is an inequality that lacks justification, because it does not give the talented the right amount of compensation (RJE: 108-109).

7.4 Scrutinizing the Cohenian Alternative

The scheme to which Cohen would agree for the regulation of social and economic inequalities and the use of morally arbitrary advantages requires a different approach to natural primary goods and an equal distribution of social primary goods. This system D3 would make everyone better-off, without making the most privileged citizens excessively well-off.

Indeed, the Cohenian critique of the Rawlsian argument about the irrationality of insisting on equality even though inequality would improve the situation of everyone is no doubt of primary importance. It highlights the "unjustified" Rawlsian defense of inequality from an egalitarian point of view. However, the state of affairs that would satisfy Cohen's egalitarianism is not excluded from the possible Rawlsian treatments of social and economic inequalities.

> [T]he two principles require that everyone benefit from economic and social inequalities. It is obvious, however, that there are indefinitely many ways in which all may be advantaged when the initial arrangement of equality is taken as a benchmark. How then are we to choose among those possibilities? (TJ: 65).

Rawls's system aims at improving or even maximizing the expectations of the different social classes of society not necessarily from an egalitarian viewpoint, but rather from a fair position. In other words, Rawls would not reject D3 if both talented and untalented people found it fair and consented to it. So D3 is a possible socioeconomic arrangement, which should maximize the prospects of everyone and thereby proves acceptable and feasible. As stated by Rawls, the difference principle does not necessarily imply one economic scheme; it however implies that the scheme maximizes the expectations of the worst-off citizens.

> According to the difference principle, it [inequality] is justifiable only if the difference in expectation is to the advantage of the representative man who is worse off [...]. The ine-

> quality in expectation is permissible only if lowering it would make the working class even more worse off (TJ: 78).

Rawls illustrates his idea with the example of an entrepreneur and the working class. The greater expectations entrepreneurs can anticipate are the incentives that motivate them to "do things which raise the long-term prospects of laboring class" (ibid.), so that the economic system is more efficient and productive. The social and economic arrangement should avoid excessive inequalities in a society or better prospects for the more fortunate, because "the even larger difference between rich and poor makes the latter even worse off, and this violates the principles of mutual advantage as well as democratic equality" (TJ: 79). Nevertheless, as Rawls says, the expectations of both talented and untalented workers should be maximized within a fair socioeconomic arrangement. It is true that an improved situation of the worst-off persons allows greater inequalities in favour of the well-off citizens; but, if the expectations of the better-off "were decreased, the prospects of the least advantaged would likewise fall [...]. Even higher expectations for the more advantaged would raise the expectations of those in the lowest position" (TJ: 78-79). If the Cohenian alternative were applied to the Rawlsian conception of justice, by choosing D3 to regulate social and economic inequalities, would the expectations of the talented people still be maximized? One could imagine, for example, a society where the talented and the untalented consented to a social arrangement that implies the maximal use of natural primary goods and the equal distribution of social primary goods. Rich and talented people would agree to increase their productivity and equally share their income with the untalented. In such a case, the expectations of the unfortunate persons would be maximized, whereas the prospects of the talented persons would not be or might even be minimized. Consequently, the Rawlsian aim of maximizing the expectations of all social classes in society seems to be unachievable within the Cohenian alternative, according to which the prospects of the least privileged are maximized at the expense of the most privileged. Does a just social system imply lowering the expectations of some citizens in order to achieve equality? If an equal share of income seems to be dictated by the Cohenian alternative to the Rawlsian conception of justice, what principles would this alternative also entail?

> [I]n a basic structure with n relevant representatives, first maximize the welfare of the worst off representative man; second, for equal welfare of the worst-off representative, maximize the welfare of the second worst-off representative man, and so on until the last case which is, for equal welfare of all the preceding n-1 representatives, maximize the welfare of the best-off representative man. We may think of this as the lexical difference principle (TJ: 83).

7.5 A Further Rescue of Equality: The Cohenian Reply to the Trilemma Objection

An affirmation of the Pareto argument for inequality implies either an abandonment of equality or a rejection of the Pareto improvements. “But if my reply to the Pareto argument [...] is correct, then the argument fails, and that corollary dilemma is escaped: we do not have to choose between equality and Pareto” (RJE: 184). Yet if equality is consistent with the Pareto principle, there might be inconsistency “when we add freedom of occupational choice to equality and Pareto: the three, it is widely thought, cannot be realized together” (ibid.).

Cohen considers a talented doctor-gardener,[8] “who is capable of pursuit and prefers gardening at £20,000 a year” (ibid.) to doctoring at the same income. This doctor would opt for practicing medicine if the reward rose to £50,000 a year. The egalitarian position, asks the doctor to give up gardening in favour of working as a doctor, however at a gardener’s wage. This would benefit the underprivileged; and “she would have a much better life than most people have (even though a less good one than she would have gardening at that salary: what is peculiar about her is not how much she hates doctoring, for she does not hate it at all, but how much she loves gardening)” (ibid.). However, the doctor and society could choose between three packages,[9] which combine job satisfaction and income in various ways. “If, [...] we freeze salaries at £20,000 and allow the doctor-gardener to choose her job, she will garden, and then both she and the rest of the community will be worse off than they could be: Pareto is violated” (RJE: 185). Thus, at an income of £50,000 for doctoring, equality is lost in favour of the Pareto principle and the freedom of occupational choice. Likewise, if the doctor is forced to work as a practitioner for £20,000, the freedom of occupational choice is lost in favour of equality and the Pareto principle.

> Unless consumer preference determines what is produced, Pareto optimality is breached. But consumer preference prevails only if labor shifts occupation in response to it. And short of allocating labor by command, and thereby violating freedom, the only way to in-

8 This example illustrates the standard case presented above.

9 Cohen distinguishes between the preference ordering of the person and the preference ordering of the community. He proposes three packages, which combine job satisfaction and income. At £50,000 the doctor is much better-off than most people in job satisfaction and income. At £20,000, as a gardener, the person is much better-off than most people in job satisfaction but not in income. At £20,000, as a doctor, the person is still better-off than most people in job satisfaction, but not in income.

> duce the desired shifts is by overpricing (relative to equality of reward) what would otherwise be underfilled jobs, and thereby violating equality (ibid.).

However, no egalitarian would give up egalitarianism, so either freedom or Pareto would fall by the wayside. "The Trilemma argument says that equality cannot be achieved, consistently with Pareto, unless people act unfreely" (RJE: 191). Yet Cohen argues against the trilemma by proposing a dilemma: either members of society believe in equality or not. If they do, they would find a way[10] to reconcile it with freedom and Pareto. But, if they do not, it can only be instituted by force and manipulation. "It cannot, in any case, be a reason for people not to believe in equality that it requires them to reject at least one of freedom and Pareto: it doesn't" (RJE: 196). To the trilemmists, who require the abandonment of equality, which sacrifices the Pareto principle and also freedom, Cohen replies: "that isn't so, because, if we were egalitarians, we should be sacrificing neither" (ibid.). Equality is therefore rescued from the trilemma objection.

> [B]oth money and quality of work experience matter to people, and [...] both should therefore enter the egalitarian reckoning. Just as individuals trade the two desiderata off against each other in their intrapersonal comparison of the work/money packages available to them, so egalitarians should bring form and amount of work, as well as income, into their conception of equality and inequality at the level of basic principle (RJE: 200).

7.6 The Rawlsian Challenge to the Cohenian Alternative

Rawls would question the move from D1 to D3, which is a Pareto-optimal equality and affirms that it is not justified by the difference principle. As already mentioned the Rawlsian principles of justice entail the liberty principle, equality of opportunity and the difference principle. Thus, the liberty principle, which is prior to the difference principle, mandates according to Rawls, freedom to choose one's occupation, which the move from D1 to D3 contravenes. Cohen argues against the Rawlsian case that it is unclear whether the freedom of choice of occupation is included in the equal set of rights and liberties mandated by the first principle of justice. Moreover, "the Rawlsian principle of freedom of choice of occupation excludes coercion but not morally inspired motivation. [...] The liberty principle, too, applies beyond the state: it targets unacceptable coercion as such, not just state coercion" (RJE: 198). Racist attitudes, for exam-

10 They could decide to work in a way that benefits others: the ethical solution.

ple, contradict the principle of fair equality of opportunity. This principle, which should apply to social institutions "cannot [...] penetrate to people's attitudes" (RJE: 199). So, it would be inconsistent for people to legislate against racism, and then practice it in their daily racist choices.

> It is of the nature of liberty that it leaves choices open, and, therefore, it is of the nature of the liberty principle that it should apply to the structure of choice alone and be indifferent to the content of choice. It is not of the nature of distributive justice that it should be silent on the content of choice within the right structure (ibid.).

Cohen stresses the importance of an egalitarian ethos that pushes people to make egalitarian choices. "Why might an egalitarian ethos be thought to be unacceptably demanding, when maximizing legislation is not thought to be?" (RJE: 203). People should believe in an egalitarian principle in order to act upon it in their daily lives. What should this egalitarian principle be?

7.7 The Rescue of Equality from the Basic Structure

In this part of the rescue of equality,[11] Cohen defends the slogan, "the personal is political", to affirm "that the principles of distributive justice, [which are] principles [...] about the just distribution of benefits and burdens in society, apply, wherever else they do, to people's legally unconstrained choices" (RJE: 116). The choices meant here are the ones that people make within the rules of coercive structures, but which are left open by those rules "because neither enjoined nor forbidden by them" (ibid.). Cohen uses the example of the feminists[12], who also use this slogan, to illustrate his rejection of the Rawlsian viewpoint that affirms that principles of justice only apply to the basic structure of society.[13]

> [T]he theory of Rawls in particular, unjustifiably ignore an unjust division of labor and unjust power relations within families [...]. But the (often mere implicit) form of the feminist critique, which we get when we abstract from its gender-centered content, is that choices

11 Chapter 3 of RJE (pp. 116-146) has been published as the article "Where the Action is: On the Site of Distributive Justice" in 1997 in *Philosophy and Public Affairs*. Vol. 26, No. 1: pp. 3-30.

12 This feminist idea about justice, on which Cohen focuses, does not mention the relations between men and women, nor sexism. It rather questions the justice of the division of labor within families from a political point of view.

13 Recall that the basic structure represents society's basic institutions. For an elaborate presentation, see chapter 1.

> not regulated by the law fall within the primary purview of justice, and that is the key lesson of the critique from a theoretical point of view (RJE: 117).

Furthermore, the argument for the difference principle depends, according to Cohen,

> on a choice enjoyed by well-placed people who command a high salary market economy: they can choose to work more or less hard, and also to work at this occupation rather than that one, and for this employer rather than that one, in accordance with how well they are remunerated (RJE: 119-120).

Talented people are thus in the advantageous position to be able to decide on their productive performance in relation to the size of their incomes. So the inequalities, which originally result from accidental circumstances,[14] justified within the difference principle, determine the productive performance of the privileged. Cohen disagrees with Rawls on the idea that the inequalities the difference principle creates, justify inequality in a conception of justice. He also disagrees with how much inequality is justified by the Rawlsian principle. As explored in chapter 5, people with talents living in a society, – based on the Rawlsian conception of justice – should integrate the principles of justice in their daily lives which means that their behaviour either reflects their affirmation of the difference principle or not. "[E]ither they themselves believe that inequalities are unjust if they are not necessary to make the badly off better off, or they do not believe that to be a dictate of justice" (RJE: 121). The second option is rejected, since all members of society should act upon and affirm the principles of justice. This means that the gifted, living in a society affirm the difference principle and believe that inequalities are unjust, unless these inequalities improve the situation of everyone. Therefore Cohen argues that the privileged cannot uphold their choice to demand financial incentives in order to maintain high productive outputs. These rewards are only necessary because necessitated by talented persons, who do not believe that inequalities are unjust, but are only acceptable if they improve the situation of poor.[15]

> Now this conclusion about what it means to accept and implement the difference principle implies that the justice of a society is not exclusively a function of its legislature struc-

14 Recall that those are morally arbitrary circumstances that play a big role in determining the initial chances in life.

15 Recall that chapter 5 presents the Cohenian critique of the Rawlsian inconsistency of his argument for the difference principle: either the behaviour of the talented people contradicts the content of the principles of justice, or they live outside the community.

> ture, of its legally imperative rules, but also of the choices people make within those rules (RJE: 123).

Cohen imagines a market economy, in which the difference principle reigns and in which all agents seek to maximize their own benefits. In this scenario the Rawlsian economic scheme would imply a tax system on income that would increase the returns of the untalented persons, "within the constraint that, because of the self-seeking motivation of the talented, a fully equalizing taxation system would make everyone worse off than one that is less than fully equalizing" (ibid.). Following the set of rules in this example, inequalities may be produced and endorsed as just, even if they are not necessary for the improvement of the situation of persons with fewer talents. Therefore citizens should receive an important role and should be able to judge the justice of social arrangements. Cohen concludes that without an ethos of justice, which informs the individual choices in everyday life, coercive rules cannot achieve a just society in the Rawlsian understanding. The required ethos should not only direct agents to obey the rules or the principles, but also guide their individual choices within these rules.

> In the absence of such an ethos, inequalities will obtain that are not necessary to enhance the condition of the worst off: the required ethos promotes a distribution more just than what the rules of the economic game by themselves can secure. And what is required is indeed an ethos [...] that inform everyday life, not only because it is impossible to design rules of egalitarian economic choice [...], but also because it would severely compromise liberty if people were required forever to consult such rules (ibid.).

Whereas Cohen highlights the importance of applying the principles of justice to the individual choices in daily life, Rawls stresses the importance of applying them to the basic structure of society. "The objection is that my focus on the posture of talented producers in daily economic life is inappropriate, since their behavior occurs within, and does not determine, the basic structure of society, and it is only to the latter that the difference principle applies" (RJE: 124). According to Rawls, the individual choices might be just or unjust irrespective of the basic structure of society, which must be just. The difference principle is thereby for institutions and not for human economic choices.

The "basic structure objection" is formulated as a reply to the Cohenian argument against the difference principle. This argument illustrates the behavioral inconsistency of the lucky ones who seek to maximize their incomes instead of acting in agreement with the underlying values of the principles of justice. Yet the basic structure objection finds the Cohenian argument inappropriate, since the principles of justice apply to the basic structure of society and not to personal choices. Therefore members of society could adhere to the difference principle whatever their economic choices are.

> My concern is distributive justice, by which I uneccentrically mean justice (and its lack) in the distribution of benefits and burdens to individuals [...]. [T]here is an injustice in distribution when inequality of goods reflects not such things as differences in the arduousness of different people's labors, or people's different preferences and choices with respect to income and leisure, but myriad forms of lucky or unlucky circumstance (RJE: 126).

Rawls's understanding of distributive justice differs when the distribution of rights, duties and benefits is in accordance with the principles of justice that rule society's main institutions. "When full compliance with the rules of a just basic structure obtains, it follows, on Rawls's view, that there is no scope for (further) personal justice and injustice that affects *distributive* justice, whether it be by enhancing it or reducing it" (ibid.). Yet Cohen believes that the just treatment of inequalities depends on the basic structure of society (coercive rules and powers) and on people's individual choices (non coercive, personal just decisions). Both components should be complementary criteria to judge the justice or the injustice of social and economic inequalities and thereby achieve a just treatment of social and economic inequalities.[16] Hence, it is not possible to realize justice without a social ethos that constantly informs personal decisions. To emphasize the role of citizens advised by this ethos, Cohen gives the example of a just distribution that occurs in an "intense Protestant" society, where citizens are motivated by "self-denial, hard work, and investment of assets surplus to needs" (RJE: 128). This society is just but not according to the Rawlsian principles of justice. The Cohenian reply challenges the basic structure objection: Is a commitment to the principles of justice possible without an ethos informing personal choices within social just rules? What should such a commitment involve? Cohen replies to the basic structure objection by highlighting the values involved within the principles of justice, whose importance hides a necessary commitment to a certain ethos in the Rawlsian conception of justice. Achieving the values of fraternity, dignity of the destitute and full compliance with the principles of justice, does not depend on the basic structure of society, but rather on the citizens living in a social group, who realize their moral powers and

16 Rawls believes that members of society must live in full conformity with the rules and the principles of justice, so that personal daily choices would not have relevant influences on distributive justice. "When full compliance with the rules of a just basic structure obtains, it follows, on Rawls's view, that there is no scope for (further) personal justice and injustice that affects distributive justice, whether it be by enhancing it or by reducing it" (ibid.).

sense of justice. But then a more fundamental reply to the basic structure objection, which is provided by Cohen, shows that "justice requires an ethos governing daily choice that goes beyond one of obedience to just rules" (RJE: 132) and goes beyond the basic structure of society. In this reply, Cohen questions the basic structure in the Rawlsian sense: What is the basic structure? It is not clear whether certain institutions, such as the family are included in the basic structure.

> [I]n this first understanding of it, [the basic structure] is, so one might say, the broad coercive outline of society, which determines in a relatively fixed and general way what people may and must do [...]. In this second reading of what it is, institutions belong to the basic structure whose structuring depend far less on law than on coercion, usage, and expectation (RJE: 133-134).

According to Cohen, the family example shows that it is difficult to separate personal choices from the scope of justice, when the line is crossed from coercive to non-coercive rules. Rawls defines the basic structure as the "primary subject of justice because its effects are so profound and present from the start" (TJ: 7).

Yet Cohen rejects the affirmation "that only the coercive structure causes profound effects" (RJE: 136). Considering the example of the family, he compares the values governing the political framework and those that govern our conduct in the family. He concludes that both values have profound effects on people's existence and affect the distribution of social benefits and burdens.

> Accordingly, if Rawls retreats to coercive structure, he contradicts his own criterion for what justice judges, and he lands himself with an arbitrarily narrow definition of his subject matter. So he must let other structure in, and that means, as we have seen, letting chosen behavior in (ibid.).

Cohen addresses another dilemma for Rawls, who must either admit the application of the principles of justice to social practices, such as personal choices; "or, if he restricts his concern to the coercive structure only, then he saddles himself with a purely arbitrary delineation of his subject matter" (RJE: 137). The application of the Rawlsian principles of justice should not only govern the basic structure of society, but also personal daily economic choices.

> [W]hy should we care so disproportionately about the coercive basic structure, when the major reason for caring about it, its impact on people's lives, is also a reason for caring about informal structure and patterns of personal choice? [...] [W]e must care equally about the ethos that sustains gender inequality and inegalitarian incentives (RJE: 138).

Accordingly, the Cohenian egalitarian conception of justice would imply that justice "is fully served only if people's access to desirable conditions of life is equal, within the constraint of a reasonable personal prerogative" (RJE: 181).

7.8 Pogge's Defense of the Basic Structure

In his article, "On the Site of Distributive Justice: Reflections on Cohen and Murphy" (SDJ), Pogge disputes the Cohenian critique of the Rawlsian conception of distributive justice, dividing it into two main claims. The first one is directly related to the difference principle, according to which the socioeconomic system should regulate socioeconomic inequalities to the greatest benefit of the least advantaged members of society.[17] The second claim concerns a conception of distributive justice that should include the four factors presented in the following.

He presents Cohen's criteria of distributive justice, which should apply not only to the basic structure but also to three other interdependent factors, namely non-coercive structures or conventions, the social ethos that informs people's behaviour, and personal economic choices. Pogge questions the point of including all these factors in a society fully devoted to the difference principle and whose citizens are ready to be committed to any social scheme that maximizes the situation of the least advantaged members of society.

> If the social product were fixed, then its equal distribution would maximize the smallest share. But the social product is in fact variable, affected by education, career, and work-habit choices, which in turn are influenced by the incomes offered for various kinds of performance (SDJ: 140).

According to Cohen, the lowest income could increase if talented persons increased their production without extra money incentives. In order to explore this moral demand, Pogge affirms that "we must reflect in some detail on how differences among persons may give rise to income inequality in the society Rawls envisions" (SDJ: 141). He imagines a society with 100 workers. 13 of them are managers who earn 120 $ per hour, while 87 are workers who earn 10 $ per hour. Depending on the taxes people pay, the pay rate ratio "g" might vary from 12 to 5. The formula to obtain the pay rate ratio is g = income of the manager / income of the worker, like for example, g = 120 $ / 10 $ = 12. Pogge affirms that

17 Pogge calls this distribution that regulates social and economic inequalities to the greatest benefit of the least advantaged members of society the goal D.

the manager's pay rate and the worker's pay rate as well as the numbers of managers and workers vary according to the tax regime applied.

> Taxing managerial work more heavily diminishes the reward multiple, n, offered for managerial work and therefore tends both to reduce the number of talented persons choosing managerial work and to increase the numbers of laborers whose pay is to be enhanced (SDJ: 142).

Pogge claims that Cohen would choose the tax regime that reduces the pay rate ratio to the maximum, which is 5 in the case at hand: If the manager earns 75 $ and pays the rest for taxes, the worker would be able to earn 15 $ per hour, considering that the number of managers decreases from 13 to 10. The responsibility attributed to talented persons is therefore decisive. Pogge argues that the Cohenian argumentation for choosing this tax regime is not clear and explores the five different ways the responsibility Cohen attributes to talented persons can be understood.

The first specification states that Cohen's critique condemns the behaviour of talented persons who act like the kidnapper.[18] They refuse to increase their productivity unless they receive special money rewards. Pogge argues that this conduct could succeed in a small-scale society but not in a real society, where "few talented persons would go against their own preference by avoiding a high-productivity career in order to reduce the tax rate for those other talented persons who choose it" (SDJ: 144).

To understand the second specification, Pogge explains that people prefer different types of jobs, influenced by different factors, such as the salary. But, there is no place in the Rawlsian theory for interpersonal comparisons. Persons who have the same job with the same salary are equally well off, because they have the same set of primary goods; even if one hates the job and the other loves it. Pogge defines certain reservation net pay rate ratio, which he calls respio, as the lowest reward multiple sufficient to let a person work as a manager. He considers for example that Clara has the optimal reward multiple of 5, while other managers have lower respios. Moreover, "if work in one (reasonably congenial) job adds much more value than work in other jobs, then its reward multiple is likely greatly to exceed the respios of most workers in this job, so that a very large portion of the special rewards they collectively receive is economic rent" (SDJ: 146-147). According to Pogge, Cohen wants to redirect this economic rent share toward maximizing the lowest pay rate. He argues that this Cohenian

18 For an elaborate presentation of the kidnapper's argument, see chapter 5.

idea is not feasible in real society because of the diversity of jobs one can choose and the complexity of calculating the rent portion of the income in every job. "A moral duty to redirect the economic-rent portion of one's special rewards cannot be defined in a plausible way and is not coherent with Rawls's theory" (SDJ: 149).

Pogge explores the third specification of the Cohenian critique that follows from the second one, in which Cohen holds that a real commitment to the difference principle implies that financial rewards should be redirected so as to maximize the situation of the least advantaged members of society. But Pogge argues that in this case, managers would give up their careers and choose to work as laborers with a respio above 1. This decision would make everyone worse off.

The fourth specification illustrates another moral duty that Cohen requires from gifted persons. According to Pogge, Cohen affirms that a true commitment to the Rawlsian difference principle imposes on Clara to choose managing over laboring, but allows Jeff, who is reluctant to be a manager and whose respio is 7, to choose laboring over managing. Someone as talented as Clara is not free to prefer laboring over managing and is also obligated to accept an equal distribution of benefits, (D3).[19]

> The talented ought to contribute as they would in the society Rawls envisions even while receiving merely an equal share of the social product. Only if they do, according to Cohen, is Rawlsian economic justice fully realized in the tax regime and in the personal choices of talented citizens (SDJ: 150).

Pogge argues that it is not clear why the commitment to the difference principle, which implies that social and economic inequalities should be regulated to improve the plight of the least advantaged members of society "should require Clara, but not Jeff, to renounce laboring for managerial work at unit pay. [...] If Clara ought to be a manager at unit pay, so ought Jeff" (SDJ: 151-152).

This leads Pogge to the last specification, which requires everyone with talents to strive for maximum productiveness in order to enhance the lowest incomes and reduce socioeconomic inequalities. Pogge finds this moral duty unfair towards talented persons, who will find themselves penalized for their special talents.

> She [Clara] must choose managing over laboring at a fraction of the reward multiple at which she would (barely) prefer managerial work. [...] she is required to render herself

19 For a further presentation of D3, see chapters 5 and 7.

> very much less happy than she would be laboring at unit pay in order to make others slightly more happy laboring at a (somewhat enhanced) unit pay (SDJ: 153).

Subsequently, Pogge defends Rawls's viewpoint of limiting the application of the difference principle to the basic structure of society. As presented, all the specifications of Cohen's critique, explored by Pogge, seem to be directly or indirectly related to the Cohenian alternative, D3, discussed in the beginning of this chapter. This alternative examines the feasibility of an equal distribution of rights, duties and benefits. But, in RJE, Cohen is aware of the difficulty of applying such an equal distribution because of human nature. Inspired by the difference principle, talented persons find socioeconomic inequalities necessary in order to advance the situation of the disadvantaged. According to Cohen, the talented persons make these inequalities necessary. He proposes an equal distribution of income and wealth but questions its feasibility and concludes that even if an unequal distribution is not just, "it's preferable on grounds of human flourishing and might therefore reasonably be chosen" (RJE: 319). Thus, although Cohen is convinced that justice requires equality, the "reasonable" choice for an unequal distribution of goods, reduces the distance between the Cohenian and the Rawlsian choices and therefore lessens the force of Pogge's argumentation. Pogge examines whether a conception of justice should apply only to the basic structure, or also to everyday human life. He compares the two ways in which our thinking about justice is structured. With reference to Liam Murphy in "Institutions and the Demands of Justice", he compares between a dualist and a monist thinking. On the one hand, the Rawlsian conception of justice is dualist, separating between applying the principles of justice to everyday human life and to the basic structure. On the other hand, Cohen's and Murphy's understanding of justice[20] is monist, insofar as there should be a fundamental principle that applies to institutions and to personal conduct alike. In his defense of Rawls's dualism, Pogge argues that personal judgements are responsible for achieving and maintaining a just basic structure. Personal dispositions, conventions, and ethos are not excluded from the Rawlsian conception, but are taken into account in the design and maintenance of a just basic structure. "Thus, while conventions, ethos, and personal choices are not governed by Rawls's criterion of justice, they are still affected by it indirectly:

20 Note that there is a difference between Cohen's monism and Murphy's monism. Cohen considers that both persons and basic structure should pursue or aim at a common goal, while Murphy thinks that both should be so shaped to promote this common goal. Pogge affirms that persons and institutions are inspirationally related to the common goal in the Cohenian case, while they are performatively related to according to Murphy.

through the influence of a just basic structure exerts upon them" (SDJ: 166). Consequently, Pogge concludes that the gap between Cohen's monistic challenge and the Rawlsian conception of justice is reduced.

7.9 Scheffler's Defense of the Basic Structure

Another focus on the merits of the basic structure is presented by Samuel Scheffler in his article, "Is the Basic Structure Basic?" (BSB). He examines the motivations behind the Rawlsian viewpoint, which affirms that the basic structure is the primary subject of justice but then reviews Cohen's arguments and objections showing that they do not succeed in undermining Rawls's position about the basic structure.

Scheffler stresses the importance of the Rawlsian reasonable pluralism about moral principles and highlights the fact that the principles of justice are inappropriate for private groups, associations, and human conduct in general. They apply to a limited scope, namely to society's main institutions. However, an essential part of Rawls's theory asserts that just institutions as well as individuals must comply with two principles: "the principle of fairness, which accounts for all of our voluntarily incurred obligations, and the principle governing the natural duty of justice" (BSB: 103). The principles for individuals are defined according to the conception of justice that regulates the basic structure of society. So the basic structure is the primary subject of justice insofar as the content of just social institutions is defined before the rules of human conduct are laid down. Scheffler cites three points of Rawls for considering the basic structure the primary subject of justice.

First, "the basic structure is the primary subject of justice because its effects are so profound and present from the start" (TJ: 7). People born into different social classes have different expectations in life; therefore, the main institutions of society should be regulated by principles of justice to avoid even more inequalities.

Second, the basic structure must be designed to shape individuals' desires and aspirations, which are influenced by the economic system. "It [the basic structure] determines in part the sort of persons they want to be as well as the sort of persons they are" (BSB: 104).

Third, the basic structure is primary in the sense that it secures and preserves just background conditions to guarantee just agreements among citizens. "Rawls argues that there simply are no feasible rules of individual conduct that are capable of preserving background justice and that do not violate these conditions" (BSB: 105). Thus, there should be an institutional division of labor between the basic structure and the rules that apply to individuals and associations. Scheffler adds that according to Rawls, if

> this division of labor can be established, individuals and associations are then left free to advance their ends more effectively within the framework of the basic structure, secure in the knowledge that elsewhere in the social system the necessary corrections to preserve background justice are being made (*Political Liberalism*: 269).

In addition to the three considerations mentioned by Rawls regarding the basic structure, Scheffler makes three observations about Rawls's theory.

First, Rawls draws two contracts between the norms for the basic structure and other norms. He distinguishes between the principles of justice that apply to social institutions and the principles that apply to individual conduct. Then he contrasts rules that are designed to preserve background justice over time with rules to regulate individual economic agreements. For example, if the basic structure includes the rules of income and inheritance taxation, the set of rules that govern people's agreements and transactions "includes the law of contract, and its function is to provide individuals with a set of clear and practical guidelines" (BSB: 106) that regulate economic transactions within the rules of the basic structure. Therefore, Scheffler refers to the first contrast as "the division of moral labor" between the principles that apply to the basic structure and the principles that apply to personal conduct, groups and associations. As for the second contrast, Rawls believes it is the "institutional division of labor" between the social forms that are required to ensure background justice and the social forms that regulate individual economic transactions.

The second observation is that rules of personal conduct are insufficient in preserving background justice; but it is essential that individuals have a strong sense of justice and a natural duty to support just arrangements, without which a just and stable society cannot be achieved.

The third idea is that principles regulating the basic structure do not replace the varied principles that apply to individuals, allowed by the Rawlsian reasonable pluralism. Rawls affirms that individuals and associations are left free to advance their interests within the framework of the basic structure. Despite this Rawlsian affirmation, Scheffler argues that "the idea here is not to relieve individuals of a burdensome but feasible task, but rather that the task in question is one that individuals are incapable of discharging" (BSB: 107). Then Rawls is misunderstood: citizens are not placed beyond the reach of justice. Without the rules of the basic structure, members of society would have to acknowledge the injustice of their economic transactions. However, this conclusion seems to trouble Cohen, who stresses the role of a moral ethos that regulates daily economic choices along with the principles that regulate social institutions. According to Scheffler, Cohen explores two main ambiguities in the Rawlsian conception of justice. It is unclear whether the difference principle should be given a lax or a strict interpretation. As seen above, the difference principle allows inequalities necessary to enhance the position of the least advantaged members of society. Whereas in the strict reading of the difference principle, money incentives are not necessary to improve the situation of the worst off people, they are essential in the lax understanding because without this extra income, talented persons might be unwilling to increase their productivity. Although elements for both interpretations are present in the Rawlsian theory, Scheffler believes that Cohen thinks Rawls is committed to the lax reading of the difference principle. It is also unclear whether the basic structure includes non-coercive structures, which affect human existence profoundly. If non-coercive structures are included in the basic structure, individual conduct cannot be excluded from the sphere of the principles of justice. This shows the importance of the Cohenian moral ethos which should impact people's daily lives. If non-coercive structures, such as the family[21], which have profound effects on human conduct, are excluded from the basic structure, then Rawls contradicts his own justification for treating the basic structure as the primary subject of justice and thus establishing an arbitrary exclusion. This dilemma that faces Rawls is discussed below. Scheffler believes that Cohen's arguments are insufficient for undermining Rawls's view of the basic structure as the primary subject of justice.

Against the legitimacy of incentive inequalities, Cohen imagines that Rawlsians would reply to his argument with the basic structure objection, saying that the difference principle is meant to apply to social institutions and not to personal choices within that structure. "Within the basic structure, the principles simply do not apply, and so they do not exclude purely self-interested economic decisions by individuals" (BSB: 111). Cohen challenges the basic structure objection by showing its inconsistency with the importance given by Rawls to the principles of justice within the lives of citizens and by highlighting the ambiguity of including non-coercive structures.

21 Scheffler argues that the grounds for classifying the family as a non-coercive structure is ambiguous because "there is a large body of family law, and all societies engage in the legal regulation of marriage, adoption, divorce, child custody, child support, alimony, parental responsibility and the like. There is, for example, nothing non-coercive about the practice of restricting marriage to pairs of adults consisting of one man and one woman" (BSB: 122).

However, Scheffler doubts that Rawls would have replied with the basic structure objection. This reply to Cohen's argument against incentive inequalities is inconsistent with the importance of the sense of justice that citizens should have in a well-ordered society within the Rawlsian framework. Furthermore, Cohen rejects the basic structure because it allows the pursuit and the maximization of economic self-interest. Scheffler argues that "Rawls does not say that individuals should be motivated purely by economic self-interest nor does he contrast his position with the view that the principles of social justice should 'appropriately inform' individual conduct" (BSB: 113). Rawls denies the fact that a single principle is sufficient to regulate both social institutions and human conduct. Although he does not say how individual economic choices should be informed by the principles of justice, he does not claim that individual motivation should be unaffected by the principles of social justice, or be beyond the constraints of justice. He equally does not endorse unlimited self-fulfillment. Scheffler then asks what else Rawls might reply.

Scheffler supposes that Rawls would endorse the strict reading of the difference principle for the regulation of the basic structure of society, which only includes coercive rules. In this case, only necessary inequalities independent on people's choices would be allowed, which means that there would be little inequality in society. In the case at hand, an egalitarian ethos would not be necessary to achieve an economic just distribution as it would be achieved by coercive structure.

> It may well be true, that if the coercive structure were regulated by the lax principle, then economic equality would be achieved only if talented had an egalitarian ethos [...]. But it does not follow that, if the coercive structure were regulated by the strict principle, the achievement of equality would depend on such an ethos (BSB: 115).

Therefore, Scheffler concludes that Cohen is mistaken when he affirms that without an ethos of justice, inequalities would arise, which would not improve the condition of the poor. "There is nothing in Cohen's challenge to the legitimacy of incentive inequalities per se that undermines Rawls's claim that the basic structure is the primary subject of justice" (BSB: 116-117). Moreover, Rawls's claim about the primacy of the basic structure does not deny the importance of a sense or even an ethos of justice.

As to the dilemma that Cohen highlights in order to challenge Rawls's basic structure, Scheffler affirms that even if this dilemma is correct, it does not undermine Rawls's position about the primacy of the basic structure. Even if the basic structure includes some individual choices, it cannot include them all, so it will always be possible to distinguish between the basic structure and the choices made within it. Thus, by emphasizing the merits of the Rawlsian basic structure, Scheffler shows that Cohen's arguments do not suffice to defeat this view.

> Once the claim that the basic structure is the primary subject of justice is decoupled from the idea that justice condones unlimited self-seeking behavior, the considerations that count in its favor need to be evaluated in their own right (BSB: 128).

Scheffler tries to show that Cohen's arguments are not sufficient to undermine Rawls's view about the primacy of the basic structure. He explores in what sense the basic structure is basic and he answers Cohen's arguments against it. He doubts the Rawlsian use of the basic structure objection proposing the application of the strict reading of the difference principle. Scheffler deduces an equal economic distribution by coercive rules without a moral ethos that informs people's choices, replying to Cohen that one moral principle cannot regulate social institutions as well as human conduct. However, this is not Cohen's viewpoint. Cohen does not affirm that one principle should regulate society's main institutions and daily economic decisions. He, on the contrary, affirms that a "society that is just within the terms of the difference principle [...] requires not simply just coercive *rules*, but also an *ethos* of justice that informs individual choices" (RJE: 123). Consequently, Cohen focuses on the equal importance of two basic and complementary principles that would achieve a just economic distribution within the Rawlsian conception of justice. In this sense, the basic structure is not basic because it is not the first and the only subject of justice. An equal role in achieving social justice is given to the members of society.

In sum, this chapter explores other points in the Cohenian rescue of equality from the Rawlsian argument. Cohen suggests that Rawls should have chosen a Pareto-optimal equality that aids the worst-off people. The social and economic inequalities should be regulated in such a way that they improve the situation of the destitute albeit to the detriment of the affluent, who are already endowed with more gifts than others. By proposing his way of regulating these inequalities, Cohen presents his own "conception of justice". However, he highlights the importance of an ethos that is expected to influence daily choices. Unlike Rawls, the important role is given to citizens (and not to the basic structure) whose decisions should be made in the light of the principles of justice and applied to social institutions. Would the Cohenian ethos complete the Rawlsian conception of social justice? Are both conceptions of justice in some manner reconcilable?

8 Disagreement on the Status of Principles

Whereas the relationship between virtues and first principles representing these virtues seems to be accepted, the question of the relationship between facts and principles has been the topic of philosophical disputes in ancient as well as in modern philosophy. The idea that principles express certain virtues is not unanimously held, but it does not seem to be much contested, in contrast to the relationship between facts and principles. Some philosophers believe that all principles that express virtues as well as all convictions rest on facts and experiences. Yet at the opposite end of the spectrum, another philosophical viewpoint refuses to agree that facts support principles. The debate between Cohen and Rawls on the relation between facts and principles extends this philosophical discourse even though it does not reproduce the traditional philosophical dispute. Rawls affirms that fundamental principles of justice should be selected by members of society in order to be put into practice. The choice of these principles depends on the factual situation in which citizens live. Cohen criticizes this selection and the way it was made in the Rawlsian conception of justice. According to him, facts reflect principles of justice, for example, as a result of fundamental fact-free principles that express the virtue of justice. Cohen's question is not traditional; it is not whether principles are grounded in facts, or whether principles are objective or subjective, but rather: What is implied when principles are grounded in facts? The Cohenian viewpoint is discussed in the following which tries to answer three questions: Should the fundamental principles be fact-free? Do the Rawlsian principles of justice depend on facts? What could Cohen's critique possibly contribute to Rawls's theory of justice?

8.1 Principles in the Rawlsian Understanding

In the Rawlsian conception of justice, the relationship between the principles and the virtue of justice should lead to the building of a just social system, which applies the principles of social justice necessary for realizing justice in society. So, "I shall begin by considering the role of the principles of justice" (TJ: 4). It is to be remembered that because society is characterized by an identity and thereby a conflict[1] of interests, citizens' rights, liberties as well as social and economic benefits are mutually interdependent. Hence, a set of principles is required for selecting the most suitable social arrangement according to which rights, liberties and wealth would be fairly distributed.

> These principles are the principles of social justice: they provide a way of assigning rights and duties in the basic institutions of society and they define the appropriate distribution of the benefits and burdens of social cooperation (ibid.).

Two remarks should be made here: firstly Rawls defines the principles as principles of social justice. They are chosen in order to be applied to society's basic institutions in order to achieve social justice. They are not meant to realize other kinds of justice, such as justice within a family, or international justice which focuses on realizing justice on a global level among all types of societies. Consequently, they are not intended to accomplish justice in a comprehensive sense. Secondly these principles are normative principles insofar as "they provide a way of assigning" rights and duties, which should be distributed according to certain social conditions. For example, material goods ought not to be redistributed arbitrarily. As a result, basic institutions of society would function in accordance with these norms, which imply – in the Rawlsian conception of justice – 1) an equal assignment of rights and duties among all members of society and 2) a fair distribution of social and economic benefits. Rawls focuses on the role of the principles of justice that should involve equal assignment of rights and liberties and fair distribution of social and material goods in order to guarantee the maximum share of rights and wealth for everyone. The maximum share is determined by the citizens, who want to preserve the most of their interests within a viable social arrangement. The fairness of these principles refers then to how applicable they are and how much liberties, rights and wealth they provide. But the two criteria seem more likely to be related to facts about human nature than to truths about the virtue of justice. How then should principles of justice be selected? In the Cohenian rescue of the virtue of justice the normative principles chosen by Rawls do not represent justice, but rather a compromise between justice and the factual human condition. Therefore, they should not be called principles of justice, but rather rules of regulation on which representative members would agree. As articulated by Rawls, the selected principles are "the object of the original agreement [...] that free and rational persons con-

---

1 Citizens "are not indifferent as to how the greater benefits produced by their collaboration are distributed, for in order to pursue their ends they each prefer a larger to a lesser share" (ibid.).

cerned to further their own interests would accept in an initial position of equality as defining the fundamental terms of their association" (TJ: 11).

As discussed in chapter 1, citizens have to consent – once and for all in the original position – on a contract, which preserves a set of rights and liberties and a maximum share of goods for all for generations to come. One of the facts about their human situation is that they live with arbitrary inequalities, which cannot be removed.[2] That is why they should be regulated by applying the principles of justice. The results obtained are normative principles of justice relative to the citizens' real life situation.

> [J]ust as each person must decide by rational reflection what constitutes his good, that is, the system of ends which it is rational for him to pursue, so a group of persons must decide once for all what is to count among them as just and unjust. The choice which rational men would make in this hypothetical situation of equal liberty [...] determines the principles of justice (TJ: 12).

Rawls does not deny the importance of natural facts about the human condition for determining the first principles of justice. Contrariwise, he affirms that "there is no objection to resting the choice of first principles upon the general facts of economics and psychology. [...] Contract theory agrees, then, with utilitarianism in holding that the fundamental principles of justice quite properly depend upon the natural facts about men in society" (TJ: 159). Furthermore, he justifies that general facts are needed to select the first principles of justice because without those elements "the whole scheme would be pointless and empty" (TJ: 160). However, he argues that first principles of justice do not merely rely on general facts, but also on ideals of justice. "Justice as fairness, by contrast, embeds the ideals of justice, as ordinarily understood, more directly into its first principles. This conception relies less on general facts in reaching a match with our judgments of justice" (ibid.). To the opposing position that refuses to ground first principles on contingencies, Rawls replies that citizens should have alternatives of social arrangements to choose from. Therefore, assumptions about general facts cannot be avoided in determining all alternatives.

2 Arbitrary inequalities derive from natural or social circumstances that favour those inequalities. The aim is not to remove them, which could lead to further injustices, but rather to regulate them and to mitigate their effects. In a just social system, those arbitrary and undeserved inequalities should neither be to the advantage nor to the disadvantage of the persons.

> Some philosophers have thought that ethical first principles should be independent of all contingencies assumptions,that they should take for granted no truths except those of logic and others that follow from these by analysis of concepts. [...] Now this view makes moral philosophy [...] an examination of the reflections an omnipotent deity might entertain in determining which is the best of all possible worlds. [...] But this would appear to outrun human comprehension (TJ: 159).

Fundamental principles of justice are grounded within the Rawlsian theory in general facts about human nature and in ideals and convictions of justice. They are also normative principles, insofar as they provide ways of assigning rights, liberties, and wealth. These principles should be the first expression of justice and they should thereby serve as a basis to achieve justice in society. According to Cohen, the Rawlsian principles of justice do not exhaust the virtue of justice since they do not tell us what justice is. They might be the most suitable principles of justice that citizens put into practice, but are definitely not the fundamental principles of justice. Accordingly, they should be considered a compromise between the human condition and justice, but not the virtue of justice.

However, as elaborated in chapter 3, it is not simply the compromise between the virtue of justice and the human factual condition that is subject to the Cohenian scrutiny and critique, but also the misleading relationship between facts and principles, and the constructivist[3] approach to justice. Unlike most philosophers, Cohen refuses to define fundamental or first principles of any virtue based on facts about this virtue. How should principles then be selected? Should all principles be grounded in fundamental fact-free principles? What about the principles of justice? The logical priority of principles over facts within the Cohenian argument is discussed in the following as well as its consequences on the close relationship between principles and facts.

8.2 Principles in the Cohenian Understanding

Whereas Rawls focuses on the role of the principles of justice, Cohen questions the foundation of these principles. He argues that the first, fundamental or most ultimate principles, which Rawls thinks represent and realize the value of justice, should not at all correspond to facts. Normative principles of justice cannot be grounded merely in the facts of human nature and the human condition,

3 Recall that the constructivist approach to social justice defines important values, such as justice or equality taking the factual human situation as starting point, such as Rawls's original position.

because facts alone cannot be the foundation of principles. Cohen elaborates that not all principles are grounded in facts and the ones that are can respond to facts or be grounded in facts “only because (they are) also a response to [...] a more ultimate principle that is not a response to a fact: accordingly, if principles respond to facts, then the principles at the summit of our conviction are grounded in no facts whatsoever” (RJE: 229). The principles are divided into two groups: the first group contains principles sensitive to facts while the second group comprises principles which are fact-insensitive. But the ultimate foundation of all principles is formed by fundamental principles or ultimate principles, which are insensitive to facts.

In one way, Cohen’s thesis denies the Rawlsian principles of justice based on facts about human nature and situation insofar as it states that all principles are ultimately grounded in principles and not in facts, even though some principles can respond to facts. Yet if the thesis denies the philosophical viewpoint, which believes facts are the basis of all fundamental principles and convictions, it does not contest that principles can be to a degree grounded in facts. Therefore, it focuses on the relationship between principles grounded in facts and the facts that ground them.

> [M]y argument, so I believe, is robust across permissible variations in the meaning of ‘fact’, and it is also neutral across contrasting conceptions of the relationship of fact and value. [...] It bears emphasis that the question that my thesis answers is neutral with respect to controversies about the objectivity of principles, the relationship between facts and values, and the ´is-ought´ question (RJE: 230).

The Cohenian thesis questions the structure of belief in principles and does not focus on what motivates people to believe in their principles. The point is not to know the reason why this principle becomes an object of belief and not that one. Cohen’s aim is to identify how principles are selected.

> At least standardly, people do arrive at all the principles to which they adhere as a result of their experience of life, which is, as it were, an experience of facts, and of their reflection on that experience. My claim is that what they thereby come to believe includes and depends upon belief in principles that are independent of anything they believed or believe about facts (RJE: 255).

Cohen does not want to prove that a fact is the foundation for a principle but wants to show that a principle is based on a fact only due to a further principle which is independent of any facts.

As described in chapter 2, whereas normative principles – called “principles” – are general directives that tell us what ought to or ought not to be done,

facts correspond "to any truth, other than (if any principles are truths) a principle, of a kind that someone might reasonably think supports a principle" (RJE: 229). Thus, one should distinguish between facts, and normative, ultimate and fundamental principles. Normative principles are principles, which might reflect facts, only because the facts are grounded in more ultimate principles. Ultimate principles are relatively "fact-insensitive" insofar as they do not reflect specific facts, such as scientific facts. However, they might reflect other facts, for example, about the human condition. Fundamental principles, however, are "fact-free", because they do not rely on any facts at all; facts do not form any component of their foundation. They "are not derived from other principles, [and] do not rest on factual grounds" (RJE: 278). Consequently, the fundamental principles have logical priority over ultimate principles and normative principles, which in turn have logical priority over facts. While fundamental principles are chosen separately from facts, normative principles – which tell us what ought to be done – respond to facts. But are fundamental principles normative i.e. general directives that are imperatives? If fundamental principles ground all other logically posterior principles, what about their nature?

Before answering these questions, it is important to emphasize that the Cohenian argument supplies grounding powers to the fundamental principles. If his thesis is true, only first principles have the power to ground principles and fact-sensitive principles. The Cohenian thesis implies that the grounding power of a fact is based on another principle unresponsive to that fact. In this case, the grounding and reason-providing power derives from the fact-insensitive principle to the fact-sensitive principle through the fact. "It is always a further principle that confers on a fact its principle-grounding and reason-providing power" (RJE: 234).

8.3 Focusing on Fundamental Principles

As explained in chapter 2, whereas Cohen provides a definition of the normative principles that emphasizes their role, he does not elaborate on the fundamental principles. He says that ultimate or fundamental principles, which are reason-providing for all other principles, even though they cannot be justified by facts, "might be self-evidently true or they might for some other reason require no grounds or they might need grounds and have grounds of some nonfactual sort [...] they might not be objects of belief at all" (RJE: 238). Fundamental principles "might not be" normative principles, insofar as they are not related to facts at all. But, they "might be" normative in the sense that they are directives which dictate what ought to or ought not to be done. Thus, normative principles can be considered ultimate principles, if insensitive to certain facts, and by the same fact, ground the principles sensitive to those facts. An ultimate principle P1, which is also a normative principle, is ultimate regarding principle P and its relation to fact F. One should imagine a logical hierarchy of principles starting at the top from the most ultimate fact-free principle, from which all principles are derived to the last fact-sensitive principle. Cohen seems to be hesitant about the nature and the structure of belief concerning the most ultimate (fundamental) fact-free principles. Indeed, it is not clear whether they need grounds or whether they are already grounded in something else. Cohen neither justifies why they are self-evidently true nor why they are self-explanatory. It is not clear whether they are objects of belief at all. Even if they are, for argumentative purposes, considered as self-evidently true, their nature and structure is nevertheless ambiguous. These confusing principles remain of primary importance in Cohen's rebuttal of the Rawlsian theory. To Cohen, Rawls cannot pretend to be establishing the fundamental principles of justice because these principles cannot depend on facts. To consolidate his thesis, Cohen examines the human structure of beliefs and convictions and its relationship to facts. He concludes that there is always a reason why a fact supports a principle. The reason is another principle, which survives the denial of the fact. This way of reasoning from one principle to another, leads to a last[4] fact-free principle. Since every person has their own way of reasoning, these fact-free principles would be different from one person to another. But if the first principles are independent from facts about human nature, would they not be universal or common amongst all persons? Do persons believe in the same fundamental principles? What about the fundamental principles of justice? If they are independent from the facts about men, would they not be the same among all persons?

8.4 Cohen versus Rawls

If the Cohenian argument about the foundation of all principles were sound, the grounding principles or the first principles would not need to be supported by facts, but rather by the virtue of justice. The Cohenian viewpoint is discussed in the following: The Rawlsian principles are questioned and whether or not they are grounded in facts.

4 The last principle in our reasoning is logically the first principle, which is not derived from any facts.

Thus, the two principles of justice selected by Rawls for social institutions "must not be confused with the principles which apply to individuals and their actions in particular circumstances" (TJ: 54). The justice to be realized within the application of these principles is the justice of social institutions and not the justice of human behaviour in daily life. On what principles or facts does the justice of social institutions rely?

As said, fundamental principles of justice exist independently from any facts. They provide their own reasons or are self-evident and represent the virtue of justice. However, human reason does not start its reasoning at the first principles of justice, but rather at the facts and fact-sensitive normative principles and ends when it reaches the fundamental principles. However, the course it takes – as Cohen describes – within the Rawlsian reasoning about justice is not the same; Cohen's hierarchy of principles does not exist within the Rawlsian framework. Human reason starts with facts about human nature and establishes the first fundamental principles of justice based on these facts. But are the Rawlsian principles of justice grounded in facts about human nature? What facts do they reveal? How should principles for social institutions be selected?

8.5 The Thesis

On the theoretical level, Rawlsian principles of justice, which apply to social institutions, are not based on facts, but on the fundamental principles of justice, equality, and fairness. This supports the Cohenian viewpoint that fundamental principles should not be fact-based. The selected principles correspond to facts about human nature on a practical level, where they need to be accepted and applied by members of society. The argument for the thesis suggests two readings of the Rawlsian conception of justice. The two readings show two levels in the Rawlsian theory, with two differing correlations between facts and principles and the importance of facts about human nature: the theoretical level on which the principles of justice are chosen and the practical level on which these principles are applied. Both levels, as well as the influence of the facts on them, are discussed below.

> It is, therefore, worth noting from the outset that justice as fairness, like other contract views, consists of two parts: (1) an interpretation of the initial situation and of the problem of choice posed here, and (2) a set of principles which, it is argued, would be agreed to. One may accept the first part of the theory (or some variant thereof), but not the other, and conversely (TJ: 15).

The principles should 1) represent social justice and 2) be agreed on by all members of society. The first level or the choices level deals with the content of the virtues of social justice and its implications, while the second level deals with the agreement and its application. To justify the choice, Rawls uses the original position device as well as the public justification argument.

8.5.1 Theoretical Level

The social principles are chosen according to fundamental principles, that is to say justice, equality, and fairness. Rawls does not justify his choice of these fundamental principles that are the criteria for selecting the social principles of justice. But within a liberal democratic society justice, equality, and fairness may be the most important fundamental principles. However, one might use the Cohenian procedure that starts reasoning from facts and ends with justice as equality and fairness at the top of fundamental principles.

There are different principles of social justice in our system of beliefs and convictions. The task is to choose the best among them and to uphold the choice to everyone within society. Whereas the justification or the acceptability is related to the application and the applicability (persons would accept the principles that they are able to put into practice), the choice is related to the virtue of justice itself. "A conception of justice cannot be deduced from self-evident premises or conditions on principles; instead, its justification is a matter of the mutual support of many considerations, of everything fitting together into one coherent view" (TJ: 21). On the level of the chosen principles, the first principle represents the idea of justice as equality, since every person within society should hold equal rights and basic liberties. On what facts does an equal assignment of rights and liberties depend? The first principle of justice is not grounded in any facts, insofar as it represents only the virtue of social justice and its tendency to equality: Rights and liberties should be equal because citizens within a just society should have the same basic rights. So, this principle is a normative principle of equality in the Cohenian sense, which favours an equal distribution of rights and liberties. The second selected principle refers to the distribution of income, wealth and social positions. Once again, equality is taken as a fundamental principle in defining the content of the social principle that should represent the virtue of social justice. "All social values – liberty and opportunity, income and wealth, and the bases of self-respect – are to be distributed equally" (TJ: 62). The first definition of justice draws a tight relationship between justice and equality. At a theoretical level, all social goods should be distributed equally according to the fundamental principle that equates justice with equality.

> Imagine, then, a hypothetical initial arrangement in which all the social primary goods are equally distributed: everyone has similar rights and duties, and income and wealth are evenly shared. This state of affairs provides a benchmark for judging improvements (TJ: 62).

Thus equality is taken as a reference point, but a reference to what? Why is this benchmark needed?

8.5.2 Practical Level

The justice of any social arrangement that aims at regulating inequalities on a practical level must be appraised, once both principles are applied. In theory, the second principle of justice has the fundamental principle of equality as a reference. In practice, this principle reflects facts about its feasibility. The Rawlsian mistake, according to Cohen, is the move to make the fundamental principles of justice, which claim the equal distribution of income and wealth, feasible and applicable. In order to become feasible, the principles should correspond to facts about human nature. But once they reflect practicable facts, they stop being fundamental principles of justice; they represent a mixture of practicability and justice.

Any social system that aids everyone's economic and social situation would be fair and thereby accepted by all members of society. Therefore, inequalities are permitted if and only if they improve the social and economic situation of everyone. On the practical level, the principle of fairness is a crucial criterion for the justice of both principles which are to be applied. Rawls did not question the concept of justice. His aim is to establish a just social system, where social institutions function in a just way. Both principles must be accepted by a society's citizens in order to be applied and to treat everyone's interests fairly. This fairness would be conducive in making the principle acceptability and applicability by everyone. How would both principles match human nature? What makes them acceptable and applicable? This is where the importance of the facts about the human condition and human nature reveals itself. To be accepted and applied, social principles of justice should meet facts about the human nature, of economics, and of psychology. On the practical level, these facts are essential to make social principles applicable. However, by the same criteria, the principles cannot be called fundamental principles of justice, since they do not only represent the virtue of justice, but also other criteria.

As a conclusion, the application of the Cohenian argument on the Rawlsian theory would indeed lead to fact-insensitive fundamental principles, related to one another, from which both principles of justice are deduced: justice as equality and justice as fairness. In order to be fair, inequalities should be to the advantage of all. "Injustice, then, is simply inequalities that are not to the benefit of all" (TJ: 62). On a practical level, facts about human nature and condition are necessary, because the social choice has to be accepted in line with these facts before it can be applied.

> So, it might be asked, 'How much difference would it make if Rawls did not call his two principles 'first principles' but reserved that designation for the principles that justify the original position machine?' [...] To our assessment of the desirability of the principles that A theory of Justice tells us to follow it might make no difference at all (RJE: 263).

8.6 A Discussion of the Role of Facts

In his interesting critique of Cohen's thesis about the relationship between facts and principles, A. Faik Kurtulmus develops, in his article, "Rawls and Cohen on Facts and Principles" (RCFP), an account for Rawls's justificatory strategy and the role of facts in this strategy. According to Cohen, the scrutiny of fact-sensitive principles will reveal fact-insensitive principles, by which facts can reflect principles. If Rawls's construction of the principles of justice is fact-dependent, Kurtulmus affirms according to Cohen, Rawls denies the Cohenian thesis that fact-insensitive principles ground the structure of beliefs. Kurtulmus argues that Rawls would not deny Cohen's thesis.

In fact Cohen does not say that Rawls denies his thesis about the relationship between facts and principles. Contrariwise, Cohen argues that Rawls does not reach the ultimate fact-insensitive principles at the bottom of all other fact-sensitive principles which make up the structure of beliefs. Rawls does not examine the relationship between facts and principles, but affirms that given certain facts about human nature and the world, principles of justice are selected in the original position. Kurtulmus is nonetheless right with his conclusion, since he confirms that Rawls has a completely different thesis.

To make the difference clear, Kurtulmus distinguishes between a "metaphysically fact-insensitive principle" and an "epistemically fact-insensitive principle".

> A principle is metaphysically fact-insensitive if its truth doesn't depend on any facts. A principle is epistemically fact-insensitive if our belief in it doesn't depend on knowledge of facts (RCFP: 490).

Kurtulmus affirms that Cohen's central claim is that there are metaphysically fact-insensitive principles, whose truth does not depend on any facts. However, he argues that Rawls's stipulates metaphysically and epistemically fact-insensitive principles need not correspond and that epistemically fact-insensitive principles, can be metaphysically fact-sensitive principles, grounded in facts. Reformulated in Kurtulmus's terminology, Cohen's thesis would say that epistemically fact-sensitive principles, which are the fact-based principles we believe in, are grounded in metaphysically fact-insensitive principles, whose truth does not depend on any facts.

Moreover, in his defense of Rawls's justificatory strategy Kurtulmus affirms that

> Cohen is defending the thesis that there are metaphysically fact-insensitive principles. Rawls, however, is defending a thesis about how we should go about our theorizing. [...] [W]hen theorizing we can assume that certain facts hold, and principles which are epistemically fact-insensitive need not be metaphysically fact-insensitive (RCFP: 496).

But what is incomplete in Kurtulmus's comparison, is that Cohen is also defending a thesis about how we reach fundamental principles, which are at the top of all our convictions. If Rawls does not provide a particular method for theorizing, other than the gathering behind the veil of ignorance in the original position, Cohen gives a method that every person is able to apply in order to discover their fundamental principles. It is obvious that the conceptual search, within the structure of beliefs, starts with principles grounded in facts. But Cohen affirms the existence of principles independent of facts, which survive the denial of fact-sensitive principles, and which are at the summit of the structure of beliefs. These principles, disregarded by Rawls, which according to Cohen, express the essence (for example, the concept of justice) itself, without any influence of facts. For both philosophers, theorizing begins from "lower-level principles" and intuitive judgements and convictions. Whereas Rawls arrives at the "higher-level principles" by employing facts, Cohen rejects the influence of facts on eminent and fact-free principles. In addition epistemically fact-insensitive principles need not be metaphysically fact-insensitive principles, as fundamental principles representing a concept, for example the concept of justice, exist independently of our acknowledgment of them. But both types of principles can correspond in the structure of beliefs, when fact-free principles are reached and accepted as true.

To summarize, this chapter explores the relationship between the facts that ground the principles within the Rawls-Cohen debate. The explanation of the meaning and terminology related to the principles in Cohen's and Rawls's theories makes it obvious that the two philosophers do not have the same approaches to social justice. According to the Cohenian argument, our fundamental fact-free principles exist at the summit of all our principles and convictions, independently from all fact-sensitive principles. According to this argument, the Rawlsian pretension of establishing the first fundamental principles of justice would be false, because these principles transcend the facts. The applicability of the principles depends on their acceptability and public justification, which would materialize once the principles were reflected by social facts. But in that case, their acceptability and feasibility would preclude their being fundamental principles of justice.

9 Disagreement on the Status of Facts

According to the Cohenian thesis presented in chapters 2 and 3 on the relationship between facts and principles, fundamental principles of any virtue should not be sensitive to facts. Fundamental principles of justice reflect the virtue of justice and stand apart from other values or facts. The two readings of the Rawlsian conception of justice, presented in chapter 5, show that there is, at the theoretical level[1], an underlying fact-free principle in the selection of the principles of justice. This is the principle of equality, according to which both principles of justice are selected. The principle that identifies justice with equality is fact-insensitive and the benchmark for choosing both principles of justice. Whereas the first principle of justice promotes equality of rights and liberties, the second principle promotes equal opportunities and does not permit excessive inequalities in the distribution of social and economic benefits, due to the principle of equality and its relation to the virtue of justice, underlying the choice.

However, Rawls emphasizes not only the reference to the principle of equality, but also the role of facts about human nature and human society in the selection and the application of the principles of justice. According to him, first principles in general, respond to facts about the human condition. Even though the fact-free principle of equality is taken as a reference in order to define these principles, the status of facts remains essential within the Rawlsian understanding of principles in general. How can a just social system be determined without facts about society's members who are going to recognize it and to live under its laws? Why are facts about human nature and human practice necessary in establishing a just social system? What basic facts exist in the original position for determining a just social system? Does the constructivist approach mislead in questions of social justice? Does a "fact-free" constructivist approach lead to justice? On the one hand this chapter explores the Socrato-platonic origin of the Cohenian philosophical position that claims that the content of justice should not be affected by mundane information. On the other hand, it shows that the pragmatic Rawlsian question about a just social system implies a "fact-sensitive" conception of justice. Why should a conception of justice that aims at establishing a just social system for man reflect facts?

---

1 The argument proposes two levels of the Rawlsian conception of justice. There is a difference regarding the importance given the facts between the theoretical level, where equality is taken as a benchmark and the practical level, where the principles of justice are to be applied.

9.1 Cohen's Search for Justice: What Is Justice?

Cohen's socialist-egalitarian philosophical position and his understanding of the virtue of justice emerge in his critique of Rawls's conception of justice. Justice is represented as an unattainable ideal that the Rawlsians, however, believe they have reached.

> The Rawlsians, who believe that the constraints of human nature and human practice affect the content of justice, are inclined to regard me as unrealistic and/or utopian in that I believe that justice is unaffected by those mundanities. But it is worth pointing out that they are in one way more utopian than I. For in believing that justice must be so crafted as to be bottom-line feasible, they believe that it is possible to achieve justice, and I am not so sanguine. It follows from my position that justice is an unachievable (although nevertheless governing) ideal (RJE: 254).

In the first chapter of RJE, Cohen disapproves of the Rawlsian theory of how to establish a just social system. He argues for a justice superior to the justice recommended by Rawls, which is a compromise with human nature and the human condition. The Cohenian socialist-egalitarian position is articulated by John Stuart Mill in his *Principles of Political Economy* (PPE).

> The proportioning of remuneration to work done is really just, only in so far as the more or less of the work is a matter of choice; when it depends on natural difference of strength or capacity, this principle of remuneration is in itself an injustice; it is giving to those who have; assigning most to those who are already most favoured by nature. Considered however, as a compromise with the selfish type of character formed by the present standard of morality, and fostered by the existing social institutions, it is highly expedient; and until education shall have been entirely regenerated, is far more likely to prove immediately successful, than an attempt at a higher ideal (PPE 2: 210).[2]

Cohen is aggravated by Rawls's constructivist[3] reasoning that builds the conception of justice on a compromise between the human factual situation and the virtue of justice. According to Cohen, principles of justice should only reflect the virtue of justice[4] and remain unaffected by realities, such as the human condition. He, therefore, believes that the Rawlsian principles should not be called

---

2 Cohen also quotes this paragraph of Mill that "nicely articulates his [=Cohen's] position". See RJE p: 85.

3 According to the constructivist view, a principle "qualifies as one of justice because it is the product of a sound procedure for selecting rules of social regulation" (RJE: 299).

4 Cohen prefers to call these principles rules of regulation, if they result from a compromise between the virtue of justice and the human nature and condition.

principles of justice, but rather rules of regulation.[5] Is this constructivist approach that starts from facts about humans and ends with the virtue of justice a legitimate approach to justice?

> I argue in what follows that the constructivist approach to social justice mischaracterizes justice both because it treats justice as sensitive to certain sorts of fact and because it fails to distinguish between justice and other virtues. [...] The present chapter is an extended defense of the claim that the constructivist approach to social justice is, for that particular, and transparently simple, reason, misguided (RJE: 275).

9.2 The Cohenian Critique of the Rawlsian Constructivism

Cohen rejects the constructivist approach to social justice because of two main errors, which result in a disfigurement of the virtue of justice. The first error is to mistake the principles of justice with the best rules to live by: "optimal all-things-considered principles are therefore not necessarily the best principles considered from the point of view of justice alone" (ibid.). The second error is that representative citizens are not asked to define justice, but to define the optimal rules of social regulation. The Cohenian criticism of constructivism is that the answer to the question about the rules of regulation is not the same as the answer to the question: What is justice? As a result, Cohen questions what makes a principle a principle of justice.

> My question is whether its being the product of a favored procedure for choosing the general rules for social existence establishes that a principle is one of justice, whether or not those who think so think it because they also think that they are describing what is, in a principle, the very property of validity itself, when they lay out what their favored procedure is (RJE: 276).

The Cohenian critique is based on two distinctions. The first is between fundamental normative principles of justice, which are not derived from other normative principles, and principles or rules of regulation, which citizens create and adopt to organize their communal life. "But we do not in the same sense adopt our fundamental principles, any more that we adopt our beliefs about matters of

5 It is very important to mention that Rawls is aware of this distinction that he emphasizes. Rules of regulation in the Cohenian terminology are what Rawls calls fair terms of cooperation. However, "the role of the principles of justice (as part of a political conception of justice) is to specify the fair terms of social cooperation" (JF: 7). Hence, the principles of justice are the criteria according to which fair terms of cooperation or rules of regulation would be selected.

fact. Our fundamental principles represent our convictions. They are not things we decide to have and that we consequently work to install" (RJE: 276-277). The second distinction is between principles that serve the virtue of justice and principles that serve other values, such as human welfare.

> Now, Rawlsians believe that the correct answer to the question 'What is justice?' is identical to the answer that specially designed choosers, the denizens of the Rawlsian original position, would give to the question 'What rules of regulations for society would you choose, in your particular condition of knowledge and ignorance?' Their answer to that question is supposed to give us the fundamental principles of justice. But in this identifying justice with optimal rules of regulation, Rawlsians breach both of the distinctions (ibid.).

For Cohen, a fundamental principle of justice is not an applied principle of justice, which is derived from justice together with something other than justice, such as empirical facts, or maybe another virtue.

> [F]undamental principles of justice reflect nothing but considerations of justice, but they may not reflect a mixture of justice considerations and other considerations, for principles that reflect such a mixture are applied principles of justice (RJE: 279).

Cohen rejects constructivism, which states that fundamental principles of justice depend to a certain extent on facts; that is, principles "derived from judgments [...] about the right procedure for generating principles of justice, together with facts of human nature and human society" (RJE: 281). But as they are fundamental, principles cannot be derived from a mixture of justice and empirical facts.[6]

As explored in chapter 2, any principle, which is sensitive to facts, is "committed thereby to a fact-insensitive principle, from which, together with the relevant fact or facts, the fact-sensitive principle (for example, of justice) that he affirms is derived" (RJE: 282). Thus, another mistake of the constructivists is to identify between fundamental principles of justice and applied principles of justice. "[T]hey assign a role to fundamental principles of justice that fundamental principles of justice are not suited to fulfill" (ibid.). The mistaken role is determined by the fact that representatives are asked to select the most suitable principles to regulate their social cooperation. Even if the principles chosen in the original position are considered by Rawls principles of justice "because of the special conditions of motivation and information under which principles that are to serve the role of regulating their common life are adopted" (RJE: 283),

6 For an elaborate discussion, see chapter 3.

they cannot be principles of justice. Indeed, they express other virtues and principles than justice, such as the practicability and stability of a social system. Moreover, they cannot be "fundamental principles of anything" (ibid.) because of the influence of the factual contingencies that prevents them from being fundamental[7] at all.

> The relevant non-justice considerations do indeed affect the outcome of typically favored constructivist procedures. My complaint is not at all that constructivism fails to take them into account, but precisely that it does take them into account, inappropriately, when purporting to identify what justice is. [T]he constructivist procedure means that what it produces is not fundamental justice, and is sometimes, moreover, [...] not justice at all (RJE: 284).

Whereas facts about human nature and society are very important in selecting the best rules of regulation, Cohen affirms that these facts are irrelevant in determining the nature and the content of the virtue of justice and thereby its fundamental principles.

> Facts of human nature and human society of course (1) make a difference to what justice tells us to do in specific terms; they also (2) tell us how much justice we can get; and they (3) bear on how much we should compromise with justice, but so I believe, they make no difference to the very nature of justice itself (RJE: 285).

9.3 Two Complementary Cohenian Theses

In reply to the Rawlsian constructivist view, Cohen affirms two theses: a strong thesis and a weaker one. He starts his argumentation against the constructivism of Rawls by affirming the weaker thesis[8] that states that fundamental principles cannot be based on facts.

> If even the weaker thesis is true, constructivism obscures how the principles it selects are arrived at, whether or not the fact-insensitive principles that it presupposes and fails to explore are properly called 'principles of justice', simply because it does not expose those fact-insensitive principles to view (RJE: 287).

The strong thesis, which Cohen does not demonstrate, but only approves, states that when the fact-insensitive principles are exposed, "we shall recognize them

7 As explored in chapter 2, Cohen believes that fundamental principles of any virtue cannot be grounded in facts, in opposition to the derived principles of justice that might be fact-sensitive.
8 The weaker thesis is explored in chapter 6 of RJE and discussed in this work (see chapter 2).

to be the fundamental principles of justice that a given constructivism latently affirms: it will be those principles that endow the constructively selected principles with whatever amount if justice they have" (ibid.). So both theses are complementary in the sense that the weaker thesis affirms the first part of the Cohenian argumentation and the strong thesis affirms the second part of it. Whereas the facts of human nature and human society cannot be the basis for fundamental principles (weaker thesis), the fact-insensitive principles – from which all other normative principles derive – are the fundamental principles of justice (strong thesis). Hence, the strong thesis recognizes the non-factual principles as fundamental principles of justice.

> Sound rules of social regulation must satisfy virtues other than justice, and must defer to factual constraints that do not affect justice itself. Accordingly, my objection is not that the denizens will not answer the question put to them [what are the most suitable rules of regulation?] correctly, but that it is the wrong question to put to them if what we want to know is what the fundamental principles of justice are (RJE: 291).

If the constructivist approach originating in facts is misleading in questions of justice, would not a constructivist "fact-free" approach lead to justice?

9.4 Cohen's Reply

Cohen imagines a revised application of constructivism for determining the content of justice, where representatives are not provided with factual information.

> Such an application of constructivism would make it immune to the criticisms of constructivism about justice, as it is currently conceived, which relate to constructivism's propensity to pollute fundamental justice with fact (RJE: 299).

In the case at hand, the considered move toward justice is constructivist, but it lacks the factual information that the selectors of the principles are generally provided with. Then, "they would produce rules of regulation for each possible world, or set of assumptions about the facts, that they can reach by formulating principled reactions to merely hypothesized facts" (ibid.). Cohen believes it would make an important difference if facts were not taken into account in the selection procedure. The principles chosen in the original position for example, "will be of a more purely egalitarian kind, since it is so often the facts that make equality ineligible (as opposed to not identical with justice)" (RJE: 300). Therefore, the lax understanding of the difference principle[9] proposed by Cohen would be "a principle, not of justice but of how to come as close to justice as possible when it is impossible to realize justice fully" (ibid.).

Finally, even if constructivism about justice would not consider any facts in its move toward justice, it does not confuse the erroneous identification of principles of justice with the best rules of social cooperation. "[T]hat remains an error even when constructivism's principles about justice are chosen in freedom from factual information, and, therefore, for all possible worlds" (ibid.).

9.5 Cohen's View: A Socratic-Platonic View

Cohen agrees with the Socratic-Platonic view that refuses to answer the question, "what is justice?" with illustrations of just behaviour.

> Until we unearth the fact-free principle that governs our fact-loaded particular judgments about justice, we don't know why we think what we think just is just. [...] Plato thinks, and I agree, that you need to have a view of what justice itself is to recognize that justice dictates P [principle] when F [fact] is true. That is how justice transcends the facts of the world (RJE: 291).

However, if justice is a reality that transcends the world and is therefore out of reach for human beings, could not an agreement about a just social system be achieved? Must we know what justice is to know what a just social system requires?

9.6 Two Different Approaches

The argument in this part presents three main ideas. It aims at showing that 1) Rawls and Cohen have asked two different questions and that thereby 2) do not employ the same concepts regarding normative principles. It puts at a final step

---

9 Recall from chapter 5, that Cohen proposes two interpretations of the difference principle: the strict difference principle and the lax difference principle. The lax interpretation of the difference principle implies that everyone within the society "gets what she can through self-seeking behaviour in a market whose rewards are so structured by taxation and other regulation that the worst off are as well off as any scheme of taxed and regulated market rewards can make them" (RJE: 74).

3) the importance of the facts into evidence for any pragmatic approach to social justice.

9.6.1 Two Different Questions

The Cohenian conception of justice presented above, which claims that justice is an unachievable ideal, is an answer to the question: What is justice? This conceptual philosophical Cohenian question about the virtue, the essence or the nature of justice is different from the concrete question asked by Rawls: What is a just social system? Indeed, Rawls did not inquire into the nature of justice, but into the justice of a social system from the practical point of view of a member of society. A just social system depends, according to Rawls, on a just social cooperation between citizens and just basic social institutions. Consequently, the Rawlsian inquiry should be directly related to facts about the interacting members of society and to facts about fundamental social institutions. Whereas Cohen's question starts from the virtue in order to deduce the principles, Rawls's question is a factual, pragmatic, and normative question disinterested in the nature of virtue; it starts from the facts in order to attain a compromise between the virtue and the facts, from which it starts. Cohen, unsatisfied with the Rawlsian answer to his (Cohen's) question about the virtue of justice (a question that Rawls did not ask), criticizes it and takes up the inquiry anew. But he actually asks a different question, viz. "what is justice?" one that was not asked by Rawls who wanted to know what a just social system is. Why are facts so important in determining a just social system?

9.6.2 Terminology

Even if the terminology used by both philosophers in designing their concepts is the same, the meaning of the concepts expressed with these terms is not the same. An elaborate discussion of both terminologies and concepts is presented in detail in chapter 10. But as an example of such discrepancies, the crucial concept of fundamental principles is presented in the following.

In the Cohenian understanding of fundamental principles, they are normative fact-insensitive or fact-free principles. They are fundamental, in the sense that they are not derived from any other principles or facts. In the Cohenian terminology the adjective fundamental refers to insensitivity to facts, which does not have the same designation or significance for Rawls. Fundamental principles that Rawls also calls first principles may rest upon facts. They are however fundamental, in the sense of most important values for a just social system. In addition to the fact that both philosophers asked two different questions, they use the same terminology for different concepts.

9.7 Rawls's Question: "What Is a Just Social System?"

Rawls imagines that citizens in a liberal democratic society ask his question of what a just social system is. This question reveals their needs to specify the fair terms of their social cooperation.

> [They] do not regard their social order as a fixed natural order, or as an institutional structure justified by religious doctrines or hierarchical principles expressing aristocratic values. Nor do they think a political party may properly, as a matter of its declared program, work to deny any recognized class or group its basic rights and liberties (JF: 6).

Adapted to the fact that citizens are free, equal, rational and reasonable, the Rawlsian question, "what is a just social system?" becomes more specific and precise:

> what is the most acceptable political conception of justice for specifying the fair terms of cooperation between citizens regarded as free and equal and as both reasonable and rational, and (we add) as normal and fully cooperating members of society over a complete life, from one generation to the next? (JF: 8).

9.7.1 A Factual Question

Rawls believes that the answer to this factual normative question on the fairness of the political conception of justice should be based on the good sense of free and equal, reasonable and rational individuals in a liberal democracy. Accordingly, the search for justice in the case at hand, concerns a precise conception of persons (free and equal) living within a particular political system (liberal democracy). But the question is already informed by factual elements about the features of the citizens as well as the characteristics of the social system. In order to be accepted and applicable, the social system should include these facts implicit in the question. The social justice Rawls seeks concerns human beings living in a world of scarce resources and conflicting interests. Therefore, it should reflect facts about human nature and the condition and understanding of the virtue of social justice. Consequently, deities and angels (who maybe live in a world already ruled by justice so they need not search for it) probably have their own understanding of justice and thereby their own principles of justice reflecting facts about their nature[10] and their living conditions. What are the facts that the Rawlsian conception of justice conceived for free and equal persons should reflect? Why are these facts important criteria for the Rawlsian conception of justice?

Before exploring the importance of the facts in the Rawlsian conception of justice, it is important to examine on what social (human) foundation a social system's justice rests. According to Rawls, a just social system should be based on a fair system of cooperation between all social classes and a just functioning of social institutions. The laws according to which social institutions work should be ordered by justice. "Then, having chosen a conception of justice, we can suppose that they [the representatives] are to choose a constitution and a legislature to enact laws, and so on, all in accordance with the principles of justice initially agreed upon" (TJ: 13). These accepted and binding social rules preserve everyone's rights, liberties, and social and economic advantages within a pluralist society. "The justice of a social scheme depends essentially on how fundamental rights and duties are assigned and on the economic opportunities and social conditions in the various sectors of society" (TJ: 7).

As a result, the justice of the social system must be fair towards all persons, thus guaranteeing its acceptability and applicability. In reference to what principles are things fair or unfair?

9.8 The Meaning of Fairness

It is the innovative idea of fairness introduced by Rawls that shows his emphasis on the role of human nature in his theory. It is not only the fairness of the conditions in the original position[11], under which the principles of justice are selected, which matters, but also the fairness of the chosen principles themselves. The human nature and condition are the ultimate reference according to which the fairness of any scheme or principle or theory is judged. A social system is fair towards all citizens when it preserves their interests thus rendering it just and providing the reason why it is accepted. For example, it is fair for free

10 Maybe they are according to their nature capable of fully realizing the virtue of justice without any compromise with facts about their nature and practice and that is why they are deities and angels.

11 For an elaborate discussion of the original position, see chapter 1.

and equal persons to have the same set of rights and liberties and it would be unfair if a group had more advantages than others. There is a tight correlative underlying relationship that starts respectively with the fairness of the principles, their acceptance and applicability, and ends with the affirmation of their justice. However, people's economic and social advantages are for the most part determined by factual situations and the social circumstances, within which they live. Hence, the idea of fairness, which is fundamental in the Rawlsian theory of justice "justice as fairness", depends on facts on man's actual real-life situation.

> Our social situation is just if it is such that by sequence of hypothetical agreements we would have contracted into the general system of rules which defines it. [T]hose engaged in them can say to one another that they are cooperating on terms to which they would agree if they were free and equal persons whose relations with respect to one another were fair. [...] The general recognition of this fact would provide the basis for a public acceptance of the corresponding principles of justice (TJ: 13).

9.9 The Autonomy of the Rawlsian Citizens

The importance of facts about the human condition and human nature for selecting the most suitable principles of justice becomes apparent with the autonomy of free and equal citizens. Spokespersons invited to agree on and put into practice the principles of justice, are – within the Rawlsian conception of justice – autonomous. They need to choose under equal conditions, within the same factual situation, "from their own understanding of the virtue of justice", the fair terms of cooperation they want to respect.

> Yet a society satisfying the principles of justice as fairness comes as close as a society can to being a voluntary scheme, for it meets the principles which free and equal persons would assent to under circumstances that are fair. In this sense its members are autonomous and the obligations they recognize self-imposed (ibid.).

In order to have a just social system, members of society choose autonomously the universally fair principles of justice substantiated by their factual reality. All social institutions that constitute the basic structure of society are based on these principles. The autonomy that characterizes the Rawlsian citizens implies that the selected principles would always reflect facts about their human condition. What facts are important for the Rawlsian principles of justice? Should all of them be available to the representatives in the original position?

9.10 Important Facts in Shaping a Just Social System

From the Cohenian point of view, facts about human nature should not affect the essence of justice. However, as presented above, in Rawls's understanding of a just social system the acceptability and applicability of principles that rule social interactions are related to life's realities. The facts that representatives in the original position know and include when selecting the principles of justice can be divided into three groups. Examples for the three groups, which constitute the human factual situation, are examined in the following.

9.10.1 Facts about the Human Condition

This group involves all facts that determine the social conditions under which members of society live. An important truth about the human condition is that persons live in a social and economic interdependence within an association which should advance the good of all of them. "Now obviously no one can obtain everything he wants; the mere existence of other persons prevents this. The absolutely best for any man is that everyone else should join with him in furthering his conception of the good whatever it turns out to be" (TJ: 119). However, liberal democratic societies are marked by a conflict of interests, since persons are not indifferent to how the produced social and economic benefits are distributed. The majority pursues their own interests and wants to obtain a larger over a lesser share.

> If men's inclination to self-interest makes their vigilance against one another necessary, their public sense of justice makes their secure association together possible. Among individuals with disparate aims and purposes a shared conception of justice establishes the bonds of civic friendship (TJ: 5).

An additional important factor which bears on the principles of justice are the (great) undeserved and thereby unjust inequalities in a society. Persons born into different social classes have different expectations of life, determined by the political system as well as social and economic contingencies. "It is these inequalities, presumably inevitable in the basic structure of any society, to which the principles of social justice must in the first instance apply" (TJ: 7).

9.10.2 Facts about Human Nature

Human nature's precise facts on which Rawls bases the choice of the principles of justice are the following. The first fact is that representatives are autonomous in the sense that "they are to decide in advance how they are to regulate their claims against one another and what is to be the foundation charter of their society" (TJ: 11). The principles are the object of a social contract between members of society.

However, citizens are also reasonable and rational. Reasonable persons are those engaged in social cooperation and who accept fair terms of cooperation for all. Rational persons are those who exploit their social position in order to attain greater benefits while disregarding that all citizens are formally equal. According to Rawls, citizens are free and equal persons. Everyone accepts the principles of justice and knows that all citizens know and accept them. They are all capable of exercising their moral powers[12] and free to pursue the conception of the good they believe in. Consequently, their society is characterized by reasonable pluralism, where every citizen is free to hold their own convictions and beliefs.

> Thus I believe that a democratic society is not and cannot be a community, where by community I mean a body of persons united in affirming the same comprehensive, or partially comprehensive, doctrine. The fact of reasonable pluralism which characterizes a society with free institutions makes this impossible. [...] But this fact is not always easy to accept, and political philosophy may try to reconcile us to it by showing us the reason and indeed the political good and benefits of it (TJ: 4).

9.10.3 Facts about the Political System

The first and most important fact is that "each person possesses an inviolability founded on justice that even the welfare of society as a whole cannot override. [...] Therefore in a just society the liberties of equal citizenship are taken as set-

12 In chapter 1 there are two moral powers. To be fully cooperating in society, citizens need to exercise both moral powers. The first one is a "capacity for a sense of justice" or the capacity to put into practice the principles of a conception of justice that specify the fair terms of social cooperation. The second moral power is the capacity to pursue an understanding of the good. Citizens are equal in so far as they possess, at least to the requisite minimum degree, the moral capacities that enable them to participate in social cooperation. While they are free to choose the conception of the good they want to pursue over their life, they have to agree on one conception of justice they should put into practice, as basis for a mutual cooperation.

tled" (ibid.). The Rawlsian society is a liberal democracy, characterized by equal freedom and liberty among all individuals. The facts about the inviolability founded on justice and the equal liberty are general facts known to all citizens. Are all these facts available to them in the original position? How can Rawls propose selecting the principles of justice that will last over time if they are affected by the present realities?

9.10.4 Available Facts in the Original Position

To ensure fair conditions for the selection process of the principles of justice in the original position, Rawls assumes that representatives do not know certain facts, such as their positions in society, their social class, or their social status. The conception of the good or expectations of an accomplished life are unknown to everyone. No one knows their natural abilities and talents or their psychological features "such as his aversion to risk or liability to optimism or pessimism" (TJ: 137). Moreover, representatives do not know the political and economic situation of their society. However, they do know particular facts, such as the fact "that their society is subject to the circumstances of justice and whatever this implies" (ibid.). They also know general facts about human society, political affairs, economic theory, the basis of social organizations and the laws of human psychology.

> Indeed, the parties are presumed to know whatever general facts affect the choice of the principles of justice. There are no limitations on general information, that is, on general laws and theories, since conceptions of justice must be adjusted to the characteristics of the systems of social cooperation which they are to regulate, and there is no reason to rule out these facts (TJ: 138).

Why are facts about the human situation important in the choice, acceptance and applicability of the principles of justice, also necessary in the regeneration of justice over time, from one generation to the next? What does in the Rawlsian theory ensure such a stability of a just social system?

9.10.5 The Role of the Facts in the Stability of Justice as Fairness

It is very essential to choose the suitable principles of justice that should inform social cooperation, but it is more significant to guarantee the just functioning of the social system from one generation to the next. In chapter 1, the question of the stability of any conception of justice depends on its acceptability by all social groups, which guarantees its legitimacy, and on its capacity to produce justice over time. The facts about the human situation, which are criticized by Cohen for affecting the content of the virtue of justice, are represented by Rawls as the "guarantee" for the stability of justice as fairness over time.

> We try to show that the well-ordered society of justice as fairness is indeed possible according to our nature [...]. This endeavor belongs to political philosophy as a reconciliation; for seeing that the conditions of a social world at least allow for that possibility affects our view of the world [...]. Our social world might have been different and there is hope for those at another time and place (JF: 37-38).[13]

As explained in chapter 1, Rawls presents within his justification of the selected principles of justice three companion ideas: the idea of public justification, the idea of reflective equilibrium and the idea of overlapping consensus[14], which should ensure the applicability and the stability of his theory. If the principles of justice meet the facts about human nature and human practice and the convictions of political justice, then justice as fairness is justified and thereby capable of regenerating.

> The point is that whatever idea we select as the central organizing idea cannot be fully justified by its own intrinsic reasonableness, as its intrinsic reasonableness cannot suffice for that. Such an idea can be fully justified (if at all) only by the conception of justice to which it eventually leads when worked out, and by how well that conception coheres with our considered convictions of political justice (JF: 25-26).

The Rawlsian conception of justice is shaped according to the convictions and beliefs about justice held by the citizens, for whom it is conceived. The principles of justice for a just social system should reflect the human situation if members of a society are to apply them.

In sum, this chapter explores the Cohenian critique of the Rawlsian constructivist approach to social justice. According to Cohen, this approach fails to lead to justice, because it involves factual information to determine the principles of justice, instead of reflecting the virtue of justice. It confuses fundamental principles of justice with applied principles of justice. It also mistakes rules of regulation for fundamental principles of justice. Cohen uses a strong and a

---

13 A well-ordered society represents the basic structure of society informed by justice as fairness: society's main institutions should function according to the principles incorporated in the political conception of justice.

14 See chapter 1 for a detailed discussion.

weak thesis to refute the Rawlsian constructivist view. Rawls's viewpoint on social justice does not object to resting fundamental principles on facts.

After exploring the difference between the two philosophers with regard to their respective questions and terminologies, the importance of the facts for accepting and applying the Rawlsian applied theory of social justice is highlighted. In view of the fact that Cohen believes that facts about the human condition "pollute" principles of justice, as they prevent justice from representing equality, one has to affirm that even if a world, where justice means equality, cannot be achieved by humans, the virtue of justice should not be adapted to man's reality, because it then simply stops being what it is. However, there is no other way for Rawls to deal with the question of a just political system. Rawls is not interested in justice as a virtue; he focuses instead on a just political system for those who choose it. His answer reflects facts about these people, as his search concerns social interactions and not the virtue of justice.

10 Different Understandings of Justice

The question of social justice, which leads Rawls to identify the "most suitable" principles for a just social system, highlights the importance of equality and fairness. Whereas the idea of equality refers to the equal distribution of rights and liberties, the idea of fairness applies to the allocation of social and economic goods. "But there is no injustice in the greater benefits earned by a few provided that the situation of persons not so fortunate is thereby improved" (TJ: 15). However, the question of (social) justice, as interpreted by Cohen, which is answered through his scrutiny of TJ, is different to Rawls's. In the Cohenian understanding, the ideas of justice and equality should be rescued from the Rawlsian inegalitarian treatment. In a society where distributive justice prevails, "people's material prospects [should be] roughly equal" (RJE: 2).

Thus, both philosophers ask different questions and answer them according to their different viewpoints, but use the same terminology while referring to different concepts. The Rawlsian question – What is a just social system? – is not the question about the idea or the concept of justice as understood by Cohen.[1] "Beyond the disagreement between me and the Rawlsians with respect to both the form and the substance of justice, there is a disagreement about how to do philosophy, or indeed philosophy itself" (RJE: 3). Whereas Rawls identifies a just "society", to which the principles of justice apply, Cohen identifies a "community". While both philosophers stress the importance of education and an ethos which impacts people's actions, they attribute different roles and meanings to that ethos. Are both philosophers simply talking at cross purposes? This chapter explores the methodological as well as the conceptual and terminological differences between the Rawlsian and the Cohenian theories of justice.

10.1 Different Treatments of Justice

Rawls focuses on the idea of social justice that should regulate society's main institutions and social relations between its members. He limits his inquiry to questions only concerning social (institutional) justice. He delineates the profile of a liberal democratic society, where his conception of social justice should be

1 Cohen remains unsatisfied with the different "compromises", with which philosophers have tried to answer the question of justice. He attributes a big role to the education that should be regenerated, so that justice would not refer to expediency or efficiency (RJE: 85-86).

applied. He then goes on to describe the citizens, who would put into practice the principles of justice. To guarantee the acceptability and the stability of his theory from one generation to the next, he imagines a justificatory position, where representatives of different social classes stand within a hypothetical situation of equality, in order to select, from their de facto situation, the most suitable and feasible principles of justice.[2] Rawls believes they would choose an equal distribution of rights and liberties and a fair distribution of social and economic goods, so that each social class from the least to the most advantaged could improve their socioeconomic situation. Inequalities would therefore not be necessarily removed within a just social system. The Rawlsian understanding of social justice does not dictate equal material prospects for everyone. Instead it implies that everyone preserves their basic rights and liberties and has the chance to pursue personal plans for life and realize their own conception of good. In his attempt to rescue the virtue of justice and the idea of equality from the Rawlsian "inegalitarian" treatment, Cohen highlights the interdependence between both values. He rejects the difference principle, which endorses the righteousness of social and economic inequalities. His critique challenges the incentives argument formulated by rich people to justify their higher incomes, and also the move from "justice as equality" to "justice as inequality" within the Pareto argument. Furthermore, Cohen contends Rawls's conception of justice that rests on facts and not fundamental principles, which are not grounded in facts. He concludes that the Rawlsian principles of justice based on facts about humankind cannot be the fundamental principles of justice, but only rules of regulation. Cohen criticizes the constructivist approach to social justice for using the human factual situation in order to select normative principles. Cohen's credo is that the virtue of justice cannot be defined by facts which "pollute" its fact-insensitive nature.[3] Therefore, justice should not be compromised by man's capability or incapability of achieving it. Principles of justice should not only apply to society's institutions, but also to daily individual decisions founded on an ethos of justice.

Rawls and Cohen not only approach questions of justice differently; they also have different conceptions of society.

---

2 For an in-depth discussion of the original position, see chapter 1.

3 See chapter 2 for a further discussion.

10.2 Different Conceptions of Society

10.2.1 The Liberal Democratic Society

According to Rawls, "political society is not, and cannot be, an association. We do not enter it voluntarily. Rather we simply find ourselves in a particular political society at a certain moment of historical time. We might think our presence in it, or being here, is not free" (JF: 4). Thus, justice as fairness applies to a fair system of cooperation between members of society, who are free and equal.[4] This is

> suggested by the fact that from a political point of view [...] its citizens do not regard their social order as a fixed natural order, or as an institutional structure justified by religious doctrines or hierarchical principles expressing aristocratic values. Nor do they think a political party may properly, as a matter of its declared program, work to deny any recognized class or group its basic rights and liberties (JF: 6).

Principles of justice correspond to the characteristics of a constitutional liberal democratic regime, where free and equal citizens live in a system of social cooperation. The basic structure of society must be supported by the principles of justice, so that rights and liberties are equally assigned and social and economic goods are fairly distributed. Although the rich have higher incomes, they still are part of society; the Rawlsian difference principle allows such inequalities. Thus, the equality of citizens is a political equality of rights, liberties and moral powers. To enlighten this idea, Rawls distinguishes between a political society and communities, such as churches.

> The members of a community are united in pursuing certain shared values and ends (other than economic) that lead them to support the association and in part bind them. In justice as fairness a democratic political society has no such shared values and ends apart from those falling under or connected with the political conception of justice itself (JF: 20).

Rawls distinguishes between a democratic society and a community. For example, one can join and leave communities voluntarily, but not a society, unless one emigrates. In a community, people share values and goals; in a democratic society, everyone is free to pursue their conceptions of the good and their beliefs as long as they do not infringe the freedom of others. "All who can be fully cooperating members of political society count as equals and can be treated differently only as the public political conception of justice allows" (JF: 21). Fur-

4 For a further elaboration, see chapter 1.

thermore, it is "a serious error not to distinguish between the idea of a democratic political society and the idea of community" (ibid.). Due to the reasonable pluralism[5], a democratic society cannot be a community, even if it is hospitable to many communities and "indeed tries to be a social world within which diversity can flourish in amity and concord" (ibid.). A society would be a community only through "the oppressive use of government power which is incompatible with basic democratic liberties" (ibid.) so that its members share a unique conception of the good.[6]

10.2.2 The Cohenian Community

In applying the interpersonal test, Cohen argues that the rich fail to justify why they need special money incentives to increase their productivity. He concludes that either they live outside the community or they live in it, but they do not behave ethically.[7] The term community is explored by Cohen in his critique of the attitude of the most privileged, although Rawls does not talk of community, but of a liberal democratic society. The importance of the concept of community refers more to its central place within the Cohenian "conception of justice" than to its meaning in the (critique of the) Rawlsian theory, since Rawls intentionally avoids using this term to refer to his political democratic society.[8] Cohen observes that the term "community", in its familiar use, covers many conditions and there is more than one kind of community. But "I shall introduce the particular condition that I have in mind by relating it to the concept of a comprehensive justification" (RJE: 41).[9]

Concerning the semantics of the term "community", Cohen compares it to the term "friendship" and explains that "it functions both as count noun and as a mass noun" (RJE: 43). Community is a count noun when it refers to groups of people connected to one another, such as the European community. It is however a mass noun "when we speak of how much community there is in a certain

5 For an elaborate presentation, see chapter 1.

6 This seems impossible in a pluralistic society, where everyone is free to pursue his/her own conception of the good and free to have his/her convictions.

7 For a further discussion, see chapter 5.

8 As elaborated above, Rawls distinguishes between those two different terms that refer to different concepts.

9 The ideas of comprehensive justification as well as the interpersonal test related to it are explained in chapter 5.

society, when we say that some action enhances or reduces, or some attitude honors or violates, community , and so on" (ibid.).

Cohen does not only compare the terms "friendship" and "community", as being both count nouns and mass nouns, but also the concepts.

> A community, one could say, is a set of people among whom there is community: that is how the count-notion and the mass-notion are linked. 'Community' is in this respect like 'friendship': a friendship is a relationship in which friendship obtains. Notice that friends can do and feel things that are inconsistent with friendship without thereby dissolving their friendship. [...] But there cannot (enduringly) be no friendship in a friendship. And all that is also true of community: there can be violations and lapses of community in a community, but there cannot be no community in a community (ibid.).

However, the form of community that concerns Cohen is the justificatory community, which is a group of people among whom norms of comprehensive justification prevail. If a certain policy is applied within a community, people are asked to justify their relevant behaviour and the choice of this policy. If they are unable to justify them, then the policy lacks the justificatory communal character "whatever else might nevertheless be said in its favor" (RJE: 44).[10]

Cohen argues that "it diminishes the democratic character of a society if it is not a community in the present sense, since we do not make policy together if we make it in the light of what some of us do that cannot be justified to others" (RJE: 45). Why is it unrealistic to expect a modern society to be a community?

> The talented rich cannot justify the fact that the minor premise of the (naked) incentives argument is true. If they cannot justify the truth of its minor premise, then they cannot use the argument as a justification of inequality. If they cannot use it as a justification of inequality, then it cannot be used as a justification within community. If it cannot be used as a justification within community, then anyone who uses it (in effect) represents society as a variance with community when he does so (RJE: 47-48).

Cohen formulates through his critique of the Rawlsian democratic society, his concept of community. The Rawlsian difference principle lacks the communal character and it should therefore be rejected.

However, Rawls and Cohen attribute certain roles for the moral feelings, which are to incline members of society to act in accordance with the principles of justice. Whereas Rawls calls this feeling "sense of justice", Cohen calls it "ethos of justice". Do both expressions refer to the same concept?

---

10 Recall that Cohen rejects the difference principle, because it fails the communal justificatory character.

10.3 Different Moral Feelings

10.3.1 The Rawlsian Sense of Justice

Rawls presents his conception of justice in a system of ideas related to one another.[11] He highlights the role of members of society in achieving social justice and distinguishes between the principles of justice that should apply to society's main institutions and "principles of another kind [...] since a complete theory of right includes principles for individuals as well" (TJ: 108). Rawls believes that one of the principles which apply to individuals is the principle of fairness.

The principle of fairness

> holds that a person is required to do his part as defined by the rules of an institution when two conditions are met: first, the institution is just (or fair), that is, it satisfies the two principles of justice; and second, one has voluntarily accepted the benefits of the arrangement or taken advantage of the opportunities it offers to further one's interests (TJ: 112-113).

The principle of fairness requires a just functioning of social institutions and just voluntary acts. Moreover, Rawls explores what he calls "natural duties", such as for example, "the duty of helping another when he is in need or jeopardy, provided that one can do so without excessive risk or loss to oneself" (TJ: 114). There are negative duties, such as not to be cruel, and positive ones, such as the duty of mutual aid. These duties imply doing something good for others, but they are not dictated by or connected to principles of justice that apply to social institutions and social practices.

> From the standpoint of justice as fairness, a fundamental natural duty is the duty of justice. This duty requires us to support and to comply with just institutions that exist and apply to us. [...] Thus if the basic structure of society is just, or as just as it is reasonable to expect in the circumstances, everyone has a natural duty to do his part in the existing scheme. [...] The principles that hold for individuals, just as the principles for institutions, are those that would be acknowledged in the original position (TJ: 115).

The importance of developing the sense of justice in order to maintain an enduring just society is presented by Rawls in his comments about the family as a basic institution, and as part of the basic structure. The role of the family is essential in reproducing the liberal democratic culture from one generation to the next. "Citizens must have a sense of justice and the political virtues that

11 The Rawlsian system is explored in chapter 1.

support just political and social institutions" (JF: 163). Even if principles of justice do not apply to the intrinsic life of the family, basic rights and liberties of its members should be guaranteed.[12]

> The adult members of families and other associations are equal citizens first: that is their basic position. No institution or association in which they are involved can violate their rights as citizens. [...] [G]ender distinctions limiting those rights and liberties are excluded. So the spheres of the political and the public, and of the not-public and the private, take their shape from the content and application of the conception of justice and its principles. If the so-called private sphere is a space alleged to be exempt from justice, then there is no such thing (JF: 166).

10.3.2 The Rawlsian Ethos of Justice

In his article "What Would a Rawlsian Ethos of Justice Look Like?" (WRJ) Michael G. Titelbaum questions the egalitarian ethos proposed by Cohen and presents his own interpretation of the Rawlsian ethos. He might agree with Cohen to the necessity of an addition to the Rawlsian theory but he disagrees with him on which addition that should be. "Although we may not be able to read the presence of an egalitarian ethos directly off of Rawls's description of the just society, [...] an individual ethos must be added to the society as he [Rawls] describes it" (WRJ: 295-296).

Titelbaum affirms that in a Rawlsian just society, there would be economic inequalities among its members, even if the inequalities were produced by financial incentives for the most advantaged members of society. The difference principle allows such economic inequalities produced by financial incentives, as long as the position of the least advantaged members is improved. Titelbaum explores Cohen's defensive stance on incentive inequalities, which he does not accept as legitimate values for a just society. Titelbaum argues that in the Cohenian just society citizens have an egalitarian ethos of justice and they thereby do not need economic incentives. "[T]heir concern for the condition of their fellows supplies all the motivation required" (WRJ: 290). Furthermore, the difference principle does not conform with this egalitarian ethos of justice because it allows economic incentives.

---

12 "Since wives are equally citizens with their husbands, they have all the same basic rights and liberties and fair opportunities as their husbands; and this, together with the correct application of the other principles of justice, should suffice to secure their equality and independence" (JF: 164).

> The most controversial premise of this argument is Cohen's claim that the citizens of the just society display an egalitarian ethos – that in the productive aspects of their lives they make choices that leave the worst-off as well as possible (ibid.).

Titelbaum explains that this claim concerns, for example, the choice of one's job, the number of hours one works, or one's retirement age. If an individual making one of these economic decisions chooses an option that does not advance the economic position of the underprivileged in society, they are exercising productive latitude. Productive latitude allows the talented persons to maximize their benefits at the expense of what would improve the position of the untalented in a society. "When Cohen claims that the citizens of the just society act on egalitarian ethos, he is claiming that they never exercise productive latitude" (WRJ: 291). Their daily economic decisions would be informed by their allegiance to the economic condition of others. In real societies however, Titelbaum corroborates, persons exercise productive latitude in accordance with their plans of life: they choose this job, or that geographic area to work in, or they work a limited number of hours to spend more time with their families.

Titelbaum questions the egalitarian ethos and tries to prove that Cohen developed this idea from the Rawlsian conception of justice. "Perhaps the source of the egalitarian ethos is the difference principle itself" (WRJ: 292), although the difference principle, according to Titelbaum, does not apply to private actions of individuals, but rather to the basic structure of society. "[T]o interpret it as mandating an egalitarian ethos for individuals would be a serious misreading both of Rawls's intent and of the place the principle occupies in his theory" (WRJ: 293). If an individual, motivated by an egalitarian ethos, considers the situation of the least advantaged members of society before making his choices, he would not be acting according to the difference principle. Titelbaum says that he would be acting on a "*correlate* of the difference principle: a principle that directs him to organize his decisions around the same goals that the difference principle specifies for the basic structure of society" (ibid.).

Titelbaum concludes that if the egalitarian ethos does not find its source in the difference principle, its requirement can be found in the Rawlsian sense of justice. Rawls focuses on the susceptibility to a sense of justice that citizens should develop and the capacity to understand the principles of justice and to act in accordance with them. "Individuals in the just society act on the principles of justice in the ordinary course of events and in the course of their daily lives" (WRJ: 294). Albeit that Cohen concludes from this idea an egalitarian ethos that should inform people's daily economic choices, Titelbaum explains it differently. Based on Rawls's example, a full compliance with just laws is exercised when people cast their vote between different political parties.

> In general, I do not think we can read an egalitarian ethos straightforwardly off of Rawls's descriptions of the just society, [...]. To argue that the individuals in the just society must display an ethos that affects their productive decisions is to argue for an addition to Rawls's theory as he saw it, and a substantial one at that (WRJ: 295).

Cohen identifies the source of an egalitarian ethos when he examines the general features of a Rawlsian just society, such as stability, fraternity, mutual respect, and psychological plausibility.

The source of an individual ethos could be located in Rawls's idea that the institutional conduct of persons should match the principles of justice. The criteria for individuals and social institutions should be compatible. Rawls insists on the importance of the stability of a just society over time, secured by the link between personal conduct and the way institutions function. Yet Titelbaum imagines a society, whose "citizens displayed a sense of justice but no individual ethos" (WRJ: 298). In this case, members of society would support the principles of justice but they could still be able to exercise productive latitude "even to the point of being wholly self-interested maximizers" (ibid.). It is not psychologically plausible that the institutional conduct of individuals, within a just society, does not correspond with the behaviour in their private lives. This contradiction between public and private life would not guarantee society's stability over time. "[F]or any set of institutional principles, one could argue that for the sake of psychological plausibility and long-term stability a society featuring those principles would have to contain individuals with a matching ethos" (WRJ: 299). Rawls believes a just society should display mutual respect and fraternity among its members. Moreover, the difference principle as one of the principles of justice "allows justice as fairness to give rise to these qualities in society" (ibid.). However, Cohen disagrees. Without an individual ethos in the just society, mutual respect and fraternity among citizens cannot be achieved. Without an egalitarian ethos, the difference principle cannot provide self-respect in society. Nothing but an egalitarian ethos would prevent talented persons from exploiting their contingent talent and social advantages. The use of morally arbitrary contingencies shows a lack of respect for others. "On Rawls's own terms, this exercise of productive latitude constitutes a denial of respect for others, and this in turn undermines those others' self-respect" (WRJ: 300). Cohen concludes that mutual respect is achieved in society, only when people abstain from exercising productive latitude. This is possible, only when their daily economic decisions are advised by an egalitarian ethos of justice.

As to Rawls's idea of fraternity promoted by the difference principle, Cohen replies that not wanting to achieve greater benefits, unless the situation of the less privileged members of society is improved "is incompatible with the drive for enrichment motivating market maximizers" (WRJ: 301). Cohen concludes that without an egalitarian ethos, citizens would undermine the value of fraternity with their economic decisions in daily life. Assuming the plausibility of such an ethos to be added to the Rawlsian conception of justice, Titelbaum asks, what would a Rawlsian ethos of justice look like?

Titelbaum argues that the Cohenian ethos is a correlate of the difference principle and he proposes that the members of a just society display a "full ethos". This ethos does not only correlate to the difference principle, but also to the first principle of justice and the first part of the second principle. In this description of the full ethos, the primacy of the first principle over the second is regarded. "Thus, for instance, an individual will be motivated by the full ethos to make productive decisions in a manner that benefits the worst-off only when that requirement does not conflict with the ethos' correlate of the first principle" (WRJ: 302). Titelbaum also explores how this ethos is structured and where it might be added to the Rawlsian conception of justice.

> To the extent possible, we should imagine the ethos as structured the same way the sense of justice is structured, and we should understand the ethos as entering into the theory of justice at the same points, [...]. Under this proposal, the individual ethos could be considered an extension of the [Rawlsian] sense of justice (WRJ: 303).

Thus, a member of the just society acting ethically would be motivated to improve the situation of the least advantaged members of society, only if this improvement were consistent with basic liberties and fair equality of opportunity. The actions and choices of an individual might be directed by the underlying ethical principles. If the first principle of justice protects the liberty of conscience, "its correlate might allow a young man to go on a religious mission before joining the productive work force" (WRJ: 304). Even freedom of occupation is protected by the full ethos allowing a talented doctor to choose another, more satisfying career. Titelbaum investigates where the full ethos finds itself in Rawls's theory and examines the role of the principles of justice behind the sense of justice in this theory. First, principles behind the sense of justice are important in the original position where citizens select the principles of justice. Their importance is even prior to the original position device.

> Before the parties can settle on principles of justice, they must check that those principles will create a society in which a motive to act on the principles behind the sense of justice will be psychologically possible and intergenerationally stable for everyone (WRJ: 305).

Second, after selecting the principles of justice in the original position, the representatives selecting the principles should consider principles for individuals.

"As part of the latter process, the parties settle on a 'fundamental natural duty' called 'the duty of justice'" (WRJ: 306). For this reason it is people's duty to act according to the principles behind the sense of justice thus implying their full compliance with just institutions. Titelbaum concludes that the parties in the original position not only select principles of justice, but also correlates of these principles as guidance in their daily lives. The principles behind the full ethos match the two principles of justice. Titelbaum affirms that this relation between the principles of justice and their correlates secures the stability and the plausibility of society. In their private lives, citizens are motivated by principles closely related to the principles regulating social institutions. Titelbaum purposes that the parties in the original position would choose a full ethos instead of Cohen's egalitarian ethos. Moreover, their priority lies with the first principle.

> Because the two moral powers are essential to our ability to participate in social cooperation in a just society, and because the basic liberties are essential to our possession of the two moral powers, the parties in the original position refuse to restrict the basic liberties for the sake of anything else (WRJ: 309).

The parties in the original position refuse to curtail their basic liberties, for example, their right to practice their religion, even if they have to forsake greater economic benefits. But Titelbaum argues "if the only principle of natural duty were a difference-principle correlate, individuals would be duty-bound to choose their religious practice in a way that maximized the economic condition of the worst-off" (WRJ: 311). However, in the Rawlsian conception of justice, the primacy of the first principle over the second forbids such exchanges. "In short, the parties select the principles behind the full ethos over the principles behind the egalitarian ethos" (ibid.).

If the full ethos ameliorates the plausibility and the stability of the just society gradually, it is also compatible with the values of fraternity and mutual respect among citizens. The most important idea in the Rawlsian conception of justice, according to Titelbaum, is that all members of society understand and accept the priority of the first principle over the second. This priority would sometimes comprise the economic advantages. "Given the primacy of the two moral powers, a plurality of religious options is more important to individuals' nature as free and equal rational beings than is the distribution of wealth" (WRJ: 313). In the Rawlsian society, the principles behind the full ethos therefore permit productive latitude without undermining the values of fraternity and mutual respect among its members. "Yet while the first principle concerns what society must leave individuals free to do, the ethos concerns what individuals do with that freedom" (ibid.). Titelbaum shows that Cohen is right when he adds an ethos to the Rawlsian theory. However, Titelbaum insists that this ethos should not be egalitarian but a full ethos that respects the lexical priority of the principles of justice. He in a way completes the Cohenian individual ethos and transforms it into a full ethos that corresponds perfectly with the Rawlsian conception of justice.

10.3.3 The Cohenian Egalitarian Ethos

Cohen believes that a just functioning of social institutions should be complemented by an individual egalitarian ethos of justice. In other words, everyone's daily decisions should be dictated by their endeavors to realize social justice so that the principles of justice apply equally to a society's members and its institutions. "A society that is just within the terms of the difference principle, so we may conclude, requires not simply just coercive rules, but also an ethos of justice that informs individual choices" (RJE: 123).

Hence, both Rawls and Cohen highlight the importance of moral feelings: in Rawls's case the sense of justice and in Cohen's case the ethos of justice. The Cohenian ethos encourages citizens to deliberate the righteousness of their actions and behaviours in all their decisions but are not obliged by that ethos to automatically obey the principles of justice. "Accordingly, as things actually are, the required ethos must, as I have argued, guide choice within the rules, and not merely direct agents to obey them" (RJE: 124). Rawls's conception of justice, secures the stability of justice as fairness, but it need not be actively exercised in every economic choice. The Cohenian citizen seems to be more involved than the Rawlsian citizen in achieving social justice. Cohen urges every member of society to constantly rescue justice from the inegalitarian "threat" which might jeopardize the nature of this justice through people's choices and actions. Moreover, Cohen, here citing Marx, shows that the political and the social spheres should not be considered separate. How could both spheres become unified?

> Only when the actual, individual man has taken back into himself the abstract citizen and in his everyday life, his individual work, and his individual relationships has become a species-being, only when he has recognized and organized his own powers as social pow-

ers so that social power is no longer separated from him as political power, only then is human emancipation complete (RJE: 116).[13]

10.4 The Role of Education

10.4.1 In the Rawlsian Conception of Justice

Education is a prerequisite for citizens of a well-ordered society to recognize one another as free and equal within their reciprocally profitable social cooperation. This education must be provided by basic institutions of society informed by the conception of justice, so that the members of society understand and internalize this reciprocity. “This task of education belongs to what we may call the wide role of a political conception. In this role such a conception is part of the public political culture: its first principles are embodied in the institutions of the basic structure and appealed to in their interpretation” (JF: 56). The educational role, however, given to the conception of justice, assures a durable regeneration of justice and fairness. This means that those growing up in a well-ordered society develop ways of thought and judgement, as well as dispositions and sentiments, which lead them to maintain the political conception.

“Their education should also prepare them to be fully cooperating members of society and enable them to be self-supporting; it should also encourage the political virtues so that they want to honor the fair terms of social cooperation in their relations with the rest of society” (JF: 156). Rawls attributes an important role to education in establishing and stabilizing his political conception of justice. However, in addition to their moral powers, members of society should share certain common sentiments and judgements, which would secure the stability of justice as fairness. Even if these feelings and judgements have to be in accordance with the principles of justice, citizens need not observe them in each of their daily decisions. If the functioning of society’s main institutions is just, this suffices to attain a just social system, which secures rights, liberties as well as social and economic goods.

---

13 This quotation cited by Cohen figures originally in Karl Marx’s work, “On the Jewish Question” p. 241.

10.4.2 In the Cohenian Conception of Justice

The role of education for egalitarian citizens, whose behaviour is determined by egalitarian considerations, is central within the Cohenian conception of justice. The educational function corresponds to the function of the original position in the Rawlsian conception of justice. In a liberal democratic society, like the one described by Rawls, people need to agree on certain applicable principles of justice. They must select them and in the original justificatory position consent to the most suitable principles on the grounds of political ideas about rights, liberties, and democracy rooted in their political culture. In Cohen's socialist-egalitarian society, people must be educated so as to arrive at egalitarian decisions and to develop and exercise an ethos of justice, which justifies their egalitarian choices and rejects any inegalitarian attitudes.

Furthermore, Cohen highlights the basic role given to education in the conclusion of the first chapter of RJE, when he explains that justice should not reflect a compromise with expediency. Consequently and "until education shall have been entirely regenerated" (RJE: 285) the Rawlsian attempt to question social justice is "far more likely to prove immediately successful, than an attempt at a higher ideal" (ibid.). Education should be reformed in order to fit into the Cohenian ideal of justice.

Summarizing the tight relationship between education and moral feelings, Rawls establishes a just social system, with institutions working according to the principles of justice. Cohen, however, attributes an important role to members of society in achieving egalitarian justice. Whereas principles of justice apply to social institutions in the Rawlsian theory, they apply to people's choices and actions in the Cohenian conception. Both theories rely on education in developing moral sentiments and judgements in order to change the human attitude, but the role of education seems to be more significant in the Cohenian world, as he believes that a just functioning of social institutions does not suffice to realize a just social system. "Philosophers in search of justice should not be content with an expedient compromise. To call expediency justice goes against the regeneration [of education]" (RJE: 86). How should justice be defined according to the Cohenian ideal?

10.5 Different Approaches to Social Justice

10.5.1 The Rawlsian Constructivist Approach

In selecting the two principles of justice, the political equality of moral powers among citizens leads to an equal distribution of basic rights and liberties. The Rawlsian question is then how to regulate social and economic inequalities in people's prospects. The methodology that he proposes is to

> look to our firmest considered convictions about equal basic rights and liberties, the fair value of the political liberties as well as fair equality of opportunity. We look outside the sphere of distributive justice more narrowly construed to see whether an appropriate distributive principle is singled out by those firmest convictions (JF: 42).

Rawls's idea is that the representatives of different social classes stand in the original position and use their firmest convictions about a liberal democratic system in order to identify the distributive principles of economic and social inequalities that accommodate these convictions.

> By going back and forth, sometimes altering the conditions of the contractual circumstances, at others withdrawing our judgments and conforming them to principle, I assume that eventually we shall find a description of the initial situation that both expresses reasonable conditions and yields principles which match our considered judgments duly pruned and adjusted (TJ: 10).

Rawls assumes convictions and ideas about democracy and distributive justice from which the most suitable principles of justice are chosen in order to achieve social justice. These convictions and ideas however are built upon facts about human nature and the human condition so that the selected principles incorporate these truths. Therefore, principles of justice are based, according to Rawls, in human reason and human attitudes. "Ideally the rules should be set up so that men are led by their predominant interests to act in ways which further socially desirable ends" (TJ: 57). As previously discussed, Cohen criticizes the Rawlsian methodology as it defines the virtue of justice in reference to facts about the human nature and condition. The Cohenian approach to social justice rejects such a factual reference and instead uses normative fact-free principles to describe the principles of justice.

10.5.2 The Cohenian Conceptual Approach

Unlike Rawls, Cohen believes that fundamental principles of justice should not consider facts about human nature, because fundamental principles in general should not be sensitive to facts. Fundamental normative principles are not reflected in facts. Cohen provides a methodology that everyone can use in order to reach fundamental principles. It consists of analyzing concepts and principles until the fact-free principle is attained.[14] The Cohenian disagreement with the constructivist theories returns to the fact that they use factual contingencies to determine justice. "The influence of other values means that the principles in the output of the procedure are not principles of justice, and the influence of the factual contingencies means that they are not fundamental principles of anything" (RJE: 283). What are the fundamental principles of justice in the Cohenian understanding of justice?

In fact, Cohen does not present a theory and its principles of his own understanding of justice. He criticizes the Rawlsian theory thereby giving an indication of his viewpoint so that it is possible to sketch his conception of justice. But he does not pretend to unveil the fundamental principles of justice. He merely analyzes their structure and nature, and applies his thesis to the concept of justice. But his approach to justice is in line with the Socratic-Platonic view that "until we unearth the fact-free principle that governs our fact-loaded particular judgments about justice, we don't know why we think just is just. And we have to retreat to (what we consider to be) justice in its purity to figure out how to institute as much justice as possible inside the cave" (RJE: 291).

Cohen encourages a further search for justice in order to reveal the fact-free principle that governs the still hidden human judgments about justice. He believes that the substance of justice "transcends the facts of the world" (ibid.), so that it is essential to question justice itself to recognize that justice dictates the principles, which are reflected in facts.

> I also happen to agree with Plato that justice is the self-same thing across, and independently of, history. But that extreme anti-relativism is no part of the doctrine here defended that justice is, ultimately, facts-free, within anyone's belief structure, regardless of her position with respect to relativism, and regardless of whether or not relativism is true (ibid.).

14 For a further elaboration, see chapter 2. But, even if the fact-free principle is not reached, the conceptual analysis method is to be applied.

Accordingly, while Rawls determines the principles of justice taking facts about men and society as a starting point in his constructivist approach to social justice, Cohen does not determine the principles of justice, since justice is not yet revealed. He affirms that the unknown fundamental principle of justice, which is the cause of all other judgements about justice, should be fact-free. So, regarding the nature of justice, which Rawls thinks feasible through the application of the principles of justice, Cohen recognizes it as an unrevealed ideal and the quest for it should therefore be revived. But, if, according to Cohen, it is not possible to identify the fundamental principles of justice, is it possible to determine the applied or derived principles of justice?

10.6 Different Conceptions of Justice

10.6.1 Fundamental Principles of Justice

If Cohen criticizes the Rawlsian fundamental principles of justice for being fact-sensitive, Rawls calls them fundamental or first or basic because they apply to the basic structure of society and regulate basic institutional arrangements. They are fundamental insofar as their application is essential for achieving a just social system. The consensus in the original position should thereby concern "the fundamental principles that specify the general structure of government and the political process; the powers of the legislature, executive, and the judiciary; the limits of majority rule" (JF: 28) as well as equal rights and liberties for all.

Thus, Rawls most likely uses the term "fundamental" in the same meaning to refer to the principles and to the ideas. He explains the relation between the fundamental ideas[15], which are all related to the central organizing idea of society as a fair system of cooperation. These ideas as well as the principles are fundamental in applying his conception of justice.

15 Recall from chapter 1 that the fundamental ideas in the Rawlsian conception of justice are the ideas of a well-ordered society and its basic structure, the ideas of the original position and equal and free citizens.

10.6.2 Rules of Regulation

However, Cohen describes the Rawlsian fundamental principles of justice as rules of regulation. He does not even call them principles, although they are applied principles according to his definition of facts and principles.[16] Cohen emphasizes the concept of rules, agreed to by members of society and intended to regulate the system of social cooperation. He does not deny the importance of such rules and laws, but refuses to call them fundamental or fact-free principles, as they merely mirror man's reality.

> The distinction between rules of regulation and the principles that justify them helps to illuminate what is at stake in normative controversy. [...] Justice is not the only value that calls for (appropriately balanced) implementation: other principles, sometimes competing with justice, must also be variously pursued and honored (RJE: 271-272).

If Cohen disagrees with Rawls on the fundamental principles of justice, this disagreement shows an underlying disagreement on the convictions of justice.

10.6.3 Justice as Fairness

Different prospects among members in a pluralistic conflicting society, who, according to the first principle of justice, share equal rights and liberties, push philosophers to deliberate social justice. The philosophical debate concerns these social and economic differences, and their undeserved causes.[17] On a practical level,[18] Rawls finds it unfair to remove inequalities even though they are unmerited. A fair treatment would be to regulate them, in a way that contributes to the improvement of the socioeconomic situation of the not so lucky. Why should the effects (social and economic inequalities) be removed if their causes (natural and social circumstances) cannot be avoided? The Rawlsian

---

16 Applied principles of justice are principles justified by fundamental principles, from which they derive.

17 Recall that social and economic inequalities result originally from morally arbitrary contingencies, such as good or bad luck, which are undeserved.

18 There is a difference in the Rawlsian text between the practical applied level of his conception and the theoretical level, where he seems more idealist and does not take into consideration its feasibility: "Once we decide to look for a conception of justice that nullifies the accidents of natural endowment and the contingencies of social circumstance [...] we are led to these principles" (TJ: 15).

solution is to derive benefits from them to improve the social situation of everyone: the difference principle as a principle of distributive justice.

> [T]he difference principle requires that however great the inequalities in wealth and income may be, and however willing people are to work to earn their greater shares of output, existing inequalities must contribute effectively to the benefit of the least advantaged. [...] The general level of wealth in society, including the well-being of the least advantaged, depends on people's decisions as how to lead their lives (JF: 64).

The Rawlsian treatment of morally arbitrary contingencies does not imply an equal distribution of income and wealth, which would "correct" social and natural disadvantages. Rawls calls for a regulation of the effects of social circumstances in a way that members of society benefit from them. Hence, he formulates justice as fairness, which should be fair for all; it implies a social improvement of the situation of the least favoured and an encouragement for the most advantaged to be even more productive. Cohen disagrees with Rawls on the treatment of morally arbitrary contingencies. He affirms that if economic inequalities were removed, the poor would always benefit. In this context he scrutinizes the Rawlsian defense and endorsement of such inequalities. Does Cohen promote a conception of justice, which dictates justice as equality?

10.6.4 An Egalitarian Conception of Justice

Although Cohen does not propose any rules of regulation or fact-sensitive principles of justice, it seems irrefutable from his critique and rejection of the difference principle that distributive justice should be egalitarian in order to avoid taking advantage of morally arbitrary contingencies. At a practical level, he considers the difference principle in its lax interpretation[19] and concludes that

> it is satisfied when everyone gets what she can through self-seeking behavior in a market whose rewards are so structured by taxation and other regulation that the worst off are as well off as any scheme of taxed and regulated market rewards can make them. On my view of what it means for a society to institute the principle, people would mention norms of equality when asked to explain why they and those like them are willing to work for the pay they get (RJE: 74).

---

19 For an elaborate discussion of the strict and the lax interpretations of the difference principle see chapter 4.

Furthermore, Cohen corroborates that there is no reason, "why the talented should earn more than the untalented" (RJE: 76). He argues that if the difference principle had mandated citizens of society to a more egalitarian distribution of income and wealth, they would not refuse to act accordingly.

> So imagine that we address the talented rich people, and we ask them why they do not give the above-average parts of their incomes to people of below-average income, when, ex hypothesi, they would have compliantly accepted the resulting post-giveaway incomes had the difference principle happened to mandate them (ibid.).

However, as presented in chapter 7, Cohen defends a hypothetical state of affairs D3, which is a socioeconomic strategy to regulate social and economic inequalities and to prevent the exploitation of morally arbitrary advantages. It implies a different use of natural primary goods and an equal distribution of social primary goods. This system D3 would make everyone better-off, without making the situation of the privileged even better. In his defense of an economic egalitarian scheme that prevents the undeserved use of morally arbitrary contingencies, Cohen promotes an egalitarian distributive principle within a conception of justice that implies the idea of justice as equality. As a result, this conception of justice counters the Rawlsian conception of justice and its principles.

10.7 Different Principles of Distributive Justice

The Rawlsian definition of a just social system reconciles justice with (certain) inequalities. The acceptance of these inequalities does not only improve the situation of the deprived members of a liberal democratic society, but also motivates the prosperous persons to increase their productivity and thereby constantly boost the economy. Thus, a just social system would be fair towards poor people, by improving their socioeconomic situation and towards the rich by motivating them with financial rewards to be more productive. The practical consequences of the Rawlsian conception of justice are that everyone would be better-off, and their expectations in life improved.

> The role of the principles of justice (as part of a political conception of justice) is to specify the fair terms of social cooperation. [...] These principles specify the basic rights and duties to be assigned by the main political and social institutions, and they regulate the division of benefits arising from social cooperation and allot the burdens necessary to sustain it (JF: 7).

Cohen criticizes this reconciliation between justice and inequality and favours an egalitarian distribution of income and wealth.[20] The practical consequences of such a system would benefit the destitute more (than within the Rawlsian economic scheme) without however maximizing the profits of the well-to-do. Moreover, Cohen believes that social and economic inequalities caused by morally arbitrary contingencies are undeserved and are therefore not legitimate in an egalitarian economic scheme. Unlike Rawls, who moves, within the Pareto argument, from equality as a starting point to an inequality[21] that improves the situation of all members of society, Cohen argues that inequalities related to morally arbitrary contingencies and caused by unfair circumstances are unfair. And they remain unfair, even if these inequalities are not removed for efficiency considerations. "Fairness fanatics will then eliminate the inequality, and sensitive folk, like me, will tolerate it, while judging it to be unfair" (RJE: 168).

As previously mentioned, whereas both philosophers agree to the first principle of justice,[22] according to which equal basic rights and liberties are to be equally assigned, they disagree on the second principle of justice, which concerns the distribution of income and wealth. Whereas the just functioning of social institutions informed by the principles of justice to achieve a just social system would be sufficient, within the Rawlsian conception of justice, an ethos of justice that informs everyone's actions and decisions is, according to Cohen, indispensable for the application of an egalitarian scheme of distributive justice.

The Cohenian conception of justice accords an important responsibility to members of society in achieving a just (egalitarian) social system by employing their ethos of justice. The aim of this moral attitude is to achieve individual or personal justice through egalitarian decisions, in the sense that the justice or injustice of every economic choice would be individually examined. Should a modern conception of justice entail a principle of justice that applies to people's daily behaviour?

---

20 See the presentation of the Cohenian distribution of income and wealth (D3) in chapter 7.

21 For an elaborate discussion of the Rawlsian move from justice as equality to inequality as well as the Pareto argument, see chapter 4.

22 Recall that principles of justice are called rules of regulation by Cohen, because he argues that fundamental principles of justice should not be based on facts about humans; rules of regulation, however, that determine the conditions for social cooperation should reflect those facts.

10.8 The Cohenian Ethos for Personal Justice

According to Cohen, the difference principle should not only apply to the basic structure of society, but also to the choices of individuals in their daily lives.

> Now, many Rawlsians resist that extension of the difference principle into the personal domain by pleading the propriety of a moral division of labor, under which the state sees to justice, and the individual, having herself willingly seen to justice insofar as the state requires her to do so, sees then to the imperatives and values of her own personal life (RJE: 8).

Cohen criticizes the position, which claims that the state is the sole representative of impersonal justice. He illustrates his point of view with the Rawlsian set of natural duties, "that lie on individuals rather [than] on the state, and that include the duty to respect others, to uphold and foster just institutions, to do a great good when the cost of doing so is not excessive" (RJE: 9). These duties on which a fair system of social cooperation is based, apply to personal life; they are principles for individuals and not principles for social institutions. Yet, "[t]he real opposition between Rawls and me, on the present issue is therefore not whether the impersonal standpoint reaches personal decision but whether the demands of distributive justice in particular do so" (ibid.).

In his examination of the demands of distributive justice, Cohen distinguishes between different viewpoints and explains that he expects the individual to be as dedicated to justice as the social institutions which constitute the basic structure of the state. Unlike the Rawlsian view of distributive justice, which considers justice as a task[23] of the basic structure of society, the Cohenian view says that "both the state, with no life of its own, and the individual, who is indeed thus endowed, must, in appropriately different fashions, show regard in economic matters both to impersonal justice and to legitimate demands of the individuals" (RJE: 10). Consequently, the basic social institutions should be informed by certain egalitarian principles in order to achieve social justice. But what are "the different fashions" according to which the individual "shows regard in economic matters"? How does the Cohenian ethos of justice in reality influence individual choices? What should well-off persons decide in order to act on that ethos of justice?

> There are many forms of motivation along the continuum between unrestrained market-maximizing at one end and full self-sacrificing restraint in favor of the worst off on the

23 "Justice is the first virtue of social institutions, as truth is of systems of thought" (TJ: 3).

> other. The first extreme is permitted by Rawls (and I regard that as absurd), but the second extreme isn't required by me. [...] [E]ach person has the right to be something other than an engine for the welfare of other people: we are not nothing but slaves to social justice (ibid.).

An economic system in favour of the most disadvantaged at the sacrifice of the most advantaged is not necessary due to the legitimate personal prerogative, which is the right to be something other than an engine for the welfare of others. However, Cohen determines the different ways, according to which the state and the individual regard economic matters. On the one hand, individuals, who support the difference principle, must observe it in their economic choices, "whatever regard, that is, which starts where his personal prerogative stops" (ibid.). On the other hand, the state must regard the personal prerogative of individuals. "It should not, should it happen to have the power to do so, legislate so invasively and so comprehensively that the individual lacks scope for the exercise of what belongs within his own prerogative" (ibid.).[24] Thus, society's basic institutions should be informed by an egalitarian economic ethos as well as citizens' economic choices so that they achieve an egalitarian just society, which is not "just by the virtue of the character of its state-legislated basic structure alone" (RJE: 344). How does the Cohenian ethos of justice, which should be in accordance with the legitimate personal prerogative, practically inform individual choices?

Cohen gives many examples to illustrate his viewpoint, such as the example of the camping trip, which he explores in *Why Not Socialism?*. On this camping trip, all persons contribute equally and enjoy equally the results of their cooperation. "We proceed communistically, under understandings of mutuality and forbearance that cannot be formulated crisply" (RJE: 352). Even if all individuals contribute through similar efforts to the welfare of all, it is very hard to "say how big a piece of effort has to be for one to have qualified as doing one's bit, or what size a share has to be" (ibid.). According to Cohen, it is sufficient for the individuals to know that everyone conforms to the rules of the camping, in or-

24 The Cohenian argument for the legitimate personal prerogative expressly defends social and economic inequalities, so why does this defense not apply to the Rawlsian argument for the difference principle? Indeed, Cohen refuses the comparison between the prerogative justification and the Rawlsian justification of inequality within the difference principle and affirms that inequalities justified by the prerogative claim "will coincide only by accident with those that the difference principle would license" (RJE: 10). A state, which respects the personal prerogative, is, following Cohen, different from a society that limits the application of the difference principle to its basic structure.

der to exercise their ethos of justice and thereby provide good faith effort, without knowing who is contributing in realizing the demands of justice and the amount of the contribution.

> There are too many details in each person's life that affect what the required sacrifice should be. [...] '[D]o your bit' was understood and applied as a principle of justice. It would have been crazy to ask for it to be carefully defined, and it would be crazy to deny that it performed a task of social regulation, in the interest of justice (RJE: 353).

But, is a "communistic" behaviour dictated by an egalitarian ethos of justice – which implies taking egalitarian decisions – not considered a compromise with the freedom of persons or their legitimate personal prerogative? Is such a communistic behaviour possible within a liberal democratic society? According to Cohen, "justice is fully served only if people's access to desirable conditions of life is equal, within the constraint of a reasonable personal prerogative" (RJE: 181). The meaning of the term "reasonable" is related to the role of an egalitarian ethos of justice that should inform people's everyday lives. To what extent has one the right to pursue one's own interests?

> If, being more talented and having suffered nothing special to acquire her talent, A produces more widgets per hour of comparably repugnant (or unrepugnant) toil than B, then justice forbids paying A at a higher rate per hour. If, then, A uses her capacity to control how hard she works to secure a higher rate of pay by refusing to produce as many widgets per hour as she could (working no more arduously than B) except at that higher rate, then she strikes a posture that sets her against just egalitarian principle (ibid.).

To explain the demands of an egalitarian ethos of justice, Cohen affirms that according to the egalitarian viewpoint, the talented need not choose a work package that makes their situation less well-off nor are they asked to produce more, because of their extra endowments. "Egalitarians ask more product or service of the talented, but no more sacrifice. It is an aspect of their greater talent that, usually, producing more product or service than others provide [,] does not mean, for them, more sacrifice than others endure" (RJE: 208). Therefore, talented persons are not forced to act in an egalitarian way; those who take egalitarian economic decisions would be, within an egalitarian society, less well-off than they would be in unequal societies. "But it is to be expected that, with more equality, those at the top in an unequal society will be less well off" (ibid.).

Cohen proposes a correction of the old communist slogan, which says "from each according to his ability, to each according to his need" (ibid.). This slogan suggests that the talented persons should give more of themselves without their needs being heeded which might then lead to frustration or contentment. "No one should be expected to serve in a fashion that will unduly depress her position, in comparison with others, with respect to what she needs to have to live a fulfilling life" (RJE: 209).[25] The distribution of income and wealth D3 suggested by Cohen and explored in chapter 7 shows his viewpoint concerning the ethos of justice and the consequences of its application. D3 is a status, in which the amount produced is maximized but with equal wages distributed to talented and untalented people alike. This particular distribution, exercised in an egalitarian ethos of justice, preserves equality, leaving the untalented citizens better-off in D3 than they are in the Rawlsian D2 state. In the Cohenian understanding of justice, the most advantaged persons should take egalitarian economic decisions, only after preserving their interests that allow them to have a fulfilling life. Despite the conflicting points in the Rawlsian and the Cohenian understandings of justice, Cohen's economic proposal gives a decisively bigger task to citizens. A just society is therefore achieved by just persons and just social institutions.

In sum, after the Cohenian critique of Rawls's TJ, and his attempt to rescue the virtue of justice and the value of equality from the Rawlsian treatment, this chapter compares both conceptions of justice. Both philosophers are indeed talking at cross purposes, because each has his own methodology to question social justice which leads them to different conceptions of justice involving different political systems, principles, concepts as well as moral feelings. Indeed, both theories of justice exist separately and are in opposition to one another reproducing yet again the conflict between socialist egalitarianism and egalitarian liberalism.

25 Cohen does not precise the conditions of a fulfilling life.

Conclusion

In sum, this work that compares the different approaches to the idea of justice as presented by Rawls and Cohen leads to several philosophical results.

Concerning the concept of justice, the Cohenian conceptual analysis method, that, when applied, leads everyone to understand the structure of their principled beliefs, belongs to the philosophical Socratic-Platonic tradition. This tradition begins unveiling the concept of justice in order to judge what is just and what is unjust. Cohen's thesis about the relationship between facts and principles aiming at reaching fundamental principles that represent the concept of justice also belongs to the Socratic-Platonic tradition. However, the Rawlsian method which implies the use of the original position device, where the conditions of the hypothetical meeting of representative members of society secure the justice of the selected principles, is a pragmatic approach. This approach starts from the facts under which members of society live, in order to define what is just and what is unjust. Cohen's process aims at questioning the concepts in order to explain the facts and not inversely. One of the significant intentions of this work is to show how Cohen takes justice back to its conceptual and philosophical roots. The Cohenian method and thesis for analyzing the relationship between facts and principles might be criticized as erroneous, and even unconvincing, but it remains subscribed in the philosophical tradition, as a philosophical attempt to determine the human understanding of justice.

Furthermore, the Cohenian rescue of justice from constructivism, which rescues it from facts, shows his endeavor to not define justice by something else than justice itself. It would be acceptable to select rules that regulate social cooperation according to facts about the economic system and the human condition. But in this case the selected rules cannot be called principles of justice. Fundamental principles of justice should not depend on facts, because facts do not represent the essence of justice but the factual world. Yet the principles of justice should only represent the idea of justice and nothing else. They are therefore fundamental in this meaning; they cannot represent a mixture of justice and something else.

Regarding the idea of equality, Cohen's critique of the Rawlsian difference principle, which at points is exaggerated, for example in the use of the interpersonal test, constitutes a rescue of the tight relationship between justice and equality. Justice cannot move that far from the idea of equality, as condoned by Rawls as just; it could be justified as efficient, reasonable, but not as representing the virtue of justice. The feasibility of the Cohenian alternative that proposes an egalitarian distribution of income and wealth depends only on the will of members of society and their just decisions. Unlike the difference principle, an egalitarian distribution does not allow anyone obtaining economic or other benefits from morally arbitrary contingencies. But even if this egalitarian distribution is not practicable, it represents the idea of justice, unlike the difference principle, which upholds the injustice of socioeconomic inequalities as just. The practicability of certain social systems of distributive justice does not make them just or unjust; their justice should be judged in agreement with the idea of justice and not according to the capability of anyone to accept them and to put them into practice. One important quality of the Cohenian conception of justice is that it defines a just society by just social institutions and just persons, while also focusing on the importance of an ethos of justice that determines people's daily actions and decisions. It is common for the criticisms leveled against Rawls's principles of justice to confound both theoretical and practical levels of his theory. This work shows that the Cohenian critique of the difference principle proves the underlying contradiction behind this principle even on the theoretical justificatory level, where the choice of this principle is made. Although it is easy to find differences, when a principle is applied and then adapted to the real world, Cohen shows a profound contradiction between the values of fraternity and reciprocity promoted by the principle and the incentives argument in the Rawlsian argument for the difference principle. The different points stressed in the present work question Rawls's input into the philosophical debate on the idea of justice. The Rawlsian approach might be in the light of the above mentioned results slightly overestimated.

References

Arneson, J. Richard (2009) "Justice Is Not Equality". In *Justice, Equality And Constructivism: Essays on G.A. Cohen's Rescuing Justice and Equality*. Brian Feltham (ed.). Oxford and Malden MA: Wiley Blackwell: pp. 5-25.

Barry, Brian (1989) *Theories of Justice*. London: Harvester Wheatsheaf.

Bentham, Jeremy (1823) *An Introduction to the Principles of Morals and Legislation*. Oxford: Clarendon Press (first published 1789).

Cohen, Gerald A. (2009) *Why Not Socialism?* Princeton: Princeton University Press.

Cohen, Gerald A. (2008) *Rescuing Justice and Equality*. Cambridge, Mass.: Harvard University Press.

Cohen, Gerald A. (2001) *If You're an Egalitarian, How Come You're So Rich?* Cambridge, Mass.: Harvard University Press.

Cohen, Gerald A. (1997) "Where the Action is: On the Site of Distributive Justice". In *Philosophy and Public Affairs*. Vol. 26, No. 1: pp. 3-30. (Here as chapter 3 of RJE).

Cohen, Gerald A. (1992) "Incentives, Inequality, and Community". In *The Tanner Lectures on Human Values*. Grethe Peterson (ed.). Salt Lake City: Utah University Press. Vol. 13: pp. 263-329. (Here as chapter 1 of RJE).

Cohen, Joshua (1993) "Moral Pluralism and Political Consensus". In *The Idea of Democracy*. David Copp, Jean Hampton, and John E. Roemer (eds.). Cambridge: Cambridge University Press.

Gauthier, David (1986) *Morals by Agreement*. Oxford: Oxford University Press.

Hobbes, Thomas (1968) *Leviathan*. C.B. MacPherson (ed.). Harmondsworth: Penguin (first published 1651).

Kurtulmus, Faik A. (2009) "Rawls and Cohen on Facts and Principles". In *Utilitas*. Vol. 21: pp. 489-505.

Locke, John (1952) *Second Treatise of Civil Government*. Thomas P. Peardon (ed.). Indianapolis, Ind.: Bobbs-Merrill (first published 1689).

Marx, Karl (1978) "On the Jewish Question". In *The Marx-Engels Reader*. Robert Tucker (ed.). New York: Norton & Company (first published 1843).

Mill, John Stuart (1965) *Principles of Political Economy*. In *Collected Works of John Stuart Mill*. J. M. Robson (ed.). Vol. 2. Toronto: Toronto University Press (first published 1848).

Murphy, Liam (fall 1999). "Institutions and the Demands of Justice". In *Philosophy and Public Affairs*. Vol. 27, No. 4: pp. 251-291.

Narveson, Jan (1978) "Rawls on Equal Distribution of Wealth". In Philosophia. Vol. 7: pp. 281-292.

Pareto, Vilfredo (1971) *Manual of Political Economy*. Ann S. Schwier (tr.) Ann S. Schwier and Alfred N. Page (eds.). Clifton, N.J.: Augustus M. Kelly (first published in Italian, 1906).

Plato (2008) *The Republic*. Robin A. H. Waterfield (tr.). Oxford: Oxford University Press (first published 380 BCE).

Pogge, Thomas (2009) "Cohen to the Rescue". In *Justice, Equality And Constructivism: Essays on G.A. Cohen's Rescuing Justice and Equality*. Brian Feltham (ed.). Oxford and Malden MA: Wiley Blackwell: pp. 88-109.

Pogge, Thomas (Spring 2000) "On the Site of Distributive Justice: Reflections on Cohen and Murphy". In *Philosophy and Public Affairs*. Vol. 29, No. 2: pp.137-169.

Rawls, John (2005) *Political Liberalism*. Expanded edition. New York: Columbia University Press (first published 1993).
Rawls, John (2005) *A Theory of Justice*. Cambridge, Mass.: Harvard University Press (first published 1971).
Rawls, John (2003) *Justice as Fairness: A Restatement*. Cambridge, Mass.: Harvard University Press (first published 2001).
Rawls, John (1999) *The Law of Peoples*. Cambridge, Mass.: Harvard University Press.
Rawls, John (1999) *Collected Papers*. Samuel Freeman (ed.). Cambridge, Mass.: Harvard University Press.
Rawls, John (1980) "Kantian Constructivism in Moral Theory". In *Collected Papers*. Samuel Freeman (ed.), (1999). Cambridge, Mass.: Harvard University Press: pp. 303-358.
Rousseau, Jean-Jacques (1913) *Social Contract & Discourses*. G. D. H. Cole (tr.). New York : E. P. Dutton & Co., Bartleby.com, (2010) (first published 1762).
Scanlon, Thomas (2000) *What We Owe to Each Other*. Cambridge, Mass.: Harvard University Press.
Scheffler, Samuel (2006) "Is the Basic Structure Basic?". *In The Egalitarian Conscience. Essays in Honor of G.A. Cohen*. Christine Sypnowich (ed.). Oxford: Oxford University Press: pp. 102-129.
Scheffler, Samuel (2005) "Choice, Circumstance, and the Value of Equality". In *Politics, Philosophy and Economics*. Vol. 4: pp. 5-28.
Stepanians, Markus (2009) "Gerechtigkeit als Fairness". In *Grundmodelle Philosophischer Ethik*. Jörn Müller, Hans-Gregor Nissing (eds.). Darmstadt: Wissenschaftliche Buchgesellschaft: pp. 145-166.
Titelbaum, G. Michael (2008) "What Would a Rawlsian Ethos of Justice Look Like?". In *Philosophy & Public Affairs*. Vol. 36, No. 3: pp. 289-322.

Author Index

Subject Index

Bei Fragen zur Produktsicherheit wenden Sie sich bitte an:
If you have any questions regarding product safety,
please contact:

Walter de Gruyter GmbH
Genthiner Straße 13
10785 Berlin
productsafety@degruyterbrill.com